MARKETING™
WITHOUT MONEY

First published in Australia in 2003 by:
Pennon Publishing
PO Box 136, Niddrie, 3042

Text copyright © John C Lyons and Edward de Bono
Marketing without Money ™

The authors acknowledge and thank the following photographers for their superb contribution: Peter Braig, Bryan Charlton, Louie Douvis, Karl Hilzinger, Paul Jones, Mayu Kanamori, Daniel O'Brien, Belinda Pratten and Robert Rough.

All rights reserved. No part of this book may be reproduced, stored in a retrieval system, or transmitted in any form or by any means electronic, mechanical or otherwise, without the prior written permission of the publisher.

Every effort has been made to ensure that this book is free from error or omissions. However, the publisher, the authors, the editor, or their respective employees or agents, shall not accept responsibility for injury, loss or damage occasioned to any person acting or refraining from action as a result of material in this book whether or not such injury, loss or damage is in any way due to any negligent act or omission, breach of duty or default on the part of the publisher, the authors, the editor, or their respective employees or agents.

The National Library of Australia
Cataloguing-in-Publication entry:

    Lyons, John C., 1943- .

    Marketing Without Money: How 20 Top Entrepreneurs
    Crack Markets with their Minds.

    Includes index.

    ISBN 1 877029 41 6.

    1. Marketing - Australia. 2. Business enterprises - Australia. I. De Bono, Edward, 1933- . II. Title.

    658.80994

Designed by Allan Cornwell
Printed in Australia by McPhersons Printing Group

www.lyonsanddebono.com

John C Lyons
and
Edward de Bono

MARKETING™
WITHOUT MONEY

How 20 Top Australian Entrepreneurs
Crack Markets with their Minds

PENNON
PUBLISHING
2003

CONTENTS

ABOUT THE AUTHORS ... 8
ACKNOWLEDGEMENTS ... 10
FOREWORD from Dick Smith ... 11
FOREWORD from Gail Kelly, St.George Bank ... 13
PRELUDE ... 15
INTRODUCTION ... 16
FORMAT OF THE BOOK ... 25

PART 1 – INSPIRATION

1. MARKETING WITHOUT MONEY ... 30
Most successful entrepreneurs build something substantial and sustainable from nothing, using conceptual creativity and courage.

PAUL CAVE – BridgeClimb ... 35
LES SCHIRATO – Cantarella Bros. ... 41
ADRIAN DI MARCO – Technology One ... 47

2. REBELS FOR A CAUSE ... 54
They pursue a cause that customers truly believe in. They get the customers' attention without even asking for it.

DICK SMITH – Dick Smith Foods ... 59
EUAN MURDOCH – Herron ... 65
PETER FARRELL – ResMed ... 71

3. UNDERSTANDING HUMAN DESIRE ... 77
Successful entrepreneurs exhibit an intuitive understanding of how to satisfy their customers' most basic, often unexpressed desires.

GERRY HARVEY – Harvey Norman ... 81
CLAIR JENNIFER – Wombat ... 87
JURGEN KLEIN – Jurlique ... 93
PETER KAZACOS – KAZ ... 99

4. CREATING OUTSTANDING VALUE — 105
The entrepreneurs' first step to success is simply the recognition that they are not in business to sell products or services, but to create outstanding value – whatever it takes.

LEN POULTER – Lenards	115
PAUL ADLER AND BRAD BOND – Invizage	121
THERESE REIN – Ingeus	127
GRAEME BLACKMAN – IDT	133

5. BUILDING A REPLICABLE FACTORY — 140
Many entrepreneurs have achieved success simply by designing a formula to deliver what previously was only delivered in a customised manner.

GRAHAM TURNER – Flight Centre	147
JIM McDONALD – MDH Pastoral	153
JOE SARAGOSSI – G James Group	161

6. BECOMING A CAUSE HERO — 168
There is a direct connection between entrepreneurs choosing a cause about which they are passionate, and their ability to make their organisation and product famous as a logical solution to that cause.

RM WILLIAMS – RM Williams	175
CARL WOOD – Monash IVF	181
MAX BECK – Becton	187

INSPIRATION SUMMARY — 194

PART 2 – EDUCATION

7. BEYOND THE FUNDAMENTALS — 202
The fundamentals of business thinking such as efficiency, problem solving, analysis of information, and competition are no longer enough.

8. BEYOND INFORMATION TO CONCEPTS — 210
Technology and information have become commodities. What now matters are the application concepts.

How Dick Smith uses concepts	218
How Les Schirato uses concepts	220
How Len Poulter uses concepts	222

9. BEYOND COMPETITION TO SURPETITION — 225

Competition is necessary for survival. It is simply part of housekeeping and establishing the baseline. Surpetition is an attitude of mind, a strategy, and a matter of concept design.

How Paul Cave achieved surpetition	235
How Graeme Blackman achieved surpetition	237
How RM Williams achieved surpetition	238
How Max Beck achieved surpetition	241

10. BEYOND PRODUCT VALUES TO INTEGRATED VALUES — 243

Business has passed through the stage of product values to competitive values. The next stage is integrated values – values that integrate into the complex lifestyles of customers.

How Clair Jennifer integrates her value	251
How Carl Wood integrates his value	253
How Adrian Di Marco integrates his value	255
How Therese Rein integrates her value	257

11. BEYOND MAKING PRODUCTS TO MAKING VALUE — 260

Assembling the building blocks for a new or vastly improved business, product or service means designing a value bundle to attract the people who will be most affected.

How Peter Kazacos makes value	274
How Jurgen Klein makes value	275
How Euan Murdoch makes value	277

12. BEYOND BRAINSTORMING TO SERIOUS CREATIVITY — 280

Moving beyond ineffectual methods of encouraging creativity, such as the release of inhibitions and brainstorming, to specific creative techniques that enable everyone to be creative, even the conformists.

How Gerry Harvey is seriously creative	294
How Joe Saragossi is seriously creative	296
How Paul Adler and Brad Bond are seriously creative	298

13. BEYOND IDEAS TO CONCEPT DESIGN   301
Concepts may be designed around defined market needs or the organisation's asset base, or they may be extracted from ideas already in use.

How Graham Turner designs concepts	308
How Jim McDonald designs concepts	310
How Peter Farrell designs concepts	312

14. BEYOND TECHNICAL R&D TO CONCEPT R&D   315
In order to take concepts seriously, there is a need for a formal concept research and development function or group. The concept function is not adequately handled by conventional corporate strategy. Concept research and development should be treated every bit as seriously as we now treat technical research and development and all other significant functions.

SUMMARY   327

APPENDIX

SERIOUS CREATIVITY: SOME INTRODUCTORY LESSONS   334
1. Look for alternatives   335
2. Focus your thinking   338
3. Challenge existing ideas   340
4. Create ideas from random entry   343
5. Be deliberately provocative   345
6. Explore using concept fans   348
7. Harvest your thinking   350
8. Treat your ideas   352
Further information and training   354

INDEX   355

ABOUT THE AUTHORS

Mr John Lyons is an Independent Non-Executive Company Director with over two decades of experience in independent corporate governance. He is Chairman of Tamawood Limited and Softlink International Limited; Director of CreditLink Services Limited, O'Reilly's Rainforest Guesthouse, and Shahmann Farms; Trustee and board member of The Royal Children's Hospital Foundation, and Jupiters Casino Community Benefit Fund.

Lyons has learned business and entrepreneurship from the ground up. He founded and spent two decades as CEO and then Executive Chairman of Marketshare Pty Ltd, which grew to become a leading national strategic research and marketing company. In 2000 he sold Marketshare to a publicly listed data-warehousing and information technology company, dedicating himself to independent directorships.

Prior to founding Marketshare, Lyons had a distinguished eleven-year corporate career with global chemical company Bayer. In each of his first three years with the company he achieved recognition as Bayer's top Australian salesperson. Then as a national product manager and national marketing services manager he researched and launched some of Bayer's most successful products in the Australian market.

Lyons holds the degrees of Master of Business Administration from the University of Queensland, and Bachelor of Business from the University of Technology Sydney. He is an Associate of the Australian Society of CPAs and a Fellow of the Australian Institute of Company Directors. He is a former Queensland Chairman of the Australian Marketing Institute and of the Market Research Society of Australia. He has authored some 400 newspaper and journal columns on entrepreneurship and marketing, most recently for *The Australian Financial Review*.

**Dr Edward de Bono** is widely regarded as the world's leading authority in the field of creative and conceptual thinking, and the direct teaching of thinking as a skill. He has authored sixty-five books translated into thirty-five languages on the topic of thinking. His sessions, invariably sellouts, are sought after by business, government and education globally.

Edward de Bono was born in Malta and graduated from the University of Malta. He proceeded as a Rhodes Scholar to Oxford, where he earned his MD, and two PhDs. He has held faculty appointments at the University of Oxford, Cambridge, London and Harvard.

He is the originator of the term 'Lateral Thinking' which has an official entry in the Oxford English Dictionary, and the extremely popular 'Six Thinking Hats' concept. Peter Veberroth, who organised the Olympic Games in Los Angeles, and for the first time ever turned a profit, attributed his success to the use of De Bono's lateral thinking tools. So did John Bertrand, skipper of the successful Australian challenge for the America's Cup. There are four million references to Dr de Bono and his work on the internet.

His corporate clients include: IBM, DuPont, Prudential, Siemens, Electrolux, Shell, NTT, Motorola, Nokia, Ericsson, Ford, Microsoft, AT&T, and Saatchi and many more. The international Astronomical Union recently named a planet after Dr de Bono in recognition of his contribution to humanity. A group of South African University professors compiled a list of the 250 most influential people in the history of humanity and included Dr de Bono. At an International Thinking Conference in Boston, Dr de Bono was given an award as a pioneer in the field of 'teaching thinking'.

ACKNOWLEDGEMENTS

Sincere thanks.

Despite having authored more than 400 newspaper columns as a hobby, this is my first book, and I am indeed honoured to have Edward de Bono as my co-author. Since I first met Edward more than a decade ago, his world-leading and seminal work in conceptual creative thinking has been an inspiration, providing valuable new insights into the true drivers of business success.

I am indebted to the generosity and support of so many people. My wife Jocelyn, and our daughters Julia, Sophie and Lucy, my extended family and many friends and business colleagues, sometimes unwittingly, have helped shape the thoughts of a passionate marketing mind, still discovering its way forward after more than thirty-five years of concentrated business experience and learning.

Edward de Bono and I are deeply indebted to the entrepreneurs whose remarkable intellectual and experiential insights we have endeavoured to reflect and interpret in this book. With their extraordinary generosity and input, we believe this book serves as a true inspiration and education for its readers.

We sincerely thank our major corporate sponsor St. George Bank, and other generous supporters of *Marketing without Money*. You have made possible the much wider distribution of this important knowledge to many individuals and companies, to the ultimate benefit of Australian business success as a whole.

To Bev Friend and Allan Cornwell of Pennon Publishing, to our editorial assistant Stephen Phillips of Jarvis Moon, and to the Australian media who have been so supportive of this work, especially *The Australian Financial Review*, Edward de Bono and I are deeply grateful for your support and confidence.

John C Lyons

FOREWORD
from Dick Smith

Dear Reader

I think success in my life has come from copying the success of others. That has meant asking advice, looking at what other companies and countries do and then following the best. In the electronics business I would travel the world learning and copying from the best of my competitors, because each had evolved into doing certain things a better way. While each company was generally about as efficient as the other, each had developed particular ways which were superior. For example, one had a very good mail-order system, so I copied that. Another had the best catalogue, so I copied that. I continually copied the best concepts and ideas and brought them together under one roof. I have made every mistake you can make but I remember and have learned from every one of them.

I had no idea that Dick Smith Electronics would ever be any bigger than just one shop. I had no plans for that because it was beyond my comprehension. I actually had quite an inferiority complex because I had always loved electronics but all my friends had gone off to university and I was simply a radio repairman. I started selling electronics in a modern way, and expanded it to around fifty shops. At that point I realised it was getting too big and difficult to run. I rang Woolworths and they bought it for $25 million. Very simple.

With Dick Smith Foods, I could see the country is being sold off and everyone is concerned about it, so I decided to take advantage of that. You satisfy people's concerns and you do something worthwhile at the same time. That makes you feel good. If I wanted to make money, I would stick to electronics where you can make a fortune. You certainly wouldn't be going into food where the margins are so low. I am an adventurer; I love having challenges and tilting at windmills.

Marketing without Money

Since I started the Variety Club Bash in Australia, Variety has raised over $70 million in seventeen years to help kids. I had to find a way to get wealthy people to part with their money because if you simply phoned them up and asked for a donation, they would say no. Also, I'd always wanted to go in the equivalent of a Redex trial following the trail of Gelignite Jack Murray, and I knew a lot of other blokes did too. So I thought how can I get people to come with me on a car trial. Then I thought of the idea of allowing adults to generally behave and cheat like kids. They had two alternatives, either drive fast to win or bribe the judges by writing a big cheque for charity.

When I went into business, I had little money – only $610. No one would lend me any money, but it taught me some wonderful disciplines. The difference between success and failure is a razor's edge in just about everything. Even though a company can make huge profits, you can turn it to losses very easily.

In *Marketing without Money*, John Lyons and Edward de Bono have captured the real-world experience and learnings of twenty of Australia's top entrepreneurs – essentially how they successfully entered markets without money. They have aggregated, then distilled this knowledge to its essence, and have packaged it so that others may follow. This is vital practical knowledge for people who want to create their own future and the future of Australia, not be driven to it by others.

Dick Smith

FOREWORD

From Gail Kelly, Managing Director,
St.George Bank

It takes a great deal of courage and a lot of hard work to become a successful entrepreneur. The insight this book provides into how others overcame their fears and used their creativity and determination to achieve their vision is invaluable.

I've always believed that listening to other people's experiences is one of the most powerful ways of gaining knowledge. Knowledge that can then be applied directly or indirectly to any business situation. That is why *Marketing Without Money* is such an important book. It allows us to experience first-hand the strategies and tactics that have worked for those who have been successful in their chosen field.

One of the key themes of the book is creativity and the importance of using innovative ideas to achieve goals and overcome problems. It is an approach that I wholeheartedly support and a philosophy adopted by St.George. We are constantly seeking ways to strengthen our partnerships with our business customers by giving them new tools to increase their chances of success.

That is why we are pleased to be associated with this book and ensuring that the insights it contains are shared across the business community. As the authors say: 'The first step to success is simply to recognise that you are not in the business to provide products and services, but to create value' (p105).

The contribution of small businesses, and the entrepreneurs who run them, to Australia's economy should never be underestimated. The people and companies in this book are familiar to all of us. As you read their stories, you'll find common themes such as a passion to succeed, a determination to overcome obstacles and the creativity to see opportunities others would miss.

The values and principles outlined in the book are an integral part of the St.George culture. We recognise the importance of listening to our customers and of thinking outside the square to provide solutions to help their businesses grow.

I'm a great believer in establishing a long-term relationship with customers, becoming a part of their business and sharing their goals and dreams. By adopting this partnership role, I believe we add value over and above that which is expected.

St.George is delighted to have the opportunity to be involved in *Marketing Without Money*, which I believe will contribute significantly to promoting the entrepreneurial spirit in Australia.

Gail Kelly

PRELUDE

There is no single, simple formula for success. Winners are constantly rewriting the rules and redefining what it means to play the game. Yet successful entrepreneurs share some defining common traits and behaviours.

'BUSINESS MUST BE RUN AT A PROFIT, ELSE IT WILL DIE. BUT IF YOU RUN A BUSINESS SOLELY FOR PROFIT, THEN ALSO IT MUST DIE, FOR IT NO LONGER HAS A REASON TO LIVE.' — Henry Ford
Successful entrepreneurs pursue an elevated cause that customers, staff and stakeholders truly believe in. A cause much sweeter than the pursuit of profit itself.

....

'THINK DIFFERENTLY AND BE DIFFERENT, EVEN WHEN YOU'RE SUCCESSFUL.'
— Les Schirato
Successful entrepreneurs are always looking for alternatives, deliberate pattern-breaking thinking that is forever seeking the unexpected move.

....

'SUCCESS IS BUILT ON TRUST. QUALITY, THAT'S A MATTER OF HONESTY WITH YOUR CUSTOMERS.' — RM Williams
Because successful entrepreneurs intuitively understand basic human desires, they are constantly inventing new and outstanding value.

....

'HAVING A BUSINESS MODEL THAT'S REPLICABLE IS IMPORTANT, BUT I SUPPOSE THAT'S JUST COMMON SENSE.' — Graham Turner
Successful entrepreneurs establish a system for their business that can be easily replicated and improved.

....

'BUILDING A REPUTATION FOR QUALITY IS VITAL. BUT YOU HAVE TO DO MORE THAN JUST SAY IT.' — Max Beck
Successful entrepreneurs build and nurture their fame and reputation for delivering outstanding value.

INTRODUCTION

'The significant problems we face cannot be solved at the same level of thinking we were at when we created them.' – Albert Einstein

'The difference between brilliant and mediocre thinking lies not so much in our mental equipment as in how well we use it.'
— Edward de Bono

In this book we reveal how twenty of Australia's finest contemporary entrepreneurs have managed to crack new markets, with little or no initial financial backing, stealing a march under the very gaze of supremely better-resourced and well-entrenched opposition.

We show how, by intuitively applying *conceptual creativity*, these entrepreneurs discover and implement new *business, product and service concepts* which remove them from the competitive rat race, and which create a new race in which they can lead.

We demonstrate that, while most business people are constrained by patterns of thinking to conformity with industry norms and practices, highly successful entrepreneurs deliberately challenge such convention, doggedly discovering and pioneering new concepts that previously either had not been considered or were regarded as unpromising.

We lift the veil on what may appear to be masterstrokes of entrepreneurial brilliance and even extraordinarily good luck, to reveal and illuminate a replicable trail of opportunity recognition, creative conceptual thinking and thorough implementation which others can follow. We expose entrepreneurial solutions which, though perfectly logical in hindsight, eluded the then conventional business thinking of the day governed largely by analysis and logic.

Marketing redefined

We define marketing quite simply as *'creating outstanding value and being famous for it'*. In our view, business and marketing are one and the same. In business, we create profits by creating value for others which exceeds the price they are prepared to pay in exchange for that value. If the value produced is outstanding, then – all other things being commensurate, especially the cost of producing that value – profit will be outstanding.

Much conventional marketing is focussed on selling what the organisation has chosen to produce. Indeed, many so-called marketing departments are effectively promotion and sales departments. Others deal primarily with advertising and communication management. Without devaluing the importance of those activities, it can be said that marketing is too important and all-encompassing to an organisation's success to be left purely to the marketing department.

If one accepts the simple definition that marketing is creating outstanding value and being famous for it, then an organisation's chief executive is its chief marketing officer, and the board is responsible for setting marketing direction and policy. Without that focus by leadership, the remainder of the organisation can hardly be expected to be focussed on the creation and communication of outstanding value at the coalface.

Marketing aligned with shareholder value

Perfectly aligned with the purpose of good marketing is the ultimate purpose of good business – to create outstanding value for shareholders. An outstanding return to shareholders rests on the creation of outstanding value for customers; value for which customers are prepared to pay an appropriate premium, not simply a commodity price. So the creation of outstanding value for customers drives the delivery of outstanding value to shareholders.

There are two ways to increase the gap between revenue and cost. You can increase the revenue per unit produced and/or decrease the cost of producing each unit. A major part of what we include in the cost of production is the cost of marketing. Hence the concept of *Marketing without Money* is designed to underscore the necessity to penetrate and serve markets as inexpensively and efficiently as possible and to maintain that penetration, and to grow it, at a lower than industry-average cost.

Learning from Australian entrepreneurs

A core skill of successful entrepreneurs is to enter markets against entrenched competition, without the resources usually already available to that competition, and to build and sustain profitable market share.

Frequently, entrenched competitors create even higher barriers to entry when they sense that a new entrant may possibly erode long-term industry profitability if allowed to get a market foothold. So, for many entrepreneurial entrants, the barriers to entry are raised even higher in the short term in order to restrict their entry to the game.

The skill of marketing without money is an imperative not only for entrepreneurial organisations, but also for established, better heeled competitors who want to improve their market position and profitability simultaneously and rapidly.

Our goal is to make that skill as simple and clear for others to acquire. In essence, we seek to equip you with the thinking processes and tools that will lead you to great success in business, mirroring the remarkable achievements of some of Australia's most successful entrepreneurs.

The competition mind trap

We show that the notion of competition is a dangerous and seductive trap which limits and restricts business thinking. Anyone involved in running a business needs to move beyond competition.

We all know about the global marketplace and that in order to survive you must be competitive. You must be able to compete. If you cannot compete, you do not survive. So what is wrong with competition?

The paradox is that you cannot truly be competitive if you seek to be competitive. The key word here is 'survive'. It is of course perfectly true that you must be competitive in order to survive. Giant retailers like Sears have to cut their costs considerably to be able to survive against other retailers such as Wal-Mart with its advanced computer systems and higher sales per square metre. If your costs and values are out of line, you may cease to survive.

But any organisation that plans just to survive will sooner or later find itself out of business. Only those organisations that plan for success will survive, while those that plan only to survive will fail. Water is necessary for soup – but soup has to be more than water. So competition is important as part of the 'baseline' for survival.

In the same way there are many things that are necessary, but not sufficient, for business to survive (for example, cost control, quality control, etc.), just like water for soup. Competition is one of the things that are necessary for business to survive, but it is not sufficient. A serious mistake that many executives make is to believe that competition is the key to success.

Surpetition

We show how sustained entrepreneurial success demands going beyond competition to 'surpetition'.

The word 'competition' comes from the Latin and means 'seeking together'. It means choosing to run in the same race as your competitors. The word 'surpetition' means 'seeking above'. Instead of choosing to run in the same race, you choose to create a new race – one in which you can lead, rather than be a 'me-too' follower and competitor.

There is serious overcapacity in car production in many countries. At one time Edward de Bono suggested to Ford in the United Kingdom that it should buy a British company called NCP (National Car Parks) which owned most of the car parks in city centres throughout the UK. If NCP became a Ford company, a notice could be placed at the entrance to all city-centre car parks indicating that only Ford cars could use them.

A car is no longer just a lump of engineering. If your neighbour boasts that his lump of engineering is better than your lump of engineering, you could point out that you can park in the city, and he cannot. The ability to park is very much part of the 'integrated value' of a car if you have to drive in a city. So is the ability to resell a car, have it serviced, and have it insured.

Ford did not take up the idea of buying NCP. They said that as an engineering company it was not their business to buy up car parks. In the future, some entrepreneurs probably will buy up or build car parks and then get the Koreans to make private-label cars for them. They will sell, park, insure and resell cars. Manufacturing will only be a service to this profit centre, and the manufacturing margins will be squeezed.

As everyone knows, the classic competitive response to oversupply, for example in cars, is to slash prices and offer rebates. Surprisingly, competitors do the same. You may succeed in shifting sales forward in time, but then buyers get used to rebates and wait for them before buying again.

The suggestion that Ford should have bought up city-centre car parks is an example of surpetition.

Surpetition is about creating 'value monopolies' – monopolising the value you have created in the new race. Some ways of achieving a monopoly are illegal, but value monopolies are not. For survival, you need competition, but for success you need surpetition and the creation of value monopolies.

Integrated values

How do you create value monopolies? Value monopolies are driven by concepts, and concepts are in turn driven by serious creativity.

In order to understand value monopolies you must realise that there have been three phases in business.

1. The first phase was simply based on making available a product or service. It was production driven.
2. The second phase was based on competition, because a lot of people were now providing the same goods and services.
3. The third phase, which we are now just entering, is based on integrated values. No longer do we live in a world of simple values where a car is just a piece of engineering.

A good example of integrated values was created by Ron Barbaro, at one time head of the Prudential Insurance Company in Canada. Using lateral thinking techniques, he came up with the idea of 'living benefits'. This was a significant change in the very traditional business of life insurance, which had been unchanged for decades. With traditional life insurance, the benefits are paid out after your death to your family or other beneficiaries. Ron Barbaro's concept was to have seventy-five per cent of the benefits paid out immediately if a policy holder was diagnosed as having a potentially fatal illness such as cancer or AIDS.

This meant that the money was now available for extra care or medical attention. The concept was immensely successful, and was one of the reasons Ron Barbaro was soon promoted to the head of Prudential in the United States.

This is an excellent example of integrated values because it integrates life insurance into the lives and values of people. There are single people, people who divorce and split up, children who grow up and become self-supporting, and many others. For some of them, many of the original purposes of life insurance are gone. At the same time there are factors like AIDS and the expense of medical care that create new purposes.

Concepts and creativity

Barbaro created a simple concept change. Life insurance is traditionally seen as related to death; his concept emphasised life, and he had the courage and drive to see the concept through.

Generally speaking, many managers are not particularly happy when working with abstracts such as concepts. There is an impatience with concepts and an urgent desire to be given 'hands-on' tools. Many want to be doing rather than thinking.

This is not surprising. For a long time countries such as Australia and the United States were pioneering societies, and in such societies action is indeed more rewarding than thinking: you need to clear a few more acres for grazing, drill a few more wells, open a few more stores, and so on.

Today however, the world is more crowded. Unthinking action is not going to be rewarded. On the other hand, a concept change may be rewarded very handsomely. A new concept is unquestionably the best and cheapest way of getting added value out of existing resources.

Concept research and development

Up to now, however, our approach to concept development has been haphazard. There has been the 'me-too' approach in which we wait for someone else to develop the concept, and then we jump in with a similar copy of it. In addition, we have assumed that as intelligent, able people we will come up with needed concepts when necessary. This attitude to concepts is not good enough today.

In the future we are going to have to take concepts so seriously that we will be setting up specific concept research and development groups or departments for the intellectual engineering that needs to take place. Car manufacturers and chemical companies, for example, spend billions of dollars each year on technical research and development. Today however, concepts are even more important than technology, and we shall have to take their development very seriously indeed.

Business schools have always taught students about how to analyse information and how to make decisions. Today this is totally inadequate. The analysis of information and decision-making are part of the maintenance aspect of management, part of the water in the soup. The emphasis must now shift to conceptual thinking, not instead of information analysis and decision-making, but in addition to them. What concepts are going to be derived from information analysis? By itself the analysis of information can never yield the concepts that are hidden in the information. What alternatives are available for decision-making? Analysis can only yield some of the alternatives; the rest must be produced by creative conceptual thinking.

Unfortunately, the approach to creativity has been very weak. There is the mistaken notion that we are all basically creative, and it is only necessary to remove our inhibitions and fears of being ridiculous in order to release that innate creativity.

We now know from the behaviour of self-organising information systems (like human perception) what we need to do. We know that the brain is not designed to be creative and that in order to be creative we have to use some methods that are not 'natural'. We must begin to develop systematic methods of serious creativity. We will be discussing these later, particularly their relevance to concept development.

Valufacture

Concepts are about value. Surpetition is also about value. The future success of any business is going to be all about value.

It is strange that although we deal so much with values, we do not have a specific word to describe the creation and formation of values. There is convenience in having such a word because it allows us to look at things in a different way and to devote much more effort to the specific creation of values. More than a decade ago, Edward de Bono created the word 'valufacture', defined as 'the creation and formation of values'. There is an analogy with 'manufacture', which has to do with the creation and production of objects.

The age of contraction

Many people in business feel that we have entered the age of contraction. There have been two recent ages of expansion. The first age of expansion was driven by traditional marketing. Traditional marketing was going to create needs and open up markets. Marketing was the main competitive tool for taking market share from others. The second age of expansion was driven by 'gobble growth'. You gobbled up other organisations in order to increase market share. During this period there were all sorts of rationalisations about market synergies and critical survival size (often provided by investment bankers who liked the large fees involved).

In many respects, these two ages of expansion have now passed. The present mood is for consolidation. Acquisitions have to be digested. Corporate executives are looking inward. There is cost-cutting and slimming. There is laying-off of people. There is divestment of unprofitable businesses everywhere.

As part of this looking-inward, there is an emphasis on cost cutting and cost control. There is an emphasis on quality management. All these things are important and necessary but they are not enough. You take aspirin when you have a headache, but you cannot survive on a steady diet of aspirin.

Figure I.1 shows that if you fall below the baseline of competition, you need to get back to that baseline. But just being on the baseline is not enough. You have to do better than that.

The purpose of consolidation, contraction, quality and all the rest is to provide a firm baseline for venture. In the end you have to provide values that customers want. Having the best quality product at the lowest price is no good if that product does not offer significant value.

There is serious danger that the current emphasis on what we would call 'housekeeping' may divert attention from the very essence of business, which is to provide outstanding value.

The essence of business can be summed up in the following four 'C' words:

MARKETING WITHOUT MONEY

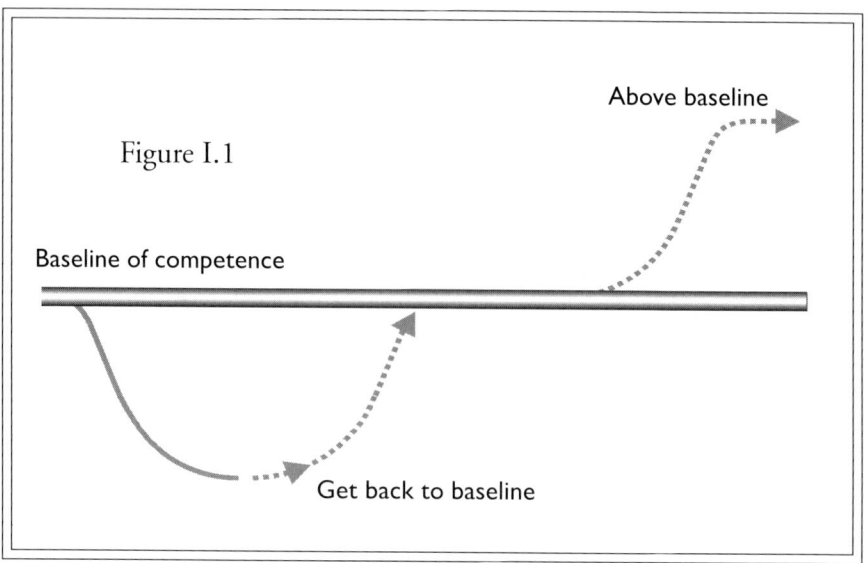

Figure I.1

- *Competence*: the quality, efficiency, effectiveness and accomplishment of what you are supposed to be doing.

- *Control*: the cost control, strategy, and knowledge of what is going on.

- *Care*: care for the customer, for the workforce, which is ultimately your most precious resource, and for the community (for example, environmental concerns).

- *Creativity*: the soul of the business. Without creativity you have a body with no soul. Creativity provides the value that is the whole purpose of any business.

So the overall message is that creative conceptual thinking is going to become ever more important. Every successful organisation is going to have a three-part strategy:

1. Get the housekeeping right.

2. Develop the concepts for surpetition.

3. Have an energetic follow-through.

FORMAT OF THE BOOK

THIS BOOK IS DIVIDED INTO TWO PARTS: INSPIRATION AND EDUCATION.

Part 1 – Inspiration

A look at the fundamental thought processes, behaviours and experiential learnings of twenty of Australia's most outstanding contemporary entrepreneurs. Most of these people were selected for inclusion in this book based on an independent assessment by a panel of experienced judges who chose them as finalists and/or winners of The Australian Entrepreneur of the Year Awards. These annual awards are sponsored by Ernst & Young in Australia and several overseas countries. The judging panel had access to the full financial history and other performance measures of the entrepreneurs' organisations, and hence was in a position to be rigorous in its evaluation process.

Each chapter of Part 1 is dedicated to a particular skill common to most of the entrepreneurs, and includes our selection of some excellent examples of that skill, very often quite intuitively rather than consciously applied.

Chapter 1 – Marketing without money is inspired by the skill of our researched entrepreneurs to develop and persist with concepts which frequently enable them to create a new race in which they can lead – *to build markets from nothing*. Paul Cave (BridgeClimb), Les Schirato (Cantarella Bros), and Adrian Di Marco (Technology One) are outstanding examples of creative conceptual thinking being applied to leverage modest resources.

Chapter 2 – Rebels for a cause shows how entrepreneurs engage public sentiment to their commercial advantage by *elevating the cause* for which they are fighting on behalf of the customer. Dick Smith, Euan Murdoch (Herron) and Peter Farrell (ResMed) are outstanding examples of this skill.

Chapter 3 – Understanding human desire examines how entrepreneurs think beyond the 'expressed' needs of customers and staff, creating concepts that respond to *higher order different needs*. Gerry Harvey (Harvey Norman), Clair Jennifer (Wombat), Jurgen Klein (Jurlique) and Peter Kazacos (KAZ) are excellent examples of this skill.

Chapter 4 – Creating outstanding value shows how successful entrepreneurs *'make'* outstanding value, going *beyond* the constraints of competition to create a new race in which they can lead. Len Poulter (Lenard's), Paul Adler and Brad Bond (Invizage), Therese Rein (Ingeus) and Graeme Blackman (IDT) are among the leading exponents of this skill.

Chapter 5 – Building a replicable factory shows how some entrepreneurs create new value just by refining and *making replicable* previously customised ways of producing value. Graham Turner (Flight Centre), Jim McDonald (MDH) and Joe Saragossi (G James Group) well exemplify this skill.

Chapter 6 – Becoming a cause hero shows how entrepreneurs who create a new race become the *acknowledged authority* or hero for their elevated *cause* using this position as a powerful communication tool for brand building. RM Williams, Carl Wood (Monash IVF) and Max Beck (Becton) are good examples of this entrepreneurial skill.

Part 2 – Education

Without exception, our researched entrepreneurs have moved beyond competition to surpetition. They have broken free from the shackles of conventional industry concepts and practice. Albeit *informally and intuitively*, they have applied creative conceptual thinking to *develop highly successful new concepts* which achieve a purpose and deliver value. With experience, they continue to refine and improve those concepts and create even stronger value monopolies. Challenging and continually changing the status quo, even that which they have created, has become a life-long habit.

This section, based substantially on the research and creative conceptual thinking principles developed by Edward de Bono, shows how you can follow in the thinking footsteps of Australia's leading entrepreneurs. It plots a course to take you *beyond* where general business focus and thinking is now *to* the new level of thinking you need to achieve surpetition. Each chapter explains an important step or thinking transition in this process. Further, we show how each of our researched entrepreneurs has in effect applied such thinking. Once the principles of concept research and development are understood and learned, achieving surpetition becomes a replicable process, rather than random.

Chapter 7 – Beyond the fundamentals looks at some of the most fundamental habits of management thinking – efficiency, problem-solving, maintenance, and error-avoidance – and shows why even these fundamental habits need rethinking.

Chapter 8 – Beyond information to concepts shows how technology is becoming a commodity. What now matters are the application concepts. Concepts are every bit as important as finance, raw materials, labour and energy. It is not enough to rely on 'me-too' copying or the haphazard use of creative intelligence. We need to take concepts very seriously. Concepts are the basis of surpetition.

Chapter 9 – Beyond competition to surpetition shows how surpetition will be the basis of success in the future, and how to go beyond competition to surpetition. Competition is necessary for survival. It is simply part of housekeeping and establishing the baseline. Surpetition is an attitude of mind and a matter of concept design.

Chapter 10 – Beyond product values to integrated values shows how the value you offer must be integrated into the complex life values of the buyer or consumer. Business has passed through the stage of product values to competitive values. The next stage is integrated values.

Chapter 11 – Beyond making products to making value shows how to assemble the building blocks for a new or vastly improved business, product or service by bundling a set of values designed to attract the people who will be most affected. We use four fundamental drivers of value as those building blocks.

Chapter 12 – Beyond brainstorming to serious creativity shows how, in any self-organising system, like human perception, there is an absolute mathematical need for creativity. We move beyond ineffectual methods of encouraging creativity, such as the release of inhibitions and brainstorming. We show specific creative techniques that enable everyone to be creative, even the conformists.

Chapter 13 – Beyond ideas to concept design shows how surpetition is achieved through integrated values, serious creativity, and concept design. Concepts may be designed around defined market needs or the organisation's asset base, or they may be extracted from ideas already in use.

Chapter 14 – Beyond technical R&D to concept R&D shows that, in order to take concepts seriously, there is a need for a formal concept research and development function or group. The concept function is not adequately handled by conventional corporate strategy. Concept research and development should be treated every bit as seriously as we now treat technical research and development and all other significant functions.

PART 1
Inspiration

Chapter 1
MARKETING WITHOUT MONEY

Like an ambitious child from a humble background, starved of the leg-up that a wealthier family might have provided, entrepreneurs' initial shortage of resources is almost certainly their most salutary and valuable lesson in developing the very skills that make them succeed. If they are to realise their ambitions, *they must use creative brainpower and guerilla cunning as a direct substitute for money.*

Most successful entrepreneurs build something substantial and sustainable from nothing, using creative conceptual thinking and courage as their main resources. Their challenge is dramatically different from the business-school-trained professional manager who enters and leaves somewhere in the continuum of an organisation's life, picking up the reins, husbanding and hopefully growing others' wealth, before moving on. Successful entrepreneurs punt their own money, and there usually is never enough to go around. Borrowing substantial money early is typically out of the question. Traditional lenders have safer pickings to pursue. Without money these entrepeneurs drive a wedge into the jealously guarded market domains of usually well-established and supremely better-resourced competitors.

They begin with no reputation or brand, and no money to build it quickly in textbook fashion. They have to win the trust and respect of potential customers who seem to have many safer choices. *Frequently they are effective in altering the criteria for selection, because they could not win otherwise.*

Prospective staff see them as an interesting though risky choice for employment, but enough are swept up by the passion and enrolled in the mission.

While words of encouragement abound from those whose commitment the entrepreneurs believe they need most, conventional sources of financial support and distribution, available to established players, are usually denied them. *Inevitably though, necessity becomes the mother of creative invention.*

The mind of the business-school-trained professional manager has been programmed to follow a pattern of thinking for which the inputs are typically situation analysis, scenario development, business case and resource allocation – a thinking pattern driven by logic and rational competitive assumptions. *By comparison, the successful entrepreneurial mind is driven by the moment, accustomed to practising deliberate pattern-breaking thinking, ever searching for the overlooked opportunity, and for concepts that might enable it to be exploited.*

Their success in marketing without money is rooted in five habits in particular:

- *Rebels for a cause* – A persistent focus on *identifying an emerging cause that will engage the customer's mind*.

- *Understanding human desire* – A persistent focus on *understanding the most basic human desires* that underpin what people will value.

- *Creating outstanding value* – A persistent focus on *creating concepts that deliver outstanding value* to satisfy future needs, not just today's.

- *Building a replicable factory* – A persistent focus on designing *systems and processes to deliver their value consistently*.

- *Becoming a cause hero* – A persistent focus on *making their company and their product the cause hero*.

Each of these habits is previewed below, and is dealt with in detail and illustrated in the following five chapters of Part 1 – Inspiration. Then in

Part 2 – Education, we show how these habits can be refined, learned and duplicated by others in the form of concept research and development.

Rebels for a cause

Being much the same as others in any walk of life is a good way to blend in and not be noticed, not a good way to build a brand. Successful entrepreneurs go out of their way, some intuitively and some deliberately, to be provocatively different, to create an individual personality for their business. Their philosophies and statements, their value propositions to customers and staff, their product and service offerings and their delivery processes are designed to make people stop in their tracks, think, and frequently change direction.

In Chapter 2 we show how entrepreneurs typically pursue a cause that *customers* truly believe in. They get the customer's attention without even asking for it.

Today, most Australians have adopted the retention of Australian-owned companies' profits and jobs as a national value and responsibility. The provocations of entrepreneurs like Dick Smith (most recently with Dick Smith Foods) and Euan Murdoch (founder of Herron Pharmaceuticals) have capitalised on and served to heighten awareness of and interest in this cause. Peter Farrell (ResMed) and his advisory board of high-profile medical practitioners have done much to raise consumer and professional awareness of the significance of sleep in a healthy lifestyle.

Understanding basic human desire

Customers are only human. They are driven by a primal quest to satisfy their most basic desires and needs. Chapter 3 introduces the foundations of what drives human desire and explores the different levels of desire, preparing you for later chapters that examine how value is created.

Successful entrepreneurs actively look for the unexpressed desires of customers. *They are focussed on what people will discover they need tomorrow,* seldom on today's expressed needs that define the current rules of competition. To rely on today's expressed needs is to be locked in to being a 'me-too' competitor, to be relegated to 'n'th place behind entrenched participants.

Instead these entrepreneurs understand that *customers can't tell you what they want until they know what is possible. If you ask customers what they want, basically they will only tell you what they already have.*

Creating outstanding value

Successful entrepreneurs recognise early that they are not in business to sell products or services, but to create outstanding value by integrating what they offer into the basic desires of customers and other stakeholders.

Chapter 4 shows how typically they assemble the building blocks for a new or vastly improved bundle of values designed to attract the people who will be most affected. Sometimes, they do not change the intrinsic value offering, but concentrate on how to radically improve the efficiency and cost with which it is delivered.

Finding integrated values is somewhat similar to looking at the spaces in a painting. You look at the customer and the relationship (or space) surrounding that customer. The customer is already integrated into the world. With integrated values we seek to integrate into existing values, taking us beyond traditional product and competitive values.

Building a replicable factory

The road to ruin is paved with entrepreneurs who discovered the value, made it famous, but then failed to deliver it well or profitably.

Chapter 5 explores how successful entrepreneurs, almost without exception, have narrowed the focus and simplified the demands of replicable delivery with systems that guide and support ordinary people in the delivery of extraordinary outcomes.

Achieving a hero reputation

Chapter 6 shows the creativity of successful entrepreneurs in harnessing opportunities to attach their products to meaningful emerging causes. This has not only guided their value creation, but also has led in many instances to millions of dollars worth of credible media publicity for their products and the causes.

Meanwhile, most entrenched players in the food and pharmaceutical industries, for example, continue to play the conventional public relations game of product-focussed press releases and publicity stunts, and wonder why they are relegated to back-seat coverage with little community word of mouth. They have not created or furthered a cause. They have not integrated themselves into what is more fundamentally important to the customer.

Cave, Schirato and Di Marco

Paul Cave (BridgeClimb), Les Schirato (Cantarella Bros) and Adrian Di Marco (Technology One), whose stories follow in this chapter, are good examples of the habits that lead to extraordinary success in marketing without money. Their seeming diversity of approach and execution of such habits, and those of the remaining seventeen researched entrepreneurs, should not be allowed to mask the definite commonalities they all share.

Paul Cave

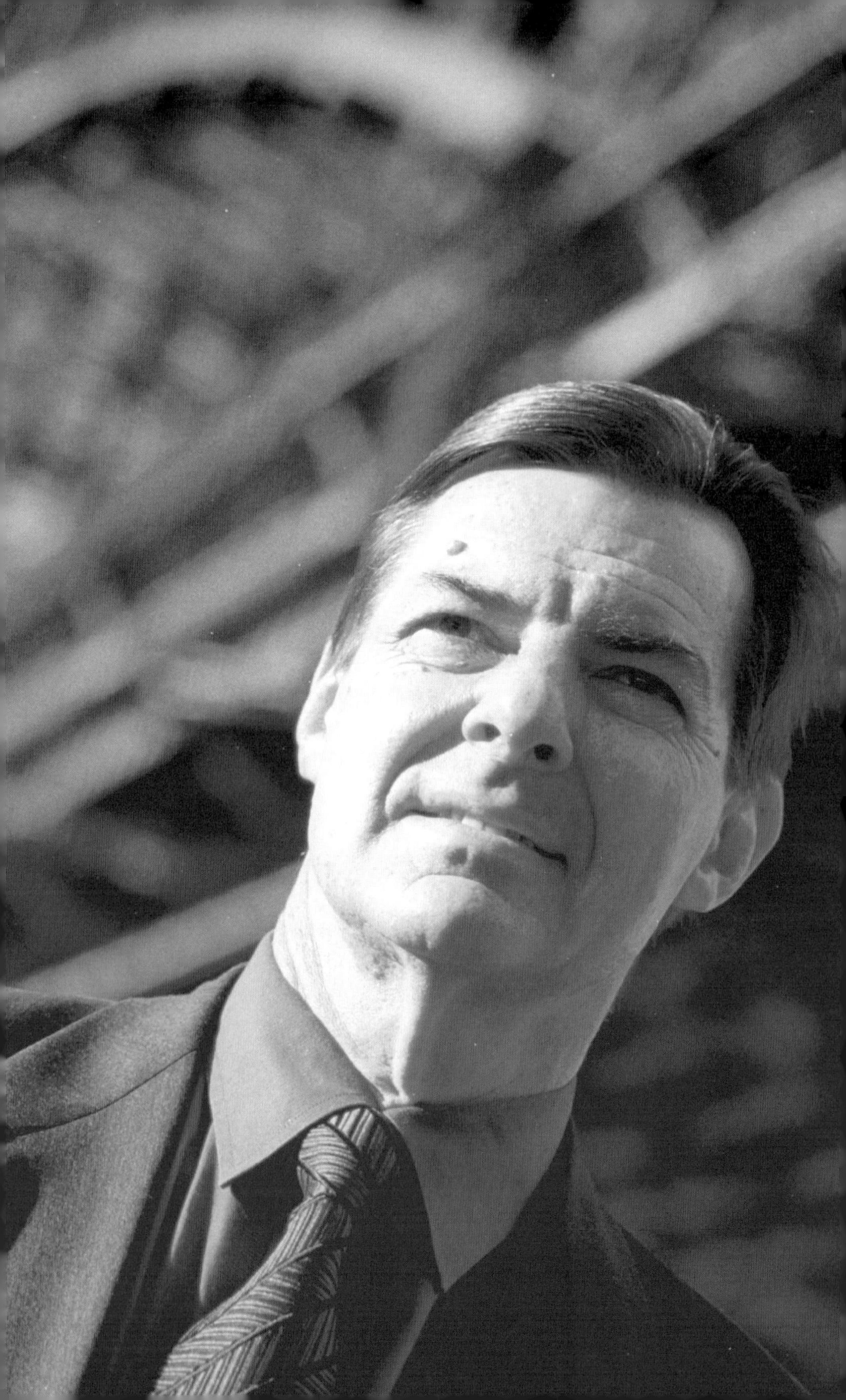

PAUL CAVE

Our job is to enable our customers to make heroes of themselves

Using creative thought and determination, Paul Cave, founder and chairman of BridgeClimb, has created a $50 million dollar business in just a few years, effectively monopolising an internationally famous Australian icon brand he doesn't own, capitalising on huge advertising he doesn't pay for, and sending a personally delivered word-of-mouth recommendation through one million customer heroes to arguably 100 million prospects around the world. And this is just the beginning.

When Paul Cave made no less than fifty-two presentations in the late 1990s in an attempt to raise $12 million to fund a business that would enable millions of people to climb the Sydney Harbour Bridge, the predominantly merchant banking targets thought it was a fascinating opportunity, but not for their money. In the end, it was another entrepreneur, Brett Blundy, who Cave says 'put money into this within sixty seconds of my telling him about it and became my first major shareholder'. Analytical minds struggle where there is no precedent to rely upon. Clearly Blundy, like Cave, searches for opportunities where there is no precedent.

Just three years after BridgeClimb opened the Bridge to climbers, Cave says the business is climbing 300 000 people per annum (two-thirds of them international visitors) and achieving a turnover of $50 million. He talks privately of a bottom line that would make Warren Buffet green with envy. Since commencement, the company has distributed over one million dollars in special thank-you bonuses to its 280 staff.

Cave isn't really surprised at the success of BridgeClimb. Since he first conceived the idea about a decade ago while on a bridge climb with his YPO (Young Presidents Organisation) forum, he was forced to take plenty of time to think the concept through.

Marketing without Money

As an entrepreneur, you couldn't have found anything more frustrating

'As an entrepreneur, you couldn't have found anything [the barriers] more frustrating. The first letter from the government gave basically sixty-four reasons why not', he says. Having been on the receiving end of so many 'No' answers has made Cave decidedly a 'Yes' man. Having now made it possible for blind and deaf people to make the climb, the next challenge to be overcome is to climb people in wheelchairs, and he is confident of success.

Fortunately, Paul Cave's analytical economics background has not masked his creative marketing ability – not only to sense a basic business opportunity that has been staring Australians in the face since 1932, but also to see beyond the simple climb to the higher order monopolisable value that is already generating extraordinary wealth for the company. BridgeClimb's projection, that it will pay an estimated $130 million to the Roads and Traffic Authority of New South Wales over twenty years for exclusive tourism rights to arguably Australia's most internationally-recognised built icon, pales into insignificance when one considers the real value of the asset 'leased'.

While the Harbour Bridge itself is perhaps worth a billion dollars as a structure, its value as an established international brand and icon is far greater, probably in the order of tens of billions. The brand is being built further and maintained by word of mouth and advertising in an extraordinary manner. Being a world-first consumerised bridge-climbing experience means of course powerful first-mover advantage. But being on an already world-famous bridge in the centre of Australia's largest and most visited tourist city is another monopoly.

But that's by no means all says Cave:

'The Australian Tourist Commission has spent some $20-30 million showing commercials featuring BridgeClimb to the rest of the world to bring people here. Eleven hundred journalists climbed the Bridge during the 2000 Olympic Games and the publicity they generated could have reached an estimated 2.5 billion people worldwide. That advertising and publicity has come to us at no cost.'

Every climber, every time, and there is no exception to that

The way Cave has harnessed so far more than a million climbers as compelling promoters of his company's message further exemplifies the man's intuitive ability to market without money through customer word of mouth. The value delivery system – company culture, defined procedures, staff training, climber preparation, climber satisfaction measures, etc. – is designed to delight the customer as Cave puts it 'EVERY CLIMBER, EVERY TIME, AND THERE IS NO EXCEPTION TO THAT'. Climbing, now permitted twenty-four hours a day seven days per week, happens as often as every ten minutes whether it its hot, cold, raining or foggy, and the customer ratings (excellent plus good) average more than ninety-nine per cent in all conditions.

Price is not an issue, but providing extraordinary value is, Cave insists. The average price per person is $145 and a further $30 is spent on merchandise. He admits that the value people ascribe to the 'Climb of Your Life' experience is a voyage of discovery for him. Once discovered, however, his mind pursues the value like a dog with a bone. For example, 400 (known) proposals of marriage have been made on BridgeClimb, with only one rejection. A technique has been devised so that the ring can be passed safely and securely down a piece of cord to seal the acceptance. Integrated value indeed!

The advice that Paul Cave offers budding entrepreneurs is deceptively simple when one considers the depths to which he has gone to implement his formula.

Find something different and unique

Be clear about what it is and don't stray from that course. Keep driving in pursuit of that goal. He admits that BridgeClimb having the Sydney Harbour Bridge is 'A DREAM COME TRUE', and his international team is working on other icon bridges around the world.

Focus your offering and recognise the unique value you deliver

Don't try to be all things. Be famous for just one thing says Cave: 'WE ARE DOING A VERY SIMPLE THING. WE ARE A FACILITATOR ONLY, TAKING PEOPLE TO THE TOP OF THE BRIDGE. OUR JOB IS TO ENABLE OUR CUSTOMERS TO MAKE HEROES OF THEMSELVES.'

Deliver quality every time – let nothing fall between the cracks

'IF PROSPECTIVE STAFF FIND THAT UNREASONABLE (I.E. THE EVERY CLIMBER, EVERY TIME, CONSTANT MEASUREMENT PHILOSOPHY), PLEASE DON'T COME HERE', Cave says.

Les Schirato

John C Lyons and Edward de Bono

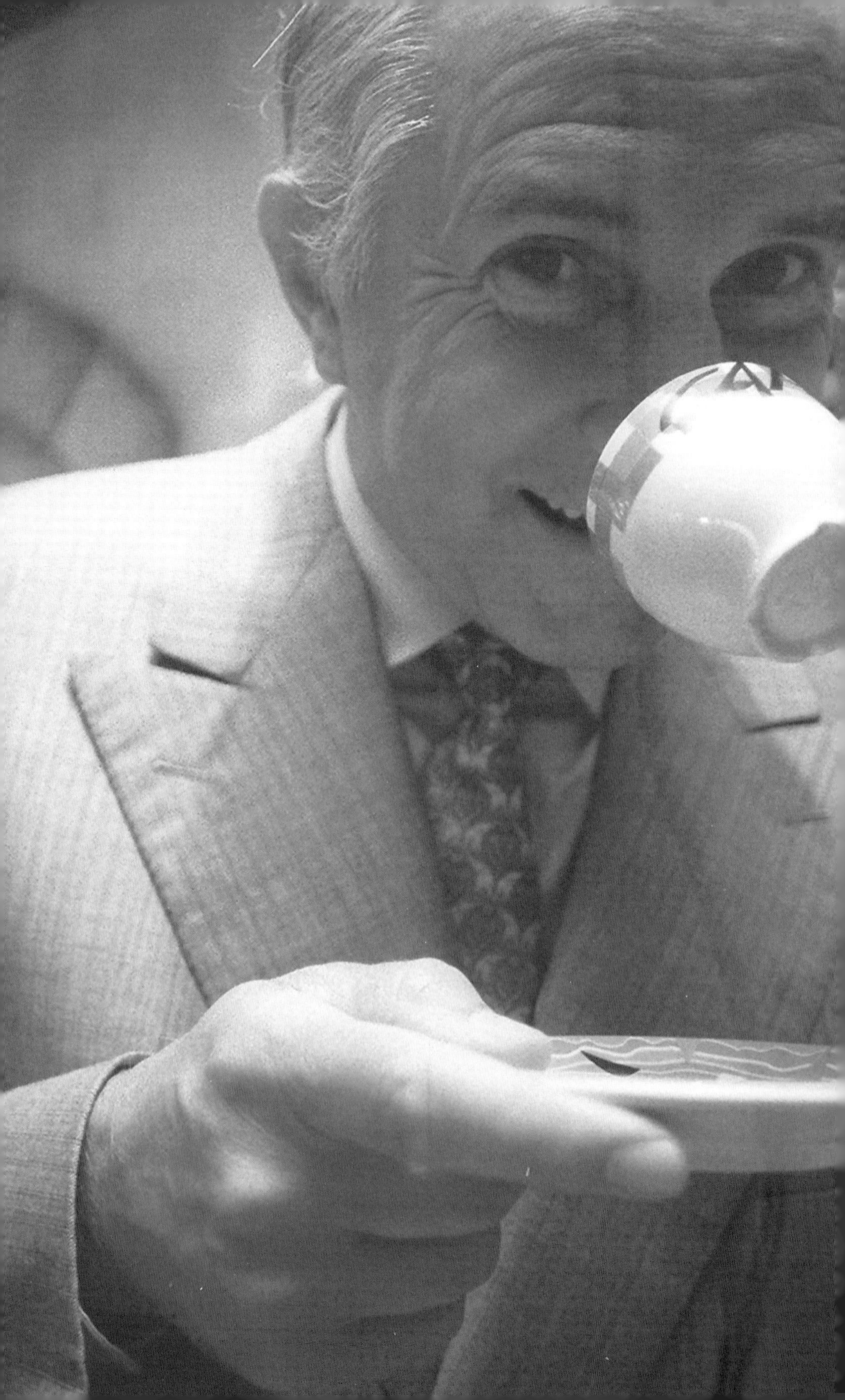

LES SCHIRATO

Australians will never drink strong coffee – you're wasting your time

Twenty-one years ago at age twenty-five, Leslie Schirato gave up his job as sales manager for Fiat, joined the small Italian-food importing business established by his wife's family some thirty-three years earlier and, tongue-in-cheek, wrote a ten-year marketing plan which he hoped would reshape and reinvigorate the business totally.

Today, much to the chagrin of global coffee companies like Nestle, Douwe Egbert, and Lavazza, the Sydney-based Cantarella Group supplies every third cup of fresh coffee drunk at home by Australians. In addition, the company sells as much coffee again into the food service trade, and its *Vittoria* and *Aurora* coffee brands are a familiar sight on café and restaurant umbrellas and cups all over the country. In addition to coffee and coffee accessories, the Cantarella Group has built a seemingly disparate collection of strong carefully-niched brands in food categories such as wine (*Santa Vittoria* and *Luigi Cavalli*), cheeze (*Jarlsberg* and *Norwegian*), sardines (*King Oscar*), mineral water (*Santa Vittoria* and *Aurora*) and tea (*Natureland*) – some imported, others locally produced.

I am going to build these products regardless

'Everyone told me why I would never be able to do it, and I guess I was trying to prove myself and my worth. So by looking at different product categories where I saw opportunities I said "I am going to build these products regardless". But we had no money, certainly not enough to market them, so I used guerilla marketing tactics which I think are the basics of marketing.'

'I WROTE THIS PLAN ON VITTORIA COFFEE WHICH SAID THAT THE WAY WE WERE GOING TO BUILD IT UP WAS BY BRANDING EVERYTHING IN CAFES — THE COFFEE CUPS, THE UMBRELLAS AND SO ON — LETTING PEOPLE KNOW THAT THE COFFEE THEY WERE DRINKING WAS VITTORIA. IT WORKED REALLY WELL FOR US, AND SOON VITTORIA WAS EVERYWHERE IN CAFES.'

But home consumption of pure coffee was still very small and so Schirato approached supermarkets. 'THEY JUST LAUGHED AT ME AND SAID "AUSTRALIANS WILL NEVER DRINK STRONG COFFEE; YOU'RE WASTING YOUR TIME". IN FACT I GOT KICKED OUT OF EVERY SUPERMARKET IN AUSTRALIA', he adds. Eventually one Coles supermarket let Schirato try fresh coffee tastings in, of all places, the fresh fruit and vegetable department. Customer acceptance eventually led to the product being put into the grocery section. Today, Vittoria is the category leader in fresh coffee sold through supermarkets, with the powerful global coffee companies' brands trailing well behind.

What are the lessons to be learned from this man's success and dogged determination that his company's core business is 'BUILDING BRANDS — IN STEP TOGETHER WITH CUSTOMERS, FOR GREATER PROFITS', flaunting the might of his global opponents?

Think differently and be different, even when you're successful

Schirato's understated manner and conservative exterior mask a powerhouse of opportunistic and creative thinking. He believes that to be noticed in the clutter of products and communication you must think differently and be different. He is not deterred, but rather encouraged by the size of his competitors because they become rule-takers, rather than actively pursuing rule-breaking which he believes has been his success.

He cites one example of running controversial full-page advertisements on *April Fool's Day* claiming that, because Cantarella had *discovered white coffee beans*, it was no longer necessary to add milk.

'WE HAD THOUSANDS OF CALLS FOR WEEKS AFTER, TRADE ENQUIRIES TOO, AND WE TOLD PEOPLE IT WAS AN APRIL FOOL'S PRANK AND SENT THEM A FREE BAG OF COFFEE FOR BEING GOOD SPORTS.' He smiles. 'WE MADE MORNING TELEVISION AND THE NEWS PROGRAMS, AND EVEN PRESS IN NEW ZEALAND AND CANADA. IT WAS AN INCREDIBLE SUCCESS FOR US.'

Chapter 1 – Marketing without money

Schirato says that this was a landmark in cementing his belief in remaining different.

'Everyone had said to me "you can't do that now you're a market leader". So we didn't for a while, and I started to hate it. If you bring in people who've worked for companies like Unilever for twenty years, they want to make you like Unilever as quickly as they can...they all want to go back to what they've learned. They don't sit back and say "this guy's built all these brands without money, and I want to learn". They want to make us like the corporations, when everything I've done that has made me successful was to be different. I used to be so paranoid about criticism.'

Narrow the focus and manage customers for profit

The road to prosperity and debt-free stability has had its threatening moments according to Schirato.

'In the late 1980s, we were staring down the barrel of financial destruction. We had huge debts. It's amazing when that happens and you're close to losing everything, you go back to taking control and you don't worry about what people say anymore, because it's survival.'

Faced with a debt of $10 million and not only losing everything for his family but affecting the families of 150 employees which were his responsibility, Schirato went on to buy out three other family shareholder groups. Today he is the major shareholder with his sister-in-law Clelia Winton.

Schirato blames accumulated debt and profitless volume from being unfocussed, and says at this point he decided to narrow the focus and manage for profit.

'I went out and chose the clients we really want to deal with, and then I went on to manage them for profit...with good internal systems that captured all the costs of doing business with that client...umbrellas, promotions, service, etc....and a good set of KPIs.

Marketing without Money

Sometimes I wish I could act like that when we are doing well. I don't make any excuses now for being a bit of a control freak because it has meant we're now successful, stable and secure.'

Work out who you are and what your competitive advantage is and stick to it

'Make sure you do something you really love. I love selling coffee and food products. The greatest work you have to do is work on yourself. Make sure you keep working on the entrepreneurs in your organisation, because if you don't let them make a few mistakes, if you don't let them be creative, I think you actually lose the whole core of what makes these people successful', Schirato says. 'Surround yourself with a good team, not simply good individuals.'

While Schirato is a great admirer of the creative flair of entrepreneurs like Dick Smith, he cautions 'If you've got four Dick Smiths in a company, you're in big trouble. You need good implementers as well. We find that people who grow up through the company are the best. They understand the culture and the company.' Doubtless Smith would agree with that.

He stresses that everyone must understand their role in the team. 'If you don't have a good loyal team, no matter how good you are, you're not going to succeed. And it's the interdependence, not the independence of each that has made us successful', Schirato adds.

American coffee giant Starbucks recently announced that it had sold its millionth cup of coffee in Australia, the Cantarella Group sells more than a million cups *a day*. Turnover today is $95 million, employees number about 200, and Cantarella is debt free.

While Schirato's has pioneered fresh coffee in Australia to a level of around fifteen per cent of home consumption, instant brands still have eighty-five per cent. He says that in most developed coffee-consuming countries, the mix is around 80/20 in favour of pure coffee, and that Australian coffee drinkers are still about as discriminating today as our wine drinkers were some ten to twenty years ago. Hence he sees large future pay-off for the 'slow and arduous' investment he's made in leading development of the market.

Adrian Di Marco

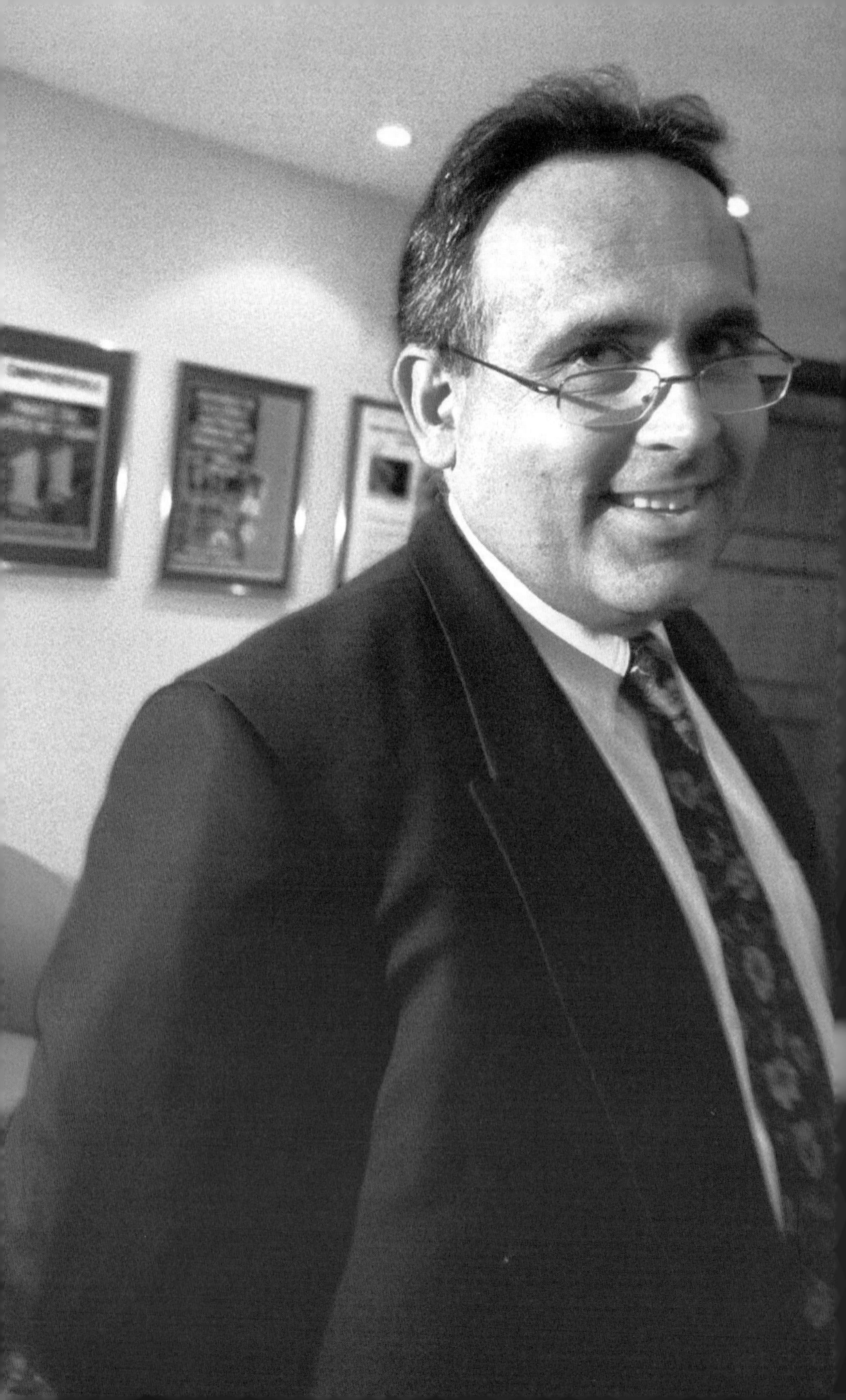

CHAPTER 1 – MARKETING WITHOUT MONEY

ADRIAN DI MARCO

We Australians undersell what we do and Americans do the opposite

How has a Queensland software developer with no money, who describes himself as a 'reluctant entrepreneur', built a technology company in a mature global market taking on the might of some of the world's biggest companies, and ended up after just fifteen years in Australia's top 200 listed companies with a market capitalisation of $150 million and sus-tained profitability which has averaged forty-five per cent pa growth since 1992?

Adrian Di Marco started Technology One in 1987 in suburban Brisbane with some financial backing from a satisfied client whose business he had computerised, because he believed he could build better software: 'I THOUGHT THAT CREATING GREAT SOFTWARE WASN'T THAT HARD, AND THAT MAKING A SUCCESSFUL COMPANY WOULD NOT BE THAT HARD EITHER. I WENT TO THE CLIENT AND SAID "I WANT TO SET UP A COMPANY AND CAN YOU GUYS PROVIDE ME WITH THE CASH?"'

The company Di Marco started announced a FY2002 net profit after tax of $8.76 million on sales of $46 million (up twenty per cent on FY2001) after fully expensing the year's R&D costs of $8.14 million. Profit before tax and after expensing all R&D has grown at an annual average rate of forty-five per cent pa since 1992.

It's marketing that will grow an organisation, because if you are giving customers what they want, then you are going to build a better product

'I HAVE ALWAYS BEEN A VERY STRONG BELIEVER IN MARKETING. IT'S MARKETING THAT WILL GROW AN ORGANISATION, BECAUSE IF YOU ARE GIVING CUSTOMERS WHAT THEY WANT, THEN YOU ARE GOING TO BUILD A BETTER PRODUCT. I AM INTIMATELY INVOLVED IN MARKETING BECAUSE MARKETING IS WHAT DRIVES

Marketing without Money

this company's product line. We look at what the market wants by talking to our sales people and potential customers. Through the marketing process, you simplify concepts, ideas or whatever, then you give that to the development team and because you have simplified it they can go and make it happen.'

Di Marco is convinced that the big American software companies have succeeded not because of their technology but because they are great marketing companies.

'When we started the business…we were so preoccupied with getting the software right we ignored the marketing, like most Australian companies do. We thought the software had to be much better before we could sell it successfully. I found it hard to accept when some people said to me that our software was better than Peoplesoft's or Oracle's because they are huge American corporations. So we actually made the switch and said we'll become more marketing driven…We Australians undersell what we do and Americans do the opposite.'

Di Marco has a rare depth of understanding of what it means to be a true marketing company, not simply a good promoter. While many Australian entrepreneurs, chief executives and boards confuse marketing with promoting and selling what you have, he clearly understands that marketing is the process of creating unique value for customers and other stakeholders, and being famous for it.

How has Technology One set about creating unique value in a very mature and competitive market dominated by huge global players like Microsoft, Oracle and Peoplesoft? Di Marco says:

'We are in the really competitive heartland of the software industry and we provide the enterprise systems that run big business. Since computers were introduced in the 1950s, these were the first applications ever developed and people have kept on reinventing and making them better and better. You can imagine the level of sophistication of software after all those years. Any industry comes down to the best players, so differentiation is becoming harder and harder.'

Adrian Di Marco is quietly confident that the formula which drives his company to such success against Goliaths in the big hard end of the enterprise system software market is not only sustainable, but is gathering strength as it goes. He stresses that the company is constantly learning from market feedback and from its mistakes, so the formula, like the proverbial road to success is always under construction: 'WE MAKE HUGE MISTAKES. WE MAKE PROBABLY ONE HUGE MISTAKE A YEAR. THE NICE THING IS THAT I KNOW WE'LL LEARN FROM THAT MISTAKE'. With the refinement that experience has now given his 'reproducible model', he believes that what has taken fifteen years to achieve could now be done in half the time!

First quantify the market, then make some friends

'THE VERY FIRST THING YOU DO IS IDENTIFY THE MARKET YOU WANT TO GET INTO, QUANTIFY THAT MARKET, AND LOOK AT WHAT A TOTAL SOLUTION WOULD LOOK LIKE FOR THAT MARKET.' Technology One's current vertical markets are financial management and accounting, local government, higher education and universities, retail and supply chain management, human resource management, and wholesale and distribution.

'YOU THEN IDENTIFY THE PARTNERS YOU WANT TO WORK WITH IN THAT MARKET – WHO WOULD WE PARTNER WITH TO PROVIDE THE TOTAL SOLUTION. THEN, USING TELEMARKETING WE WORK OUT WHO IS GOING TO BE BUYING SOLUTIONS OVER WHAT TIMEFRAME.' Di Marco stresses the importance of using partners not only to provide missing, usually vertical-market-specific parts of the total solution, but also because they provide deep market knowledge and often relationships that are essential to success. He adds: 'WE BRING TO THE PARTY THE ORGANISATIONAL STRENGTH AND A WORLD-CLASS FINANCIAL MANAGEMENT ACCOUNTING SYSTEM – EVERYONE NEEDS THAT; WE BRING SKILLS IN MARKETING, SALES AND SUPPORT AND WE TAKE ON THE CLIENT CONTRACT RISK. BUT ONCE WE GET THAT INDUSTRY KNOWLEDGE AND EXPERTISE FROM OUR PARTNERS, WE EITHER ACQUIRE THEM IF THEY PERFORM, OR REPLACE THEM WITH OUR PEOPLE.' And Di Marco says that this is understood by both parties at the outset of the relationship.

Own the customer then go deep

In dramatic contrast with most of his global competitors who have chosen to use major consulting firms as their distribution and service channel to customers, Di Marco believes that dealing directly with the customer has advantaged Technology One, especially given its vertical markets and total solutions approach:

'WE LET THE MARKET DRIVE THE COMPANY. WE DEVELOP THE PRODUCTS, AND THEN WE MARKET THEM OURSELVES, WE SELL THEM, WE IMPLEMENT THEM AND THEN WE SUPPORT THEM. WE ALMOST OWN THE SUPPLY CHAIN. WE'VE NOT IMPOSED THIRD PARTIES ON OUR CUSTOMERS AND UNLESS YOU TURN A BLIND EYE YOU WILL HEAR PROMPTLY AND VERY CLEARLY WHAT THEY LIKE AND DON'T LIKE ABOUT YOUR PRODUCT.'

This direct customer connection Di Marco says delivers huge value to the customer and his company across the board – in customer satisfaction, retention, growth and referral – and in learning and improving things all the time. 'WE KEEP OUR CUSTOMERS FOREVER – OUR CHURN RATE IS ALMOST ZERO. OUR MAJOR COMPETITORS' PRODUCT DEVELOPMENT TEAMS ARE TEN TO TWENTY TIMES THE SIZE OF OURS.'

Great processes supporting great people.

'ONCE YOU'VE GOT THE INDUSTRY KNOWLEDGE, THE MARKET AND THE FUNDING SORTED OUT, THEN THE REST OF IT JUST BECOMES A MANUFACTURING PROCESS – GETTING THE PEOPLE, THE PROCESSES, THE STRATEGY IN PLACE AND THE ORGANISATIONAL STRUCTURE. YOU INCENTIVISE THE PEOPLE. EVERYTHING HANGS AROUND THE PEOPLE THING. YOU NEED TO BUILD A BUSINESS THAT IS PROCESS-ORIENTED. GREAT PEOPLE NEED THE SUPPORT OF GREAT PROCESSES. WRITING SOFTWARE IS A VERY COMPLEX BUSINESS. MILLIONS OF THINGS HAVE TO COME TOGETHER. SO WE ARE VERY PROCESS ORIENTATED.'

Technology One's creed

- We are in a dynamic market place and we must continually innovate, work quickly, decisively and with determination to remain competitive.

- We innovate to provide solutions and services that will make our customers successful.

- If competitors are doing things a certain way, let us learn from them, but there is always a better way.

- We do our own thinking. We do not allow others to do it for us. Answers come from our own ingenuity.

- Invent different and better ways of working. We strive and are passionate to find a better way.

- The better way is always the simpler way.

- Look past the traditional way. Look for the logical solution.

- Think outside the square. Radical ideas can create great innovative solutions.

- We are flexible and adaptable. We believe that change is good. We embrace change.

- Anticipate – do not be reactive, be proactive.
  Just do it!

Chapter 2
REBELS FOR A CAUSE

When a charitable organisation, like the Salvation Army or the Red Cross, approaches you for a small donation, it is seldom that you would refuse to give them a helping hand, unless of course you are inundated with such approaches. Frequently, people will explain their generous action by describing the charity as a 'good cause'. In this situation, you have responded to a cause and let your emotions be engaged. It is as if you can imagine how perhaps they might help you one day or someone close to you.

Many people believe that the act of selling something is based on persuading others to buy. As a result, and especially when pushy sales people attempt to persuade reluctant buyers, there is frequently a natural reaction of resentment on the part of the buyer. The effect of this resentment is frequently to turn the buyer off, even though the buyer may have been interested in the product (or service) had such tactics not been employed.

Had the salesperson instead anticipated or elicited the desire or cause which the product values may well have been able satisfy, and chosen as a result to concentrate on the customer's priorities, rather than the product itself, the outcome may well have been not only the sale of the product but the creation of a long-term customer.

The difference between the two approaches, the attempt to sell by persuasion versus engaging the prospect in the cause, has a dramatic effect on the outcome. *If the customer buys the cause, you may be assured that the product will follow.*

Chapter 2 – Rebels for a Cause

Thinking about your business as a cause changes your offering, how you deliver that offering and especially how you communicate. Taking a persuasive approach, as many suppliers and advertisers do, means that you will generally spend more and take a lot longer to achieve your objective of market penetration. *Taking a cause approach means that you will immediately be aligning yourself with what is important to the customer.* You will have tapped into the customer's priorities and values. You will have the customer's attention without even asking for it.

The founder of Revlon cosmetics, Charles Revson is quoted as saying 'IN THE FACTORY WE MAKE COSMETICS, BUT IN THE DRUGSTORE WE SELL HOPE.' Revson recognised the difference between his cause and his product. The effect of this insight on the success of his business was immense. Product packaging became the focus of differentiation. Beautiful product presentation was the first step on the ladder to success. The second step was to create a retail environment focussed on beauty and glamour. Movie stars were used as presenters in advertising and point-of-sale material. Store fit-out in cosmetics departments today typically costs more per square metre of floor space than in practically any other part of the store. Attractive people are recruited to staff such departments. Handsome men are often shown giving more than a second glance to women wearing a particular brand of cosmetic.

If the cause we are pursuing on behalf of customers and other stakeholders is truly worthy in the eyes of the community at large, then *not only will the customer become engaged in our cause, but so will the media*, which strives to be of interest to its readers, viewers and listeners. Indeed, there is nothing more engaging to most of us than a person who seems to understand our desires and genuinely offers solutions that we believe can address those desires constructively.

So *the benefit of pursuing a valuable cause is that many others will carry your message with real impact to your market*. If your cause and your solution are truly newsworthy, then the media will pursue you because they will know that their audiences will want to hear about it. If the media are talking about your cause, then the community will most likely start talking about it too. Your first customers will buy into your cause and will want to tell their friends, not because they want you to sell more product but because they want to do a favour for their friends.

If this prescription is so obvious, why don't more people follow it? The reason seems to be twofold.

Firstly, many people are typically so passionate about their product or service that their minds and communication are product-centred rather than cause-centred. They are trapped in product values and competitive values, and have not moved to integrated values. Hence, they are locked in a persuasion mode, not a cause mode.

Secondly, many people do not seem to realise that the media are constantly searching for news and information that will appeal to audiences. Hence they overlook or ignore the possibility of making themselves truly interesting to the ultimate audience and hence to the media.

Ironically, even public relations agencies typically write their clients' media releases around products and services rather than what will make compelling viewing, reading or listening. They ignore the readily observable fact *that customers are interested in themselves*, and their clients' products and services are simply a means to an end – a desire or cause.

Smith, Murdoch and Farrell

When value is expressed in the context of a cause on behalf of the customer, it takes on a very different complexion. Dick Smith started his entrepreneurial life as a radio mechanic. In 1968, he went on to develop the now famous retail chain Dick Smith Electronics, which he subsequently sold to Woolworths a decade later. The cause he promoted was focussed on bringing interesting and useful electronic componentry and know-how to Australian consumers at a time when electronics was taking off in this country.

Smith's next cause was to bring to Australians a magazine about their own country. The product that followed is *Australian Geographic Magazine* which he founded in 1986. He sold this business to Fairfax just a few years later. Importantly, Smith is passionate about Australia and the wonderful natural experiences that this country can deliver. Certainly he was not unaware of the large profit potential in appealing to the desire of Australians to know more about their own unique country, and to experience it.

CHAPTER 2 – REBELS FOR A CAUSE

Reaching well beyond the need for financial gain, but clearly driven by the desire to achieve more in his life, Dick Smith created a new cause in 1999 captured in the words 'FIGHTING BACK FOR AUSTRALIA' – the cause he created for his then new company Dick Smith Foods Pty Ltd. Smith took on the formidable task of harnessing Australian farmers and food manufacturers to wrest back ownership of the contents of Australia's supermarket shopping trolleys, eighty-five per cent of which he claimed was being made by non-Australian-owned companies.

Smith knew that if consumers bought into his cause of fighting back for ownership of Australian companies, Australian brands and the retention of profits in Australia, then his groceries would follow them out the door of the supermarket.

Why would Australians want to support the retention and profitability of Australian-owned companies and build the value of Dick Smith Foods Pty Ltd? In essence, Smith connected his product with the future of Australia and the jobs of our children. While most other manufacturers are competing on the benefits of their products, Smith elevated the cause and began competing on what many Australians would regard as a fundamental value we all should strive to uphold.

Some would argue that Smith was being deceptive in presenting his businesses as if they and he are national heroes. Regardless of how much or how little Smith makes from his ventures, or for that matter how much or how little others following his footsteps make, if the cause being pursued is perceived as valuable to the customer and other stakeholders, then we would argue it is a legitimate approach. Those who argue against such an approach would appear to deny that people who create value for Australia in business should not do so if at the same time they are creating value for themselves.

Euan Murdoch, founder of Herron Pharmaceuticals, not unlike Smith, is fired by the cause and the challenge to do his part in not selling off Australian-owned production and brand assets. Like Smith, Murdoch's commercial interests were of course one important driver. However, his belief that 'AUSTRALIA EITHER MAKES ITS OWN FUTURE OR IS DRIVEN TO IT', underpins a broader conviction.

Peter Farrell's cause is a good example of people not knowing what they want until they know what is possible, or even what is really

John C Lyons and Edward de Bono

happening. Understanding by the medical profession and consumers of the huge damage caused by sleep-disordered breathing is still in its infancy, even in the developed world. Hence, despite ResMed's outstanding commercial success, adoption of Farrell's cause by these audiences is still his greatest challenge. The words of an early sleep-apnoea patient are a powerful example of a cause statement, articulated by a highly involved sufferer: 'It [ResMed's product] saved my life; I can function again; I'm back in the land of the living; it saved my marriage; I'm actually in the same bedroom as my wife; it saved my job.'

Dick Smith

John C Lyons and Edward de Bono — 59

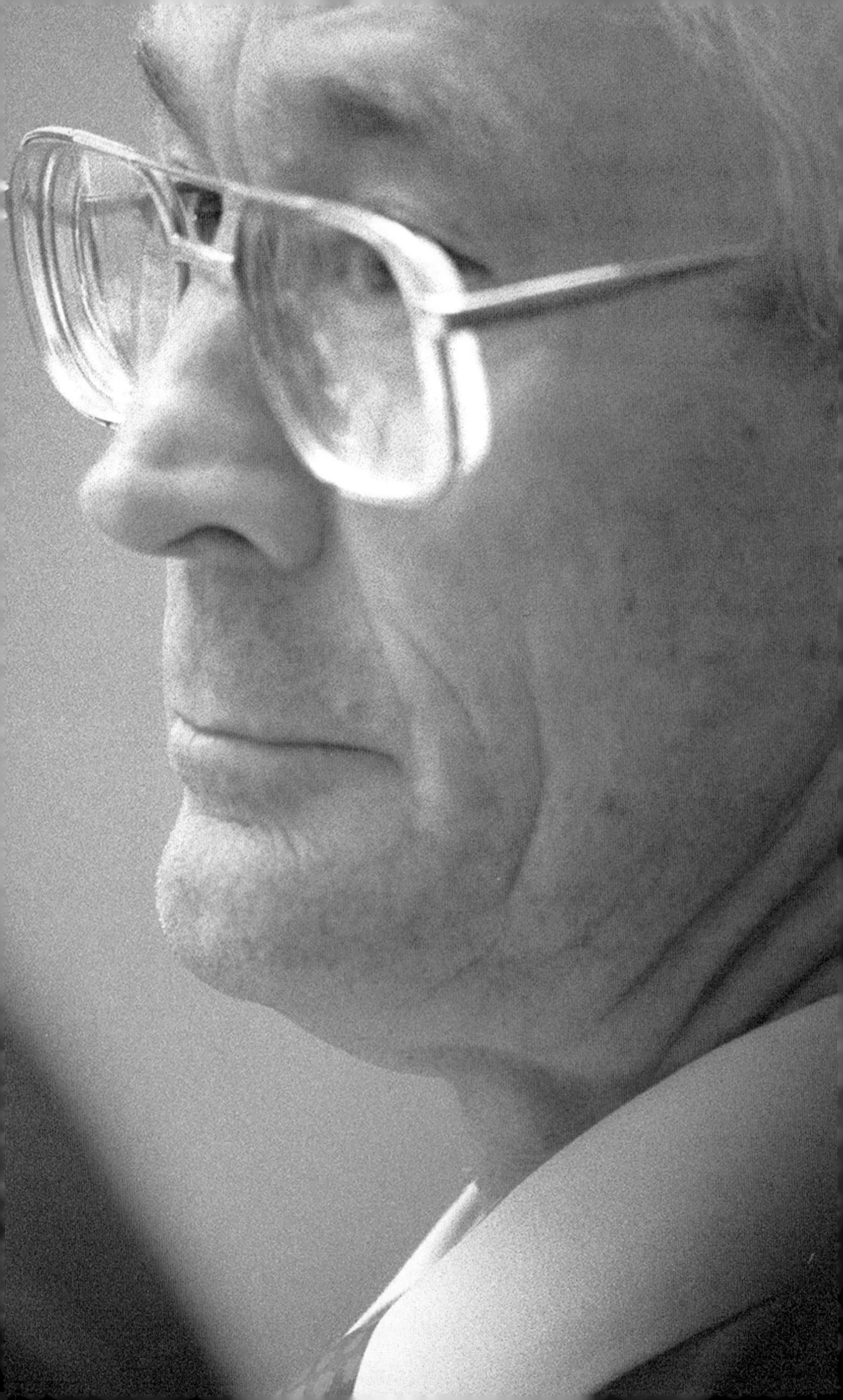

DICK SMITH

Forget the Joneses – just try keeping up with Smith

For the third time in little more than thirty years, Dick Smith has created a new category of business in which he can lead, not be a follower. His proven formula for business design, start-up and on-sell is established, and is one which most of Australia's enterprising individuals and companies could benefit from imitating.

'Ya gotta give Dick a go, I reckon', was the last thing John Lyons expected to hear from the lady on the other end of the line when he telephoned Telstra simply to ask the number for Dick Smith Foods Pty Ltd. 'Do you regularly buy his products?' he asked. 'I try at least one each time I do my grocery shopping', she eagerly replied.

While the sample response is admittedly one-off, it is typical of many others to be heard from ordinary Australians in response to the extraordinary marketing campaign, some would say 'publicity antics', of a company that claims as its fundamental value promise to be *fighting back for Australia*.

Stirring the positive passion of customers to this extent is surprising indeed, especially given that Smith began his crusade barely four years ago, provocatively taking on the might of the major grocery manufacturing companies, and appealing to the oligopoly power of Australia's supermarket distribution system.

It would be easy to dismiss Smith's exceptional ability to whip up publicity for his commercial ventures as being his key to success, and thus to categorise his strategy as purely a public relations stunt – the sort of thing a public relations company's creative think-tank could dream up on a good Monday morning in response to a client's publicity brief.

Dick Smith Foods is a business start-up using the same clever blueprint learned and honed in his start-ups of Dick Smith Electronics (1968) and *Australian Geographic* (1986).

Starting a new business and creating an asset of substantial capital value is hard going and risky; the probability of success is arguably less than one in one hundred. That is why large corporates usually prefer to grow through acquisition rather than start-up. Woolworths acquired Dick Smith Electronics and Fairfax acquired *Australian Geographic,* though the latter has since changed hands in a management buyout.

So the Dick Smith start-up blueprint formula ought to be worth bottling, if it can be, and reselling to Australia's budding entrepreneurs.

Invent a new game and make your own rules

Many start-up entrepreneurs imitate their competitors, claiming a marginal benefit on variables such as quality, price, convenience, etc.; they become simply another competitor, another runner in an established race. Dick Smith, however, invariably seems to create a new category, a new perceived need, a new race in which to become the undisputed and difficult-to-outpace leader. In all three of his high-profile start-ups Smith has narrowed the focus and yet enhanced the value of the offering: to electronic componentry and advice retailing; to an Australian geographic magazine combined with retail outlets and products; and to 'fair dinkum' Australian foods spanning a growing number of product categories.

Believe in a cause

There could hardly be a more cluttered market than grocery, nor one more difficult for new entrants. Most players compete on brand strength, advertising muscle, access to distribution and economies of scale and scope in production. Smith stepped outside the square and chose to compete on *Aussie ownership and a future for Aussie kids* – to create a cause he obviously believed many Australians would find appealing. The products are quite secondary in the value proposition – if you buy the cause, the products will follow provided they prove of reasonable quality and value.

Copy the best ideas from around the world and bring them together under one roof

Like all talented entrepreneurs, Smith's mind is open to the probability that there is a better way to do anything, and his mind is always in active search mode to find, copy and improve on it. Copying the best from around the world is his primary stock in trade. Dick Smith Electronics, which he sold to Woolworths for $25 million in the 1970s was not only a copy of the Radio Shack concept he had observed in the USA, but an improvement in that he incorporated, for example, catalogue ideas from Henry Radio in London and business system ideas from McDonald's.

To create *Australian Geographic*, which he sold to Fairfax in the 1980s for $42 million, he copied the best from Alaskan and Canadian geographic magazines, and then added subscription systems copied from Readers Digest magazine. Smith's first rule of business is to honestly and earnestly seek advice, copy the best bits wherever you find them and bring them together in your new business.

Design a replicable business system

How often do entrepreneurs' businesses die before them or with them. Once their hand moves from the guiding tiller or their face from the customer, things fall in a heap. Dick Smith clearly chooses his category and designs his business concepts with care. He is close to but separable from the product offering. Others can pick up and run with it. The business design is replicable. Those Australian manufacturers supplying the Dick Smith branded products have a vested interest in supporting them, not wiping them out.

Surround yourself with like-minded people to help duplicate your success

Smith says that while he created the idea and the system for Dick Smith Electronics and *Australian Geographic*, it was Ike Bain who duplicated them and really made the businesses valuable. 'ONCE I'VE COME UP WITH THE IDEAS BY COPYING THE SUCCESS OF OTHERS, I LOSE INTEREST VERY QUICKLY.' Bain, who started with Smith as a radio mechanic in the 1960s, has shared in the wealth he helped Smith create, and is now retired. 'THE REASON I HAVE SUCCEEDED AT TIMES IN MY LIFE IS BECAUSE I HAVE ALWAYS BEEN ABLE TO SURROUND MYSELF WITH ONE OR TWO LIKE-MINDED CAPABLE PEOPLE. THAT'S ALL I NEED, AND I ENTHUSE THEM AND NEVER LET THEM GO.'

Smith acknowledges that had Bain been on board to roll out Dick Smith Foods, things would have been easier and the company's growth faster. Indeed, Smith may not have chosen in 2002 to grant a ten-year licence to Sanitarium to manage the marketing, distribution and product development of the Dick Smith Foods business.

Think differently and work out how to do things better and at a lower cost

Smith's penchant for thinking creatively is almost his trademark. His different thinking and resultant approach have created new businesses, and often controversial notoriety in business and elsewhere. His initiative in starting the Variety Club Bash has raised $70 million over seventeen years to help children. 'I HAD TO GET WEALTHY PEOPLE TO PART WITH THEIR MONEY, SO I THOUGHT OF THE IDEA OF ALLOWING ADULTS TO GENERALLY BEHAVE AND CHEAT LIKE KIDS. TO WIN, THEY COULD EITHER DRIVE FAST OR BRIBE THE JUDGES BY WRITING A BIG CHEQUE FOR CHARITY.'

Become the cause hero

The power of word of mouth is immense simply because of its multiplier effect and credibility. Contrary to popular misconception, hero brands just like human heroes are built mainly by word of mouth. Advertising plays a supportive role. A hero usually becomes newsworthy, admired for an important cause or deed; a hero brand shares the same position – it delivers important new value. Smith is a master in the art of recognising important emerging causes, promoting the cause controversially and, along with his product, becoming the cause hero. A visitor to the www.dicksmithfoods.com.au website is focussed on the cause and the hero; the products are almost incidental.

Euan Murdoch

John C Lyons and Edward de Bono

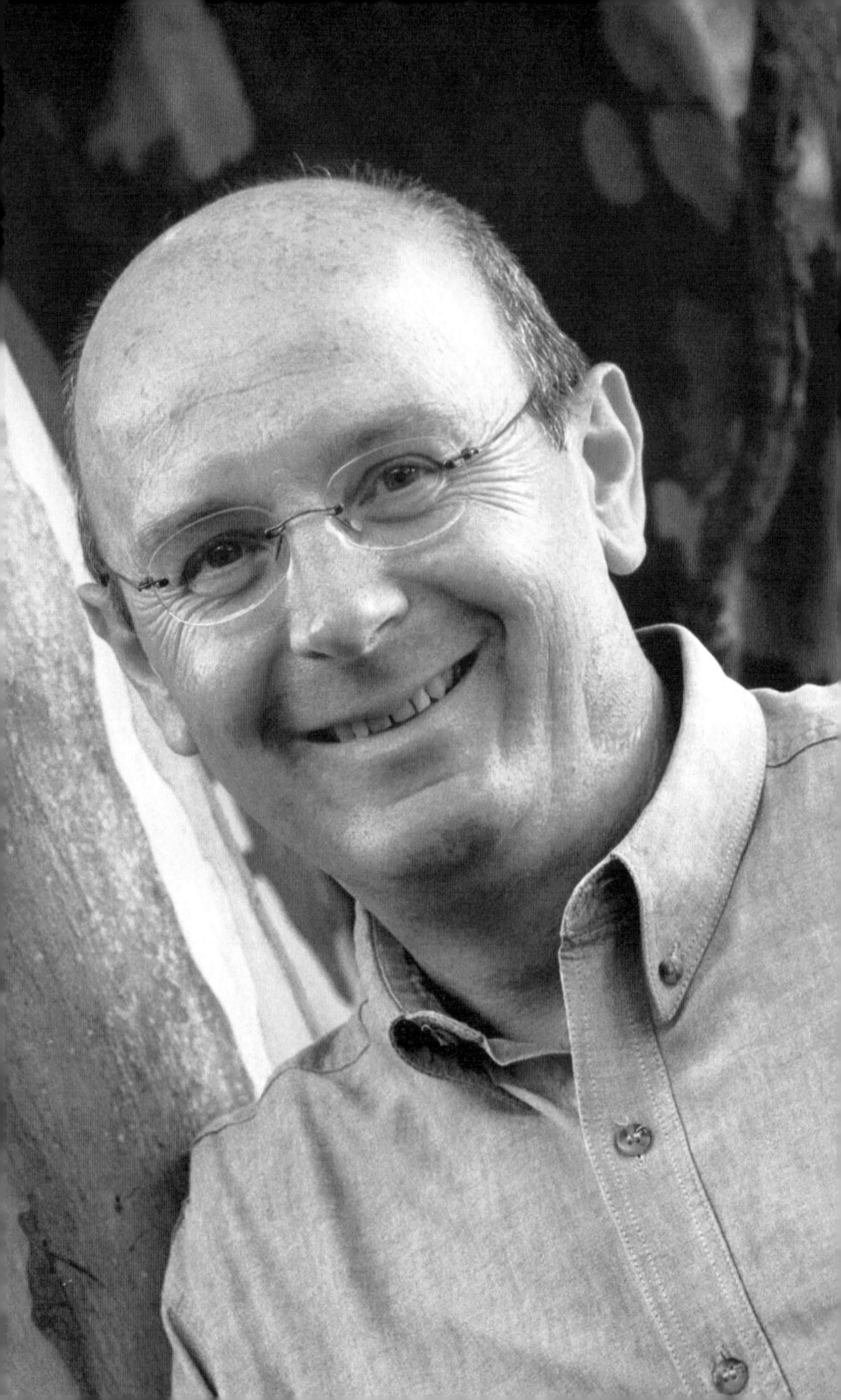

EUAN MURDOCH

We actively try to do it differently; we want to challenge convention, challenge normal business practice

Euan Murdoch built an Australian privately-owned pharmaceutical success story against powerful global pharmaceutical companies who he says outspent him ten-to-one in Australia.

It was probably fortunate that Murdoch failed veterinary science at university, but the exposure that he gained to the pharmaceutical industry whilst doing so was almost certainly one of the best things that happened to him. Together with his wife Kaye, Murdoch went on to found Herron Pharmaceuticals Pty Ltd in 1984, a pharmaceutical manufacturing and marketing company that now employs around 250 people. In April 2003, he sold the company to Australian-owned Sigma Pharmaceuticals for $123 million, and was appointed to the board of Sigma.

Herron manufactures over-the-counter pharmaceutical and natural healthcare products which it markets throughout Australia, the Middle East, New Zealand, the Pacific, Sri Lanka and Asia. The company manufactures 600 products at its head office, R&D and manufacturing facility at Tennyson in Brisbane. Murdoch says he has built the company's flagship brand, Herron Paracetamol from nothing to around thirty per cent of the Australian paracetamol market in a fierce and successful battle against global Smith Kline Beecham's previously dominant Panadol brand which has lost substantial market share. The victory is all the sweeter according to Murdoch because Panadol he estimates outspends Herron on advertising and promotion more than ten-to-one supporting its brand. Despite the David and Goliath gulf in resources, Murdoch is confident Herron will surpass Panadol's market share *within a year or so.*

Without doubt, Herron's struggle to become a major player in analgesics reflects the challenge faced by many Australian entrepreneurs – perhaps even more so in Herron's case because the active ingredient in its paracetamol product is identical to that of Panadol. Murdoch, a commerce graduate, is quite analytical and clear about the factors he believes enabled the privately financed Herron to succeed in an industry typically dominated by Goliath-like global pharmaceutical companies.

A 'why not' approach, not constrained by mindset

Murdoch says that at first he was intimidated by the sheer size and resources, both technical and financial, of his mostly global pharmaceutical adversaries. 'FINANCIALLY WE ARE NOT IN THE SAME LEAGUE, BUT INTELLECTUALLY AND CREATIVELY WE CAN MATCH IT WITH THEM AND PROBABLY CHALLENGE THEM.' On an early study tour of the United States, he was stunned by the sheer scale of the manufacturing plants of some of his rivals. 'YOU WALKED THROUGH THE PRODUCTION AREA AND IT WAS SO BIG YOU COULD SEE THE CURVE OF THE EARTH, LOOKING FROM ONE END TO THE OTHER. I EVENTUALLY THOUGHT "WHY COULDN'T WE BE LIKE THIS ONE DAY? WHY DO WE HAVE TO BE CONSTRAINED BY OUR MINDSET?"'

Murdoch believes that Australian companies, and indeed Australia as a whole, have two choices in the face of global competition – you either create your future or be driven to it. He has struggled to imbue his management team with the conviction that the company can create whatever future it chooses. To this end, in 1996 Murdoch took his management team on a tour of some of the world's most entrepreneurial, high-growth, export-oriented companies, with a bias towards those that are still privately owned:

'WE ARRIVED IN OUR AKUBRAS AND DRIZABONES AND SAID "LETS SHARE SOME LEARNING". AT THE END OF IT WE SPENT A WEEK WRITING OUR VISION 2002. JUST PLANNING FROM ANOTHER PLACE WAS A GREAT WAY OF SHIFTING THE MINDSET. WE ACTIVELY TRY TO DO IT DIFFERENTLY. WE WANT TO CHALLENGE CONVENTION, CHALLENGE NORMAL BUSINESS PRACTICE…BUT ONE OF THE THINGS WE THINK ABOUT IS THE BIGGER WE GET, THE MORE WE GET LIKE OUR MULTINATIONAL COMPETITORS, AND THAT'S NOT A GOOD PLACE TO BE.'

Doing things differently, flanking rather than going head-to-head

'IF YOU ALWAYS DO WHAT YOU'VE ALWAYS DONE, YOU'LL ALWAYS GET WHAT YOU'VE ALWAYS GOT' is another of Murdoch's passionate beliefs. 'YOU NEVER TAKE ON A MAJOR COMPETITOR HEAD-TO-HEAD. YOU DON'T DO A FRONTAL ASSAULT AND THAT'S PART OF THE FUN', he stresses. Herron's unrelenting drive into the paracetamol market has not been fought on technical product differences such as drug efficacy – there are none. Nor has the battle, focussed primarily on the grocery distribution channel which, according to Murdoch accounts for around eighty-five per cent of category sales, been fought with marketing dollars because, he says 'WE JUST CAN'T MATCH OUR MULTINATIONAL COMPETITORS'.

Herron Paracetamol has flanked Panadol using price and Australian owned as the two principal consumer weapons. According to Murdoch, the battle for recognition of Herron's Australian-owned status has provoked a favourable reaction from Australians, especially given the currency that Dick Smith and others have given to the issue.

Murdoch devoted his limited resources to playing up this difference, using Hazel Hawke as the company's advertising presenter, and revealing Smith Kline Beecham's foreign ownership in advertising and publicity. Smith Kline unsuccessfully challenged Herron's advertising claims in court. Dick Smith took time off to sit through much of the hearing. Smith says he glared at the judge during the proceedings.

Murdoch says that the retail trade has been sympathetic and supportive of Herron's stance. One would expect this to be the case simply on the grounds that retailers would want to foster a credible alternative source of supply, thus minimising the market leader's bargaining power. However, Murdoch says that trade support for Herron has increased markedly since the widely publicised extortion attempt which threatened the very existence of the company in March 2000, later followed by a similar threat on Smith Kline's Panadol. He considers Herron's immediate national product recall and destruction of all stock, and rapid introduction of tamper-evident packaging, created a good impression of the company in the trade. Murdoch believes it was influential in regulators deciding against moving the whole category behind the counter, which in Murdoch's words 'WOULD HAVE BEEN A CLASSIC EXAMPLE OF THE EXTORTIONISTS WINNING'.

An unrelenting focus and a passion for the planning process

Murdoch recalls a couple of events that dramatically sharpened his company's focus.

'IN 1989, WE'D BEEN GROWING QUITE QUICKLY AND A COUPLE OF MY YPO [YOUNG PRESIDENTS ORGANISATION] MATES WROTE ME A RATHER FORMAL LETTER SAYING THEY BELIEVED I WAS IN GREAT DANGER…THAT I HAD TOO MUCH ON…THAT I WAS DOING TOO MANY DIFFERENT THINGS, AND THAT I NEEDED TO PUT A BIT OF FOCUS INTO MY BUSINESS.'

Concurrently, the company undertook its first major strategic planning project and decided on a 'five on five' plan, basically that it would seek to increase in size by a factor of five times over the ensuing five years. 'WE ALSO ELECTED THAT WE'D CONCENTRATE ON PHARMACEUTICALS AND GET OUT OF ALL THE OTHER THINGS WE WERE DOING.'

Having achieved both goals by the next major planning session in the mid 1990s, Murdoch says the company was confident and optimistic, and basically decided 'LET'S GO FOR IT WITHIN THE BOUNDS AND CONSTRAINTS THAT CURRENTLY APPLY WITHIN OUR INDUSTRY'.

The company recently completed its third major planning round and according to Murdoch moved from puberty through early maturity to basically the 'old bull' stage.

'THE QUESTION NOW IS HOW CAN THE COMPANY REINVENT ITS INDUSTRY AND ITS BUSINESS MODEL. I THINK HERRON IS NOW IN A POSITION WHERE IT CAN REALLY MAKE A FUNDAMENTAL DIFFERENCE. THERE IS A REALISATION THAT THE COMPANY CAN PROBABLY DELIVER INTELLECTUAL PROPERTY GLOBALLY EVEN THOUGH IT PROBABLY CAN'T BUILD GLOBAL BRANDS. THAT'S REALLY QUITE CHALLENGING AND EXCITING.'

One example of this is the strong possibility of Herron licensing to overseas companies the whole production and marketing concept behind some of its products, from formulation through to the consumer. He says this will add value and enable speed to market, which he claims is a big issue in an environment where product life cycles are shortening dramatically.

Peter Farrell

John C Lyons and Edward de Bono

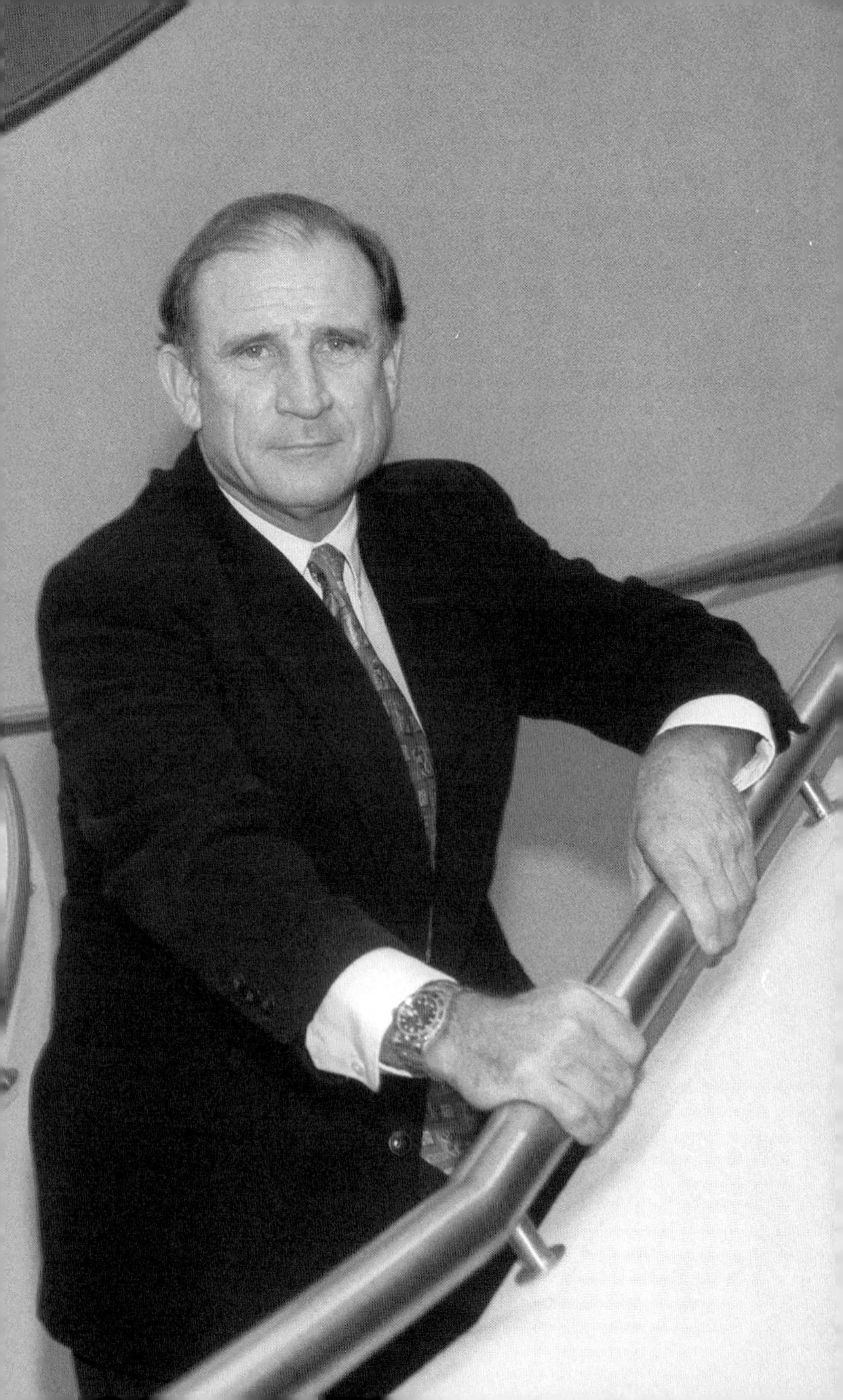

CHAPTER 2 – REBELS FOR A CAUSE

PETER FARRELL

You've got to make sure people know that you are not going to give up, ever

Dr Peter Farrell, founder, chairman and CEO of ResMed, tells what it is like to start a company that has already skyrocketed beyond his wildest expectations, but which he now realises is just beginning to tap its global potential.

The extraordinary success of ResMed, a medical technology company founded in Australia just fourteen years ago and now capped at around $1.9 billion, feels more like a corporate fairytale than the factual account of how a former Australian university engineering professor proactively stumbled on an idea that literally has the potential to save the lives, relationships and jobs of an estimated ten per cent of the world's population. Since its NASDAQ IPO in 1995, ResMed has had twenty-nine consecutive quarters of record growth, and in FY2002 made a net profit of $68 million on sales of $371 million. Now with a dual listing on the New York and Australian Stock Exchanges, seventy per cent of the company's stock is held by Australian investors.

'WHEN I WAS TOLD BY ONE OF MY COLLEAGUES THAT SOMEONE AT THE UNIVERSITY OF SYDNEY WAS TREATING SNORING SICKNESS WITH A REVERSE VACUUM-CLEANER I ROLLED ON MY BACK LIKE A COCKROACH THAT HAD BEEN SPRAYED. I SAID "SNORING SICKNESS? YOU MUST BE KIDDING!"' Farrell says.

But Farrell was shown a videotape of the man sleeping and snoring. First he stopped snoring, and then he stopped breathing. He repeated that 400–500 times a night, experiencing dangerous high blood pressure and a racing heart rate. When an experimental mask, which regulated air flow, was placed on his face he slept comfortably.

At the time of his fortunate encounter with the inventor of the idea, Professor Colin Sullivan of the University of Sydney Centre for Advanced Medical Technology, Farrell was vice-president of research and development for US-based Baxter Healthcare Inc., and honorary professor

John C Lyons and Edward de Bono — 73

in biomedical engineering at the University of New South Wales, where he had previously served as a full-time academic in the engineering faculty. Holding degrees in chemical engineering and bioengineering, Farrell was fascinated by the idea of applying engineering principles to medicine.

'COLIN SULLIVAN SHOWED ME THIS MASK LIKE A HOUSE BRICK ON YOUR FACE CONNECTED TO A MACHINE YOU COULD HAVE RUN YOUR SWIMMING POOL ON AND SOUNDED LIKE A FREIGHT TRAIN IN A TUNNEL. BUT IT COMPLETELY NORMALISED THE GUY'S BREATHING. EVERY NIGHT IT WAS GLUED ON. IT TOOK A COUPLE OF LAYERS OF SKIN WHEN YOU TOOK IT OFF. BUT THE PATIENT SAID "IT SAVED MY LIFE; I CAN FUNCTION AGAIN; I'M BACK IN THE LAND OF THE LIVING; IT SAVED MY MARRIAGE; I'M ACTUALLY IN THE SAME BEDROOM AS MY WIFE; IT SAVED MY JOB". SO I DECIDED TO SPEND SOME OF BAXTER'S MONEY ON THIS. MOST PEOPLE HAD A LAUGH, BUT I'D SEEN THE RESULTS.'

In 1986, Farrell convinced Baxter Healthcare to acquire rights to the invention. Subsequently, however, Baxter underwent a corporate restructure and Farrell was able to lead a management buyout of the still fledgling sleep-disordered technology. In 1989, Farrell founded ResMed with the express purpose of developing the market and the technology, which by now he was convinced had huge potential.

At the time, it was thought that chronic sleep-disordered breathing (SDB) affected only two per cent of population. Today, research shows that figure is at least ten per cent, making incidence of the disease comparable to that of asthma, diabetes and the effects of tobacco smoking.

Untreated, SDB-related diseases are debilitating and cause both premature morbidity and mortality. It has been discovered that SDB is profoundly connected with hypertension which in turn is the number one risk factor for both stroke and congestive heart failure. Heart disease and stroke are respectively numbers one and three causes of death. Further, people with SDB are fifteen times more likely to be involved in a traffic accident. Alarmingly, seventy-eight per cent of long-distance truck drivers suffer from the disease.

What are some of the learnings from Farrell's experience in pioneering the growth of a global market which is still in the early stages of development?

If you are not technologically literate, you are stuffed

At a time when it is perhaps not fashionable to be a technology company, Farrell describes his company as just that. He says a Massachusetts Institute of Technology study found that over a sixty year period in the United States only twenty per cent of the growth could be explained by classical economics, inputs and outputs.

'What's the other eighty per cent? It's technology. We have just come out with a new machine which is half the cost and twice as good. That's technology. You've got to love it. You've got to get into it. If you are not technologically literate, you're stuffed.'

Proactively shaping your own future

While Farrell is a lover of Australia, he is very critical of what he sees as the lack of leadership in deciding what we want this country to be famous for, and the lack of motivation, direction and management in setting and pursuing our goals as a nation. He cites as a scientific example the lack of focus of CSIRO saying:

'We are the only country in the world covering every branch of science with just one institution. Does this make any sense? The problem is there is no accountability and responsibility. What we really want this country to be doesn't occur to people. We back every horse and none of them get up.'

He says that he has learned from experience the value of being absolutely focussed, scoping and evaluating what you plan to do, and measuring results as you go. 'There's a checklist that I have built up over the years:

- Do we have a market that's accessible?
- Can we get the right people?
- Do we have the money to play the endgame?

- Does the timing make sense?
- Do we really understand the technology and what the competition and potential competition is, and the intellectual property terrain?
- Are we comfortable that we have something we can manage?'

People don't know what they want until they know what's possible

Farrell describes himself as a missionary for the cause of healthy sleep: 'You've got to have a long-term game plan. You've got to be totally consistent. You've got to make sure people know that you are not going to give up, ever.' His passion for the cause is infectious; the scientific evidence compelling.

However, the impressive growth of his category and his company, and the realisation of what he says are his social objectives, are constrained by the effective communication and adoption of the importance of healthy sleep. This depends on acceptance by the medical profession and in turn consumers of the reality and significance of sleep-disordered breathing as the primary cause of several other debilitating and life-threatening diseases. He says that many general practitioners and specialists, unaware of the symptoms and effects of sleep-disordered breathing, are diagnosing a symptom (such as hypertension or cardiovascular disease) and attempting to treat that, blissfully unaware of the need to identify and treat the real cause.

Farrell's primary job is to be an ever more effective missionary in bringing converts to the cause, because the reality is that customers don't know what they want until they know what is possible.

Chapter 3
UNDERSTANDING HUMAN DESIRE

Customers are only human. They are driven by a primal quest to satisfy their most basic desires and needs. This chapter introduces the foundations of customer desire and explores the different levels of need preparing you for later chapters which examine how outstanding value is created.

Maslow's hierarchy of needs

In the early 1900s, eminent psychologist and behavioural scientist Abraham Maslow greatly advanced the world's understanding of what people desire and need.

One of the many interesting things Maslow noticed while he worked with monkeys early in his career is that some needs take precedence over others. For example, if you are hungry and thirsty, you will tend to try to take care of your thirst first. After all, you can do without food for weeks, but you can only do without water for a couple of days. Thirst is a 'stronger' need than hunger. Likewise, if you are very thirsty, but someone has put a chokehold on you and you can't breathe, which is more important? The need to breathe, of course. On the other hand, sex is less powerful than any of these. Let's face it, you won't die if you don't get it!

Maslow created his now famous hierarchy of needs. He exposed five broad layers of needs: the physiological needs, the needs for safety and security, the needs for love and belonging, the needs for esteem, and the need to actualise the self, in that order.

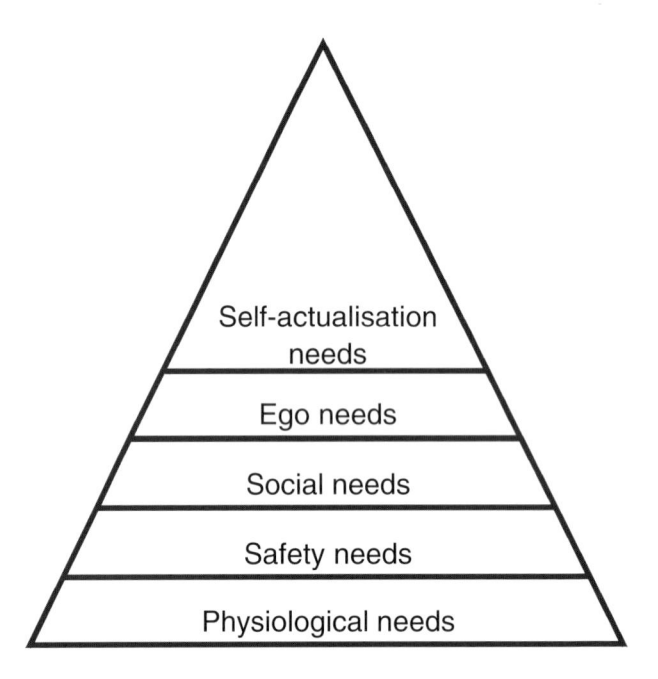

```
                    /\
                   /  \
                  /    \
                 /      \
                /        \
               /Self-actua-\
              / lisation    \
             /   needs       \
            /─────────────────\
           /    Ego needs      \
          /─────────────────────\
         /    Social needs       \
        /─────────────────────────\
       /      Safety needs         \
      /─────────────────────────────\
     /      Physiological needs      \
    /─────────────────────────────────\
```

Figure 3.1 – Maslow's hierarchy of needs

Physiological needs include all the basics of air, food and water. Also there are the needs to be active, to rest, to sleep, to get rid of wastes, to avoid pain and to have sex.

Safety and security needs, the second layer, come in to play when physiological needs are largely taken care. We become increasingly interested in finding safe circumstances, stability and protection. We develop a need for structure and order. This set of needs manifest themselves in our urges to have a home in a safe neighbourhood, job security, a nest egg, a retirement plan, some insurance and so on.

When physiological and safety needs are by and large taken care of, a third layer appears, the *social needs* of love and belonging. We begin to feel the need for friends, a sweetheart, children, affectionate relationships in general, and a sense of community. We become increasingly susceptible to loneliness and social anxieties.

The next layer to appear is *esteem (ego) needs*. One dimension of esteem is the need for the respect of others, status, fame, glory, recognition, attention and the like. The other dimension of this is the need for self-respect, including such feelings as confidence, competence, achievement, mastery, independence and freedom.

The last level of needs at the top of Maslow's hierarchy is *self actualisation*. This represents the desire to fulfil one's potential, to be all that one can be, becoming the most complete individual one can be. Self-actualisers have taken care of their lower-order needs at least to a considerable extent.

Maslow's work illustrates clearly that what we value is context-sensitive. Because people find themselves in different contexts, and because those contexts change over time, the job of marketing is to be ever sensitive to changes in people's priorities. When survival is threatened, we frequently regress to lower-order needs. When society flounders, people start clamouring for a strong leader to take over and make things right. When bombs start falling, they look for safety. When food stops coming into the stores, their needs become even more basic.

Valuable causes are based on emerging human desires and needs – the priorities which people feel are important and achievable in a given context. Sir Richard Branson launched Virgin Airlines in Australia on the cause of "Keeping the air fair" – a priority most Australians were able to buy into because of the oligopolistic behaviour of the airline industry in Australia over decades, and the fear this might be perpetuated.

Elevating a cause to prominence and providing a logical solution (value) is in effect integrating one's value into the complex values of the customer. The principles of integrated value are discussed in detail in Chapter 10 – Beyond product values to integrated values.

Harvey, Jennifer, Klein and Kazacos

Gerry Harvey is focussed on helping ordinary people, many of whom are limited in aspiration by self-imposed glass ceilings, to become the very best they can be and to achieve exceptional rewards commensurate with exceptional performance. With his personal and organisational skills in retailing and promotion, and the buying and financial muscle his company now commands, Harvey is able to offer a complete value bundle to his franchisees – one that is truly surpetitive in his categories.

Like Gerry Harvey, Clair Jennifer is faced with the reality that giving customers a valuable in-store experience is probably the biggest challenge in a retail business, yet is probably the single most important factor in making a sale on the day, and in creating repeat and enthusiastic referral by delighted customers. Mastering that challenge means mastering the people issue. Beyond product and merchandising, important factors the added value of which she can directly control, Jennifer has harnessed the right staff to provide the other major component of value – how the customer feels.

Jurgen Klein's value bundle aims to go well beyond the basics for people who see their health and wellbeing as a means of preventing illness, and thus minimising the need for cure. More than that, Klein also recognises that such people want to enhance the health and beauty they have. Despite the positive value of natural remedies, evident in Chinese medicine, for example, from which he has drawn significant inspiration, Klein has had to fight the negative value of the "quackery" label commonly associated with broad-brush perceptions of his category. Trust had to be built.

Peter Kazacos is open and opportunistic as to where his company should participate in an industry value chain, and at what time it should expand up or down from its present location, or even exit parts. In common with many entrepreneurs studied, he is constantly in search of applications in which to harness emerging technology in order to do things better and at a lower cost. Like Farrell, his is another good example of customers not knowing what they want until they know what is possible. Finding out what is possible can in some instances reinvent his client's business formula.

Gerry Harvey

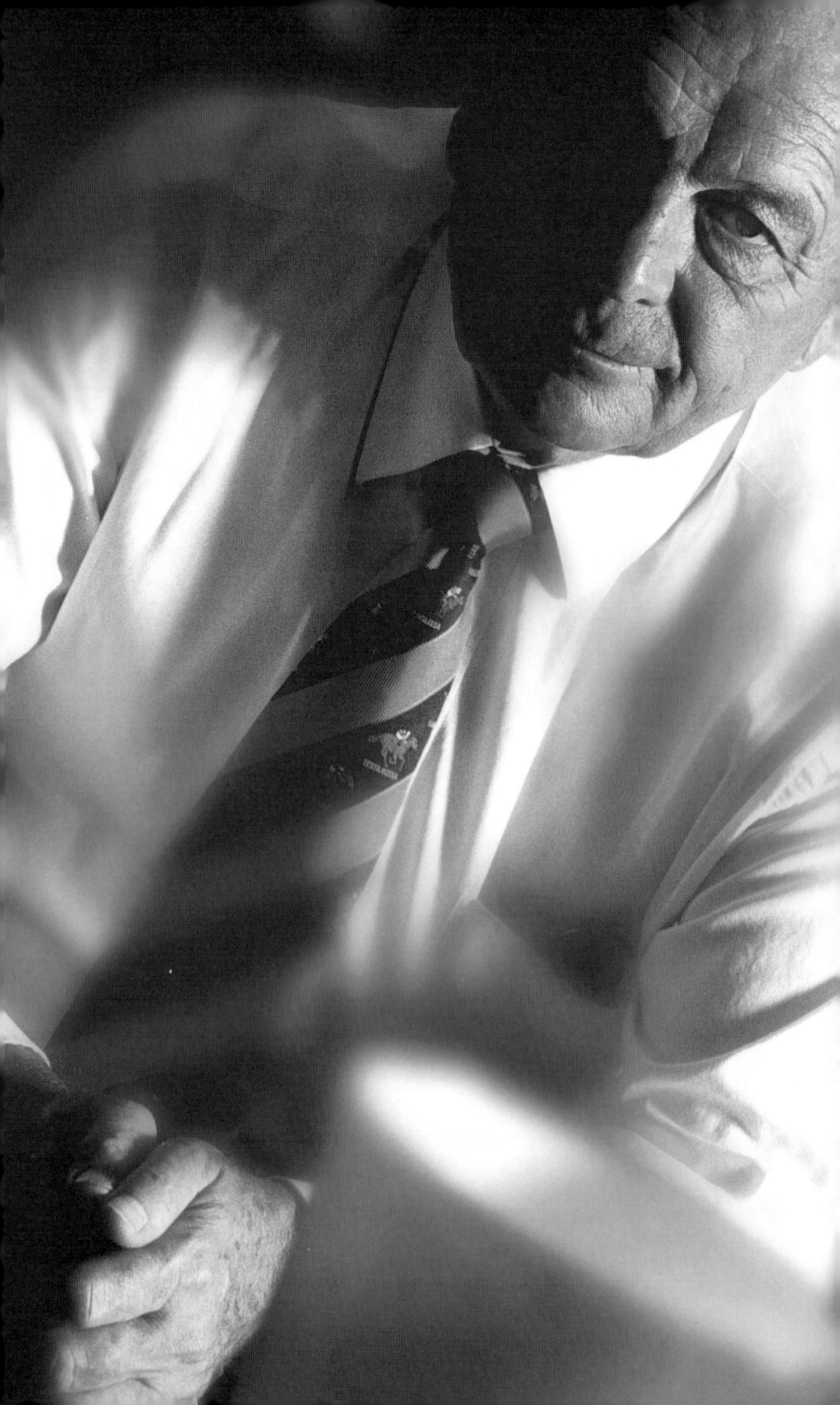

GERRY HARVEY

I don't think you go out with a grand plan; when the opportunities come, take them

At age sixty-two and with over four decades of retailing experience behind him, Gerry Harvey reckons he could still end up a failure.

'MOST BLOKES MY AGE SHOULD BE SMART BY NOW. I HAVE SPENT FORTY-THREE YEARS GETTING EXPERIENCE, AND WHEREAS ANOTHER BLOKE AT SIXTY-TWO YEARS IS LOOKING AROUND TO SEE WHERE HE WILL RETIRE, I'M LOOKING AROUND SAYING "I'VE GOT ALL THIS KNOWLEDGE, HOW CAN I EXPLOIT IT". NOW IF I DON'T EXPLOIT IT OVER THE NEXT TEN YEARS I'M BASICALLY A FAILURE.'

Behind a media façade tinged with brashness, there is a clever brain and an armory of intuitive business skills that enabled Harvey to build Norman Ross with very little money, and are currently driving Harvey Norman and Rebel Sport to success. Each of Gerry Harvey's business formulas reflects his ever learning personality and the drive of an ordinary bloke who started from scratch, without money, and has become an icon of Australian retailing, and the envy of many a so-called professional manager.

Since the days of Norman Ross, Gerry Harvey has continued to do much the same thing but, as he experiments and learns, he improves the way he does things. Today, Harvey's company has the money to do things on a grander scale, but if you stripped away that money and he had to start again from scratch, our guess is that he'd be back where he is in no time. His basic formula for starting and growing large is simple. The skill and will with which he applies it is impressive.

Know yourself before you start a business

A keen racing man, Harvey clearly believes in horses for courses. First you need to work for the best people in the business to find out whether you're any good at something.

'I don't think you go out with a grand plan. If people are good when they start a business, when the opportunities come up they take them. The opportunities are there with all of them, but very few want to take those opportunities…they get comfortable…they don't want to grow to a huge business.'

Harvey doesn't think university management education and books help much. 'There are so many views and so many books written on this. Most of the best people I know didn't do these courses.' Glancing at the array of management books on his bookshelf. He said: 'I don't read them. People just send them to me.' He continued:

'What happens a lot is that a bloke comes in with all the qualifications, but he doesn't know how to grow the company and he stuffs it or injures it. They've got the qualifications in their view, but they really haven't.'

Help your people get the most out of themselves

Harvey says that small businessmen can't become large businessmen if their people skills don't allow them to delegate and lead a team of people, but it's more than that. He says you have to help people get the most out of themselves.

'You build up a culture in the place where everyone knows you're trying to get them there all the time. I have my managers mentoring others. If a manager is having problems, then I tell him to go and work or talk with another person. I'll tell them these are the best blokes I've got, so go and spend time with them. Don't spend time with idiots…you won't learn anything.'

On the other hand, says Harvey, when someone is really good, a bit like an artist, you have to give them freedom to move, and work with them, and then you both benefit.

'I'LL GO OUT OF MY WAY WITH VERY TALENTED PEOPLE, WHEREAS A LOT OF PEOPLE WILL CLASH WITH THEM AND WON'T GIVE LATITUDE. IT'S LIKE A HORSE WHO NEVER WINS AND ONE DAY YOU LET HIM WIN, AND FROM THEN ON HE WINS ALL THE TIME. THEY HAVE GOT TO GAIN THAT CONFIDENCE. MOST PEOPLE HAVE AN OPINION OF THEIR ABILITY AND THEY ACCEPT THAT AND LIVE WITH IT…THEY DON'T ASPIRE TO GREATER THINGS BECAUSE THEY THINK THEY ARE NOT GOING TO MAKE IT.'

Find the best way to do it and keep on searching

Harvey says he changed from company-operated stores in Norman Ross to franchisee-operated in Harvey Norman because:

'I WAS NOT GETTING THE MOST OUT OF PEOPLE. IF YOU GAVE THEM A PIECE OF THE BUSINESS, SUDDENLY THEY REACHED NEW LEVELS. THEY [THE FRANCHISEES] EMPLOY THE PEOPLE AND BUY THE STOCK, BUT THEY HAVE THE WISDOM AND STRENGTH OF A HEAD OFFICE STRUCTURE. IT HAS BEEN FANTASTIC – BY FAR AND AWAY A BETTER SYSTEM.'

Harvey Norman Holdings Ltd recently acquired Rebel Sport Ltd. 'THE INTERESTING THING FOR ME AT THE MOMENT IS THAT I'VE TAKEN OVER REBEL AND IT'S GOT A FEW PROBLEMS BUT IT'S EASY TO SEE HOW IT CAN BE FIXED. IT WASN'T OPERATING PROPERLY.'

Forever searching for a better way, however, Harvey adds:

'IN REBEL, I'M GOING THE OTHER WAY FOR A WHILE – GOING BACK TO THE NORMAN ROSS SYSTEM BECAUSE I WANT TO PLAY AROUND WITH IT IN MY HEAD TO SEE WHETHER I SHOULD STICK WITH THAT…SO I MIGHT HAVE A HYBRID WITH ONE RUNNING THIS WAY AND ANOTHER DIFFERENTLY.

'MY ULTIMATE AIM AT THE MOMENT IS TO TAKE OVER POORLY PERFORMING PUBLIC COMPANIES. I HAVE THIS VIEW THAT AT LEAST TWENTY PER CENT OF

Marketing without Money

public companies are badly run. They probably don't need a whole change in direction to make them right. That's a great indictment of the management of public companies in Australia. We have a lots of very poor managers out there, and boards as well.'

clair Jennifer

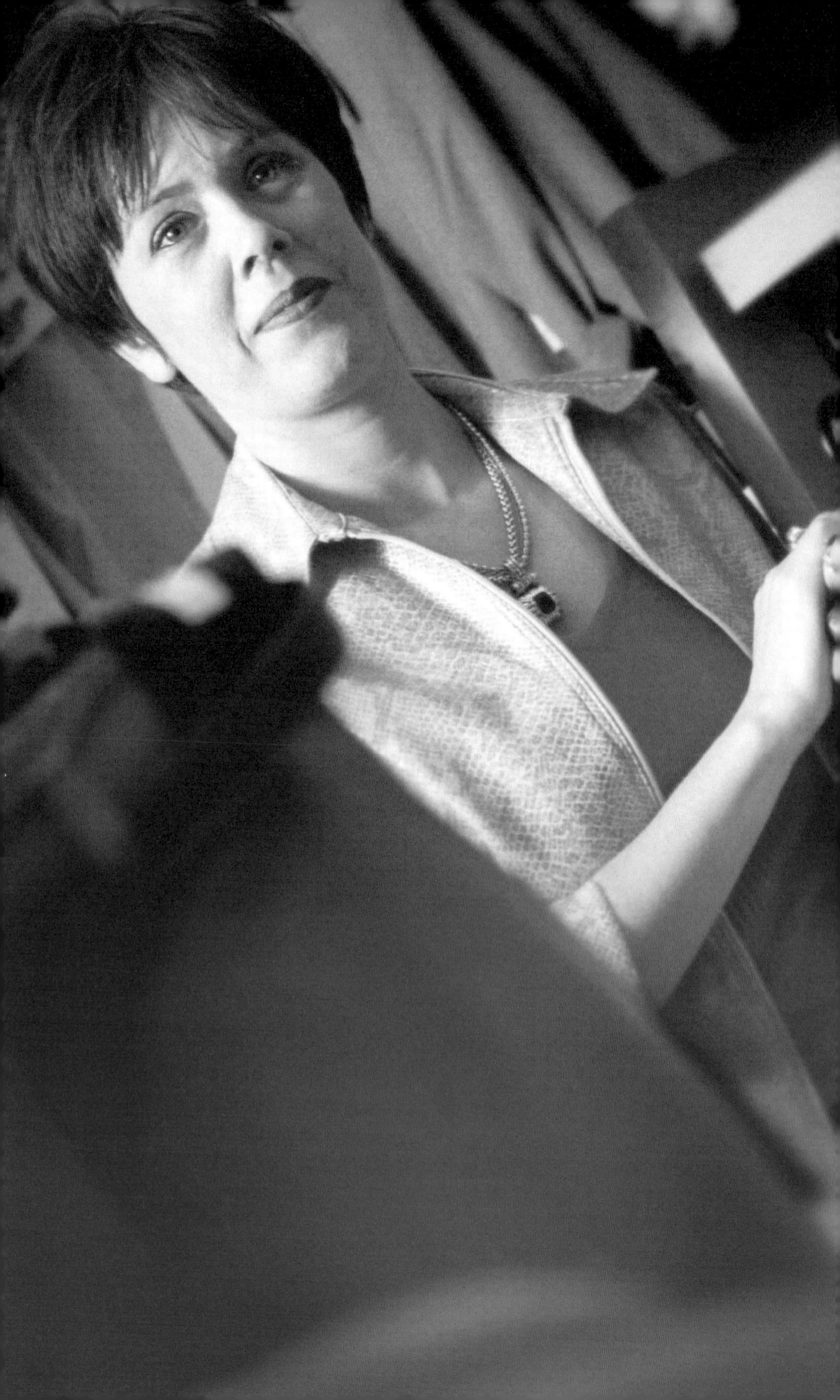

CLAIR JENNIFER

Winning handsomely without spending a cent on advertising

What does the future hold for a thirty-two-year-old fashion-retail entrepreneur who negotiated her first shopping centre lease at the age of nineteen, and now has fifty company-owned stores and a turnover in excess of $40 million?

Clair Jennifer has successfully fought for the hearts and minds of a huge market segment that arguably has not been recognised or catered for in the fiercely competitive and famously fickle female fashion market. And she is winning handsomely without spending one cent on advertising – a promotional tool she says she does not believe in.

Her childhood dream of creating a chain of ladies fashion stores developed her entrepreneurial spirit. At age fourteen she was making wedding dresses, and at seventeen she was operating market stalls. In 1988 at just nineteen years of age, with $2000, Jennifer created Wombat Enterprises, now a fashion chain spanning Australia's mainland eastern states with fifty stores and 240 staff, seemingly well on its way to her ambition of at least one hundred stores.

Closeness to her customers is the first hallmark of Jennifer's success formula

The beauty of Clair Jennifer's success formula is in its simple architecture. The challenge she has mastered ahead of most retailers, however, is clearly in its implementation. Three things in particular stand out – deep and genuine empathy for her chosen customer, a unique value proposition for "conventional" Australian women, and absolutely painstaking staff selection, systems and training.

A sort of Dick Smith of the female fashion industry, Clair Jennifer discovered her market opportunity whilst mixing it with the ruck as a stallholder at markets in Sydney and Canberra in the late 1980s. She saw past the plethora of fashion offerings trying to satisfy the desire for visible difference in fashion, to the not-so-fashion-conscious woman – whom she describes as "a fashion follower, not a fashion leader".

Jennifer talks about her primary customer typically aged 30 to 60 years:

'WHILE SHE LIKES TO LOOK BEAUTIFUL, SHE IS A REAL WOMAN WHO DOESN'T HAVE A MODEL FIGURE, SO SHE GENERALLY LIKES TO COVER THAT UP. SO WE PUT A LITTLE BIT OF ELASTIC IN THE WAISTBAND FOR TUMMIES EXPANDING, MAKE THE SLEEVES MORE FLATTERING TO HER ARMS AND THAT SORT OF THING.'

Jennifer's deep understanding of and empathy with her chosen market values, refined by over fifteen years hands-on experience, is evident in her passionate tone of voice when she says:

'THE CUSTOMER HAS DEVELOPED THE WHOLE CONCEPT FOR THE BUSINESS. SHE IS A SUBURBAN LADY, A MOTHER OR A YOUTHFUL GRANDMOTHER WHO WANTS COMFORTABLE, EASY TO WEAR AND CARE FOR CLOTHING THAT SUITS HER LIFESTYLE...SHOPPING, PICKING UP THE KIDS, GOING TO ART CLASSES AND THAT SORT OF THING.'

A uniquely Australian vision is the second key ingredient

Delivering special value to her carefully chosen customer is the second key ingredient in the Wombat business formula. 'THEY LOVE THE CLOTHING BECAUSE THEY LOVE THE FIT OF IT BECAUSE IT IS DESIGNED TO FIT REAL AUSTRALIAN WOMEN.' Jennifer claims that for the most part the Australian fashion industry only know how to copy what they see overseas:

'WE LOOK OVERSEAS MORE FOR INSPIRATION ABOUT WHAT'S HAPPENING. THEN WE TRANSFORM THAT INSPIRATION INTO WHAT WE BELIEVE THE AUSTRALIAN WOMAN WANTS TO WEAR. AND THAT IS WHY AUSTRALIAN WOMEN COME TO US TO SHOP. I SET THE DESIGN DIRECTION AND MY RANGE DEVELOPER PUTS IT INTO PLACE. SHE THEN CONTRACTS IT TO VARIOUS MANUFACTURERS.'

Jennifer's focus on unique value delivery extends to the in-store experience which she describes as:

'An Australian sort of theatre – a fantasy using soft pastel colours and wood finishes…posters of natural Australian rustic settings…fitting rooms (in addition to changing cubicles) where we offer an old-fashioned fitting room service which you don't get in most fashion stores.'

Hire your customers to deliver a credible experience

Painstaking staff selection, systems and training to deliver the in-store experience and keep the customer coming back is a third key ingredient. Jennifer believes that 'courtesy and a smile' are the same old thing that most retailers will tell you to have. Jennifer says: 'It's having real women in the store who can relate directly to our target customer…similar lifestyle and similar needs so she can discuss those with the customer.'

Make staff accountable, then appraise and reward them

Like Dick Smith, who pioneered electronics retailing in Australia, Jennifer places huge emphasis on systems which drive her business:

'I've set systems in place…policies and procedures documented down to every task so that staff know exactly what they are to do and how they are to do it, and how they are accountable for doing it as well. And then we train and train and train them all over again, and appraise and reward them.'

Unlike Gerry Harvey, Jennifer has chosen to employ staff, not to franchise her stores – a confident move given the mobility of industry staff in her widely dispersed locations. In every store there is a full-time manager and the rest of the women are part-time, usually because, like their customers, they have other family-centred commitments.

Marketing without Money

Once Clair Jennifer has achieved her one hundred store goal, which she believes will be easy, and funded entirely from reinvesting profits as has been her policy to date, she has another passion – to develop natural health supermarkets as seen in the United States. 'We have much smaller versions of health food stores here, but you can't get everything, and not at a reasonable price.'

Jurgen Klein

FOR JAPAN ONLY
THIS WAY UP
JURLIQUE
SUN CREAM
SPF 30 +
Batch No.31 Exp12/04
48 X 100g
Small
Welcome
Packs
Total: 100
THIS WAY UP
JURLIQUE
SUN CREAM
SPF 30 +
Batch No.31 Exp12/04
48 X 100g

JURGEN KLEIN

I call it heart reading, not mind reading

Dr Jurgen Klein and his wife Ulrike have pioneered the growth of scientific natural remedies and therapies, substantially overcoming the 'quack' label, and have built a large vertically integrated business that exports half its output.

In 1983, Jurgen and Ulrike Klein uprooted their four children and emigrated from Germany to Mount Barker in South Australia, having searched the world for what they describe as 'THE CLEANEST, MOST UNPOLLUTED ENVIRONMENT TO GROW HERBS AND FLOWERS, AND A PLACE TO PURSUE THE ANCIENT PRACTICES OF ALCHEMY, HERBAL MEDICINE AND HOMOEOPATHY USING MODERN TECHNOLOGY'.

Today, their company Jurlique International, enjoys revenue of around $90 million, reaps net profits in the order of thirty per cent of sales, and exports around half its sophisticated range of natural health and beauty products to thirty countries.

Jurgen Klein graduated in chemistry and naturopathy, Ulrike in horticulture. Together they established first a herb farm, then a licensed herbal therapeutic products factory, and gradually a network of now some fifty Jurlique retail and 'wellness spa' outlets spanning twelve countries – many company owned, some franchised. These Jurlique-branded outlets account for only twenty-five per cent of product sales, but they are essential for selling the experience and creating long-term loyal customers and an upmarket, scientific image. The remaining seventy-five per cent of product output is sold through resorts, department stores, pharmacies, beauty salons and health food stores – totalling some 5000 outlets worldwide.

With the concept now well-established, the Kleins expect export sales – currently about fifty per cent of revenue – to grow rapidly. The business has been largely self-funding and even today carries little external debt.

However, the spirited rise of this unique manufacturer, now employing some 300 in Australia and 100 in the United States, has been anything but a simple dream according to Jurgen Klein. He and his wife began pursuing their passionate, science-based approach to natural remedies in the early 1970s, marketing their first range of products long before aromatherapy and natural remedies became fashionable, or even acceptable in countries like Australia and the United States.

Pioneering the credibility and growth of the category has had many challenges which have not daunted the Kleins' missionary zeal. Jurgen Klein's characteristically German dedication to task and penchant for quality based on scientific research, appear to have bulldozed through consumer scepticism to broad acceptance. Further, he estimates that, while the majority of store traffic is female, males probably consume as much as forty per cent though many are shy to admit it.

Jurgen Klein says his fascination with the category began when he was fourteen years of age, and since then his life has been devoted to studying ancient and modern knowledge of natural remedies and therapies, both Eastern and Western, and the science that underpins them.

So what is the essence of the Jurlique success in building a market and a company from humble beginnings down on the farm? What are the lessons for others wishing to gain first entrant advantage in emerging markets?

Anticipating and shaping customer preferences, not following them

There is no doubt that, like many entrepreneurs, the Kleins' success lies firstly in anticipating and shaping customer preferences – not following them. Klein says: 'I CALL IT HEART READING, NOT MIND READING, BUT YOU HAVE TO GET THE TIMING RIGHT; YOU MUST CONSTANTLY DO REALITY CHECKS ON YOUR VISION.'

Some thirty years ago, Klein recognised before most that an increasingly urbanised and stressed 'civilised' society would eventually value and turn to improved quality of life as a priority, focussing increasingly on their health and wellbeing as a means of preventing illness, and thus minimising the need for cure. More than that, he recognised also they would want to enhance the health and beauty they have.

Further, Klein accurately anticipated that urban artificiality would lead to increasing interest in more natural remedies and therapies as a pathway to improving health and wellbeing.

Importantly too, Klein was convinced that a scientific, research-based approach to natural remedies and therapies, would eventually be sought after and more highly valued than what he regards as the trendy and superficial approach adopted by established chains such as The Body Shop, and emerging players such as Aveda, Hauschka, Weleda and Aubrey Organics.

Promoting the experience, not the product

Klein says that promoting products generally does not work in his category. Initially, people have to be exposed to the experience. Then they usually buy the concept and become loyal product customers prepared to buy at other outlets or via mail or the company's call centre. A very substantial investment in "day spas and wellness sanctuaries", integrated into many Jurlique retail outlets and designed to deliver that experience and create dedicated long-term customers, is tangible evidence of Klein's conviction to this consumer adoption process.

He says of the potential customer:

'YOU HAVE TO GO SOMEWHERE AND GO THROUGH THE RITUAL AND FEEL IT AND SO ON. I THINK IT'S THE SAME WITH FOOD. YOU CAN TALK ABOUT FOOD AND HAVE IT IN YOUR HOME, BUT WHEN YOU CAN GO TO A RESTAURANT WHICH HAS AMBIENCE, IT TASTES BETTER AND EVERYTHING IS FINE AND IT'S AN EXPERIENCE. SO WE NEED AN EXPERIENCE AND THAT EXPERIENCE IS MULTIFACETED. WHEN I CAN GIVE THAT TO A CUSTOMER AND IT'S HONEST, IT'S NOT FAKE, THEY WILL TAKE IT AND THEY WILL REWARD US BY BECOMING A LOYAL CUSTOMER. AND I CAN BUILD ON THAT. IT'S A SLOW PROCESS ACTUALLY, AND FOR ME IT'S HARD TO BE SO SLOW. BUT I'M GRATEFUL ALSO, FOR I SEE THE OUTCOME.

'SO WHEN WE EDUCATE PEOPLE, WE WIN THEIR TRUST AND GIVE THEM SOMETHING THAT THEY CAN KEEP AND USE LIKE A YARDSTICK.'

Looking for delivery concepts, not simply distribution channels

Though this consumer interface in Jurlique's business is essential to the value delivery process and to the creation of long-term product customers, it is clearly the most challenging and costly end of the business. This is definitely work-in-progress for Klein's honed scientific mind, now applied to his business process.

The service is very personal. Referral is the source of half Jurlique's new customers. Customer expectations of a truly uplifting experience are high. Many customers are quite passionate and demanding. The scientific rationale behind the concept and the products, Jurlique's essential point of difference, is complex. If the experience is not good and convincing, a long-term customer is not created.

Exceptional staff and franchisees with the right attitude and skill are hard to find. For example, from twenty-five carefully selected retail recruits who enter training, the company can expect to distil only two or three at best into long-term positions. Klein has experimented with different sources of staff, basically recruiting from retail and therapy backgrounds, but has found little difference. However, experimental variations in the training and induction methodology are gaining more promising results.

'WE ARE ON THE TRACK LESS TRAVELLED. SO THE HARDEST THING IS TO GET QUALITY STAFF, AND TO RETAIN THE GOOD ONES. THE DOWNSIDE OF RETAIL IS THAT, WITH GOOD EXCEPTIONS, MOST PEOPLE ARE THERE BY DEFAULT. WE HAVE EXPERIMENTED BY TAKING PEOPLE WHO ARE ALREADY THERAPISTS. DO YOU KNOW WHAT THEY HATE MOST...SELLING!'

Peter Kazacos

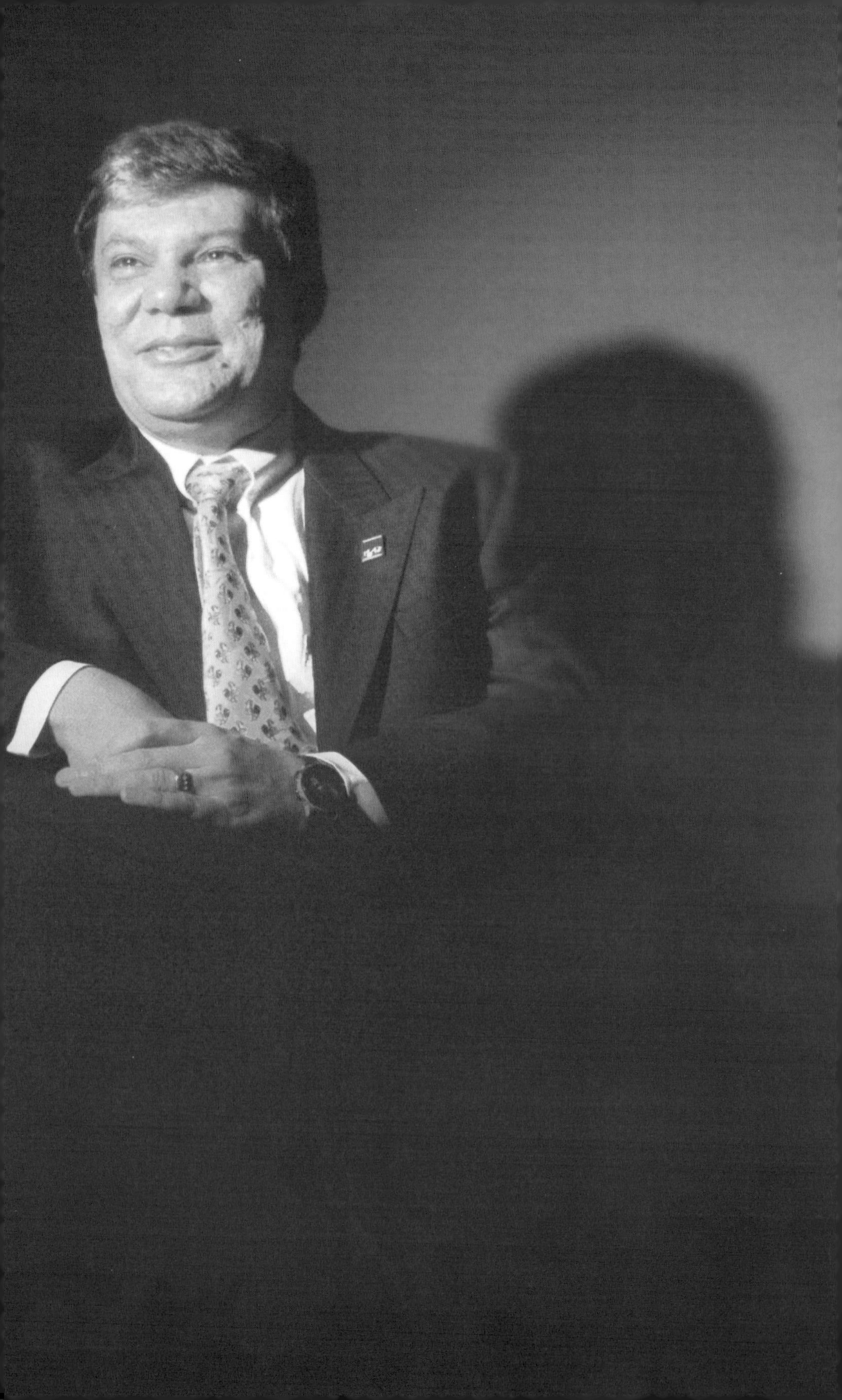

PETER KAZACOS

My success has not been the result of any grand plan, but a voyage of opportunity, discovery and learning

In 1988, Peter Kazacos and his then business partner each put up $5000 as working capital, and founded a company which recently announced a profit before tax of nearly $10 million for FY2002 and which, two years after ASX listing, is ranked among Australia's top 200 companies.

Kazacos came from a humble though industrious background. As a boy, he learned the reality of commercial life very early, helping his mother in the family fish and chip shop. This early experience of face-to-face selling and hard work he says was his first and an enduring lesson in business.

To fund his way through university science and engineering degrees in the 1970s, he and some mates began coaching high-school kids in their spare time.

Believing there must be a better way to coach than one-to-one, he taught his mates programming and cut his first commercial hand at software development, writing an automated coaching program to sell to schools. The venture failed, though the product worked – hardly any schools had computers. This was Kazacos's next lesson – picking markets and getting the timing right, a lesson which he says has served him well ever since.

What I don't do is get caught up with the excitement of a certain technology

'WHAT I DON'T DO IS GET CAUGHT UP WITH THE EXCITEMENT OF A CERTAIN TECHNOLOGY. I LIKE TECHNOLOGY, BUT IF I SEE THERE'S BEEN A SHIFT, I'LL

SHIFT. I'M NOT GOING TO BE DOGMATIC ABOUT STAYING IN THAT SAME PROCESS BECAUSE I BELIEVE THAT PRODUCT'S GOING TO WORK NO MATTER WHAT EVERYBODY ELSE SAYS.'

Still needing to fund his studies, Kazacos decided that software distribution might be a better way to go. He was an early and relatively rare reader of US computer magazines, and, taking advantage of this market imperfection, applied to become the Australian distributor of some significant software products. He grins when he recounts how one of these US companies came to Australia and tried to find his office – then a tiny room above Bankstown railway station used also for coaching high-school students.

I decided then that this is not the business to be in

The software distribution sideline was a mediocre success helping to pay university bills. Later, Kazacos was to learn again the mediocrity of being a distributor of someone else's software when KAZ took on software distribution and in one tender found itself against eighty-three other tenderers. 'I DECIDED THEN THAT THIS IS NOT THE BUSINESS TO BE IN', says Kazacos.

Finishing university, Kazacos scored a graduate job in computing with OCAL, now part of P&O. This turned out to be his next fortuitous lesson in the interface between technology and the realities of business. In addition to gaining valuable exposure to the detailed operational and technical areas of business computing, Kazacos was exposed to the full IT review process being undertaken by OCAL of its computing needs, leading to the company selecting the then latest available hardware and software.

The young Kazacos was given a newly-created position of database administrator, and the task of writing a query language, which was not only used internally by the company with success, but at his suggestion became a revenue generator itself when he managed to sell it to several other companies. 'THE LESSON THIS TAUGHT ME WAS THAT I COULD BUILD SOFTWARE THAT PEOPLE WOULD BUY', says Kazacos, reflecting the importance of this lesson on his self-confidence as well.

In the early 1980s, Kazacos was approached by a friend to join a software development and training company, Aspect Computing. At the time, Kazacos's single-minded goal was to further hone his skills in software development and to gain experience in hands-on sales and consulting as an employee. He accepted the offer. Ironically, nearly twenty years later, KAZ acquired Aspect in 2002 in a $210 million deal.

Start by finding a solid foundation customer

While employed by Aspect, Kazacos made two further discoveries that were to impact on his business approach.

First, having found a foundation customer for the development of a new database query tool, he put a business plan to the company's board to leverage off this opportunity to develop what he believed would become a significantly broader market opportunity. 'THE PLAN SCORED THE LOWEST OF ANY SUBMITTED, AND I SAID TO THE DIRECTOR "I SUPPOSE THE ONES ON YOUR SHELF THAT HAVEN'T SOLD ANYTHING ARE THE ONES THAT SCORED HIGH". TO THE DIRECTOR'S CREDIT, HE SAID "OK WE'LL DO IT ANYWAY".' Kazacos admits that even today he does not place much emphasis on formality in business plans, and tends to be put off by glossy brochures.

Use that customer to win more

For Kazacos, the second lesson of that experience was the value of having a foundation customer. His attitude today is very much one of looking first for the right customer, then shaping what he does for them and others based on their experience and needs. 'THAT'S AGAIN PART OF A FORMULA THAT I'VE CONTINUED TO USE – TO LOOK AT THE RIGHT TYPE OF CLIENTS, AND THEN LOOK AT THE RIGHT TYPE OF SPACE TO BE IN.'

Discovering the right kind of client was really the genesis of KAZ Group Limited. KAZ's foundation customer was AMP which in the late 1980s was in the market for a new superannuation system, an area in which Kazacos had had some prior experience. He made a decision to leave his job with the software company, joining a former business colleague who had told him about the AMP opportunity.

Not only did the fledgling KAZ win the bid to develop the new AMP system, but that grew into the broader role of actually running AMP's system for them, possibly the birth of the then concept of 'insourcing' in this country. According to Kazacos, the next real turning point and lesson occurred when the company won a contract to totally run the computing for three companies formed to continue the business of the then-failed JRA Group. The IT industry insider who tipped Kazacos off about the opportunity said 'I THINK ITS CALLED OUTSOURCING'. Kazacos emphasises that having such a substantial and credible foundation client as AMP made it possible to win this new contract. That was another important lesson for him.

The ultimate compliment

Last financial year, KAZ Group Limited grew sales eighty-one per cent over the previous year to $252 million, and the company now employs in excess of 2400 staff. Part of that growth has been fuelled by the ultimate compliment. KAZ was offered and accepted the opportunity to buy out its first major customer's computing arm, Australian Administration Services (AAS), which it acquired from AMP Life in January 2001.

Core to the now expanded business process outsourcing activities of KAZ is the administration of superannuation funds for nearly four million Australians. The AAS business model has some similarity to the now well-accepted public company outsourced share registry model. It encompasses call centres to take enquiries about superannuation, the receipt and processing of application forms, paying benefits and all related processes. This acquisition has opened Kazacos's horizons and he speculates on how the company may well turn its attention to other large outsourcing opportunities in the public utility and healthcare sectors.

KAZ earns about fifty per cent of its income from business process outsourcing, thirty per cent from information technology outsourcing and twenty per cent from software sales. Kazacos is open-minded as to the future, perhaps a lesson in itself for budding entrepreneurs who seek to imitate his 'voyage of discovery and learning' approach to business.

Chapter 4
CREATING OUTSTANDING VALUE

VALUE CREATION IS THE SINGLE MOST IMPORTANT FOCUS IN BUSINESS. We usually only get value if we first give it. And human beings are never satisfied with the value they have. This spells opportunity.

Our ability to create new value is limited only by our imagination. The purpose of creative thinking is to stimulate our imagination in the pursuit of new value opportunities and ways to deliver value. The remarkable and often overlooked fact of life is that we all observe new value being created every day, but we so seldom recognise that this is what is actually happening.

When a new convenience store is located closer to our place of work or living, we seldom think that the developer is actually creating new *convenience* value. We tend to focus more on the product than the value it creates, and how this value could be maximised.

MARKETING WITHOUT MONEY

Locating a store geographically closer is simply one dimension of the convenience value able to be created. Imagine if the store proactively tailored its range of merchandise and services to other convenience needs and preferences of people in the area. Certainly this happens over time in a very basic way by evolution, but instead this value could be designed and featured by the store from the outset. Most stores limit themselves to proximity and ease-of-access values. They seldom offer other convenience values. The very reason corner stores originally existed was because people needed to walk there because there were few or no cars. That need persists today for very young and very old age groups. Most stores do not look beyond convenience to the potential to strengthen their value monopoly with other value drivers such as quality of life, self-importance and distraction. In many instances, walking to the corner store and talking to the storekeeper forms part of essential social interaction for those living on their own, for example, contributing significantly to their quality of life, self-importance and distraction values. These fundamental value drivers are explained in full in Chapter 11 – Beyond making products to making value.

The first step to success is simply to recognise that you are not in business to provide products or services, but to create value. This simple paradigm shift alone is enough to start the mind on an exploration of possibilities it otherwise may not have contemplated. Terms like 'customer focus' and 'customer service' do not embrace the concept of designing a business to create and deliver value.

The second step is to begin the search for the value that is missing – the value that will make your value bundle outstanding.

In the early 1980s, Woolworths recognised the now somewhat obvious consumer desire for quality fresh food. The company at that time was in the doldrums, but set about the subsequently very successful process of re-inventing itself to become famous as Australia's 'Fresh food people', a label and place in the mind that others have tried to copy with little or no success.

The mastermind of the reinvention, Reg Clairs, who subsequently became group managing director of the company, recognised a further not so obvious value – that Woolworths' fundamental role is to be a conduit to bring customers what they want from wherever it is available. Not earth shattering you may say, but this paradigm shift revolutionised the way the company sought to integrate its buying with growers' production activities so that the two partnered in providing genuine outstanding fresh food value to Woolworths' customers.

The company's early recognition and successful exploitation of the fresh food value *concept* became almost certainly the major driver that more than doubled Woolworths's overall grocery market share and revived its economic performance to a dominant market position and profitability.

Franklins on the other hand, a significant challenger to the dominant full-range food retailing players at the time, was focussed only on dry groceries with limited range, spartan stores and a strong price-fighter appeal. In its early years the company recognised that it was better to flank strong competition with a deliberately different and focussed value offering, rather than confront them.

The Franklins strategy as a dry grocery specialist worked well for the company, and Woolworths and Coles seemed to adopt a live and let live attitude during the 1980s.

In the early 1990s however, Franklins appeared to get itchy feet and decided it too should seek to offer fresh food as a central competitive platform. This decision, and its subsequent expensive implementation, to change or at least dilute the value for which the company had become famous, proved a fatal strategic miscalculation. The fresh food value space was now filled with an entrenched leader. The move was ineffective not only as a value for which Franklins could become famous, but also because the attempt to deliver on a 'me-too' fresh food promise literally turned the Franklins operation upside down. It lost focus on the one thing that had made it famous – great prices on dry groceries.

It is reasonable to argue that Franklins could not afford to ignore the growing fresh food preferences and demands of consumers. However, it would have been far better for the company to have entered the space by capitalising on its proven skill and reputation as a price-fighter, offering a limited range of fresh foods in its then familiar, earthy, 'bulk buy and save style'. To be different and to save money, the Franklins merchandising concept could have employed pallets and bulk bins in a market style, contrasting with a highly polished merchandising approach – territory now owned by Woolworths and copied by Coles.

The search for outstanding value for which an organisation, product or service could become famous, and maintain its reputation, lies at the heart of its strategic choices. Most companies are focussed on what they produce, despite giving well-intentioned lip service to being customer-focussed. They do not consciously live out the role of being proactive creators of outstanding value.

In the search for opportunity to provide greater value, many companies use market research to ask their customers what they want.

These companies wonder why customers usually tell them that what they want is pretty much what they are getting, but maybe at a somewhat lower price and with some added service 'bells and whistles' for which the customers are usually not prepared to pay.

Of course, most such companies have employed much the same business and marketing graduates who follow much the same processes and invariably arrive at much the same conclusions. Is it any wonder then that most players in most categories end up competing largely on price, because there is little value difference between their offerings? Instead of becoming famous for a particular outstanding value offering, they eventually get run out of the market by the certain demise of price-based competition between companies who typically are not true low-cost producers, and who do not have a cost advantage.

Creating focussed value

The saying "You can't please all the people all the time" is true in business as it is in personal life. The goal may be to please some of the people all of the time. *The reality for most business is to please some of the people some of the time.* This is not meant to imply that companies should displease customers; rather they should select customers and use occasions as the main focus of the business. The question arises: 'For whom are we creating outstanding value?' If we try to be all things to all people, we may be successful short term, but soon we will be undermined by competition. A new wise competitor will attack our weakest offering. One of the reasons specialty stores survive against major department stores and supermarkets is that they create more value in specific niches and for specific usage occasions.

So what are the boundaries in choosing for whom you will provide outstanding value?

1. Your specific expertise

The mistake most people make starting out in business is in the choice of the business they enter and the way they choose to compete. Most choose to do something that many others do. They also tend to imitate those with whom they will compete, adopting much the same operating policies and procedures. Is it any wonder then that the customer tends to see them simply as an alternative supplier, rather than a provider of outstanding value?

The first step therefore is to choose a group of would-be customers to whom you could provide a value bundle better than practically anyone else could provide it. This usually means choosing something about which you are knowledgeable and passionate. If you don't feel a missionary zeal about improving something (your cause), then almost certainly you should not enter this market, because you will not be driven internally to provide outstanding value.

2. Your profitable delivery

It is usually easy to provide outstanding value in any marketplace: better quality, better service, lower price, etc. People with passion do it all the time, but most of them fail financially because they haven't worked out beforehand how to deliver the extra value profitably.

Profitable delivery means that you either extract a premium from the customer for the extra value created, or that you produce the same amount of value at a lower cost. The important and obvious prerequisite is that it costs less to produce your value than the price at which you can sell it, and that this is sustainable as the business grows.

3. A sustainable (monopolisable) position

If the outstanding value bundle you create is easily imitated by your competitors at roughly the same cost, it becomes a commodity and is no longer outstanding. In the longer term you will be famous for it no longer.

You need to decide how you can protect or *monopolise* the value that you deliver. This certainly means you will have developed an exceptionally efficient system (a formula) for providing your value, and for building and maintaining your 'famous' reputation for that value.

Marketing without Money

It is, however, true that quite often companies and products manage to sustain the perception of outstanding value long after the reality has been lost. The duration of this 'brand lag' depends on the intensity of competition and customer propensity to trial alternatives.

It is also true that the value bundle offered should be refreshed over time to include other values which in turn strengthen your value monopoly. For example, the familiarity and convenience values of a now multi-store retail chain may well overtake the original outstanding values which at first made it very attractive as a single-store operation.

4. Customised or standardised

Making your choice as to customer and value leads to the question, what level of customisation will you deliver and become famous for.

McDonald's is a rigidly standardised business design. You can only order what they have chosen to offer. Staff are rigidly recruited, attired and trained so that the service level is just as specified as the tangible product. Site selection, layout and presentation are standardised within different store category classifications. Customers are "trained" to work within this system, and are happy to do so on those usage occasions for which they perceive McDonald's is appropriate.

Importantly, McDonald's does not try to appeal to all your eating out occasions or to all people. It knows that its value bundle appeals strongly in just a few situations and, while the company constantly experiments with products and offers to expand the envelope, it also knows that to broaden dramatically would dilute and weaken its powerful "outstanding value" market position. One size is designed to fit the optimum market; virtually no customisation is offered.

At the other end of the spectrum, a one-off a la carte restaurant delivers a very customised experience. It is as if there is a large shock absorber between what the customer might like and what the restaurant delivers. The typical customised restaurateur endeavours to deliver as much choice and flexibility as possible in order to match what the customer would like. Outstanding value, if it exists, is more likely to be in the way the food, ambience, service and experience are customised from one customer to the next. The skill and disposition of key staff, such as waiting staff, chefs and so on, determine for the most part whether exceptional value is delivered. Individuality and appeal of variables such as food, ambience, view and comfort are obviously quite important. There are many variables to manage that are difficult to specify and control.

McDonald's has designed a system for delivering predetermined outstanding value, albeit very basic, whereas a customised restaurant is endeavouring to make and deliver outstanding value "on the run on the night".

Anticipating new value

Intuitive advertising man John Singleton once said that the best way to make money is to know where people are going, anticipate what they will want when they get there, be there to sell it to them when they arrive, and then go off and do the same thing somewhere else.

It typically follows that the more anticipatory the value created, the more outstanding it will become. The more efficiently provided, the more profitable it will be.

One of the serious limitations of conventional market research is that customers cannot tell you what they want until they know what is possible.

Most success stories arise where people have delivered what customers want before they even knew they wanted it. Most of us have televisions, VCRs, mobile telephones and many other products and services which we value but which we could not have imagined we would want before we knew they existed.

What we did however know beforehand is that we would like products and services that would:

➲ Make our lives easier (convenience value)

➲ Provide us a healthier, less stressed and happier family and work life (quality of life value)

➲ Provide escape from boredom or too much to do (distraction value)

⊃ Make us feel good about ourselves and cause others to admire us (self-importance value).

The more values bundled into such products, the more attractive they tend to become. For example, the world's largest mobile telephone manufacturer, Nokia, recently announced that it had decided to become the world's largest camera company – redefining and increasing the now commoditised value of its mobile telephones to include inbuilt cameras.

In the process of value bundling there is a need to look beyond the average person. An average is only an assortment of different people with different circumstances, tastes, and needs. Every teacher knows that there is no 'average' student in the class. If there are characteristics of intelligence, discipline, laziness, energy, troublemaking, boredom, troubles at home, and so on, then a teacher knows that every possible combination of these factors will be exhibited in an individual.

The trick is to recognise that individuality as a source of value, while not ending up with a market that is so small that it is of little or no interest.

The great thing about the value bundling approach is that most humans have similar desires and ultimately want the same values, albeit in differing combinations, basically depending on context. Just as a house is built from very few basic materials, so human needs and wants are also quite basic. Remember however, as Abraham Maslow discovered, *when one need is satisfied, another inevitably and quickly appears in its place.* So knowing where people are at and where they are trying to go, and anticipating and shaping their emerging priorities, is the key to designing an outstanding value bundle.

It is the concept we use to shape and combine basic values that will lead us from competition to the achievement of surpetition. This process is discussed in Chapter 9 – Beyond competition to surpetition.

CHAPTER 4 – CREATING OUTSTANDING VALUE

Poulter, Adler and Bond, Rein and Blackman

Len Poulter (Lenard's), like other top franchisors, learned early that his job is to provide a value bundle to his franchisees which they cannot provide economically or easily for themselves.

Poulter sums up this value bundle as 'SERVICING LENARD'S FRANCHISEES BY ENSURING:

- THEY [THE FRANCHISEES] ARE MOVING FORWARD AS A BUSINESS
- THEY ARE MATCHING THEIR CONSUMERS' NEEDS
- THAT OUR SYSTEM IS REFINED
- THAT OUR BUSINESS STRUCTURE IS SOUND
- THEY HAVE A GOOD, PROFITABLE FRANCHISOR TO LOOK BACK AT'.

Paul Adler and Brad Bond (Invizage) are blunt about their strategy which aims to deliver worry-free, cost-controlled and productive technology that SME (small to medium enterprise) clients say they want and need. The partners claim such businesses need to decide whether to manage IT systems by crisis, continually putting out fires, incurring regular business disruption, and allowing users to become more frustrated and work less effectively…or whether to take a proactive, long-term approach, by investing in a support plan. The value bundle delivered to stakeholders – clients, staff and the company – is potentially much greater all round. It should result in increased productivity, less stress, greater predictability, and a longer and mutually more profitable relationship between Invizage and its clients.

In injury cases Therese Rein (Ingeus) provides a value bundle which is carefully integrated into the anticipated needs of seemingly disparate stakeholders: 'IF WE FIND A SOLUTION THAT MEETS THE NEEDS OF THE INJURED WORKER, THE EMPLOYER AND THE INSURER, THAT'S THE VALUE. LET ALONE THE IMPACT ON THEIR FAMILIES. SO THERE ARE LOTS OF WINNERS.' A key stakeholder in employment services, Rein says, is the taxpayer who wants a highly accountable, effective service that is delivered in a humanitarian manner with respect towards people.

Graeme Blackman (IDT) knew that if he could ease and expedite United States Food and Drug Administration approval of his clients' anti-cancer drug active pharmaceutical ingredients – which together with expedited efficacy and safety approvals is the gateway to early market entry and first-mover advantage – the value to his pharmaceutical company clients could be immense. He achieved surpetition by enhancing and monopolising his company's value bundle in this one key move.

Len Poulter

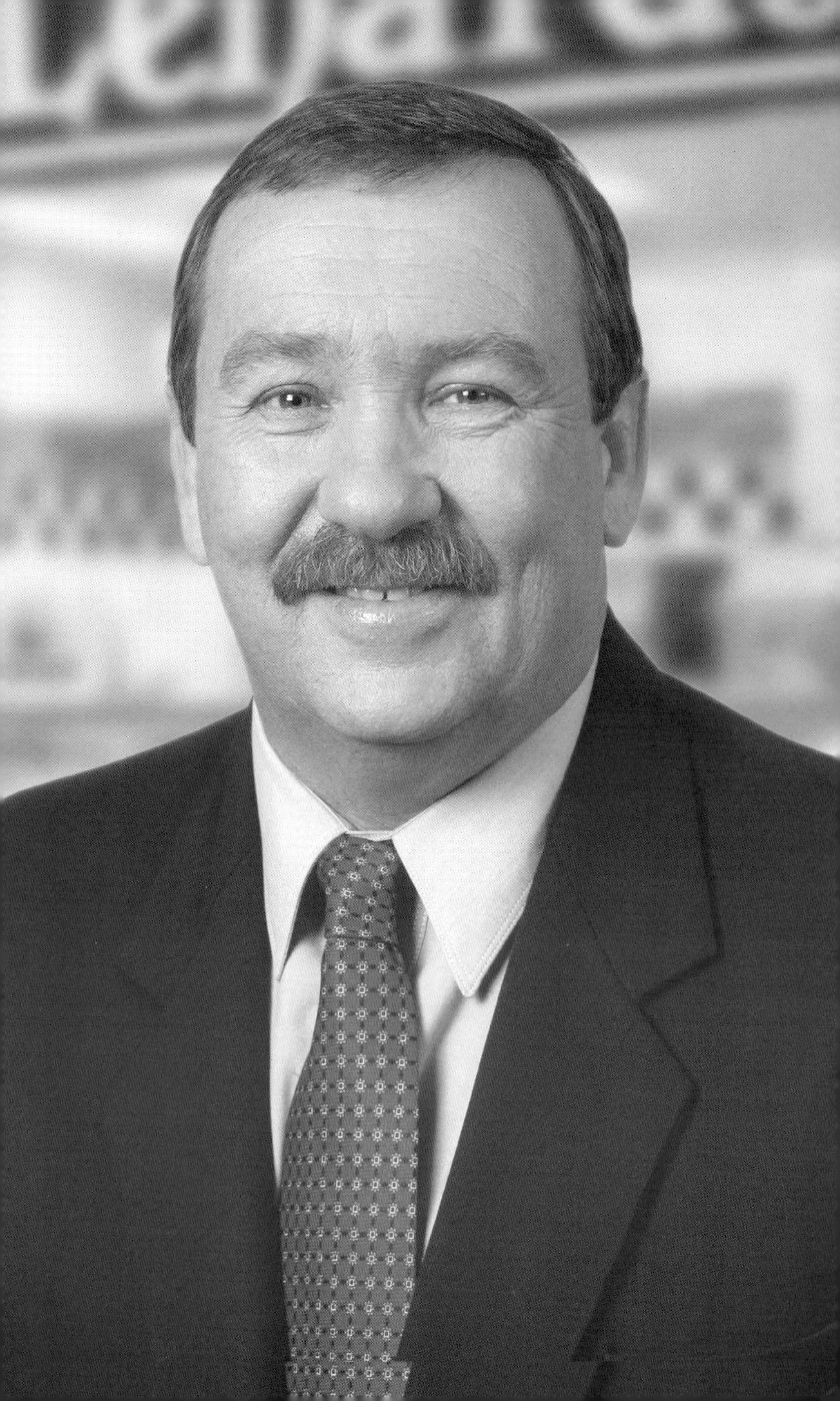

LEN POULTER

I think a lot of people know the problems of their industry, but they don't know how to step outside the norms

Len Poulter has built one of Australia's most admired retail franchise chains, successfully pioneering the development of fresh added-value chicken. He now has ambitions to reinvent and reclaim independent butcher shop retailing in Australia.

In the 1970s and in his mid-teens, Poulter earned his stripes as an apprentice butcher in a city he describes as having one of the toughest and best food markets in the world, Melbourne. In 1987 he gave up the red meat trade and moved to Queensland where he started Lenard's Pty Ltd, today a clear leader in independent specialised fresh chicken meal retailing in Australia. In 2003, the company's 167 franchised stores will serve more than 10 million customers, add value to around 11 million chickens, and earn revenue of $117 million. About twenty per cent of revenue will be in red meat meals.

Early in his career as a butcher, and with a modest loan from his father, Poulter's ambition and nose for opportunity drove him to buy a run-down butcher shop in inner suburban Melbourne. What he discovered while rejuvenating this shop, and others he subsequently bought and sold progressively, was to change his life.

'BEEF AND LAMB PRICES WERE MOVING UPWARDS AT THE TIME. BUT MORE IMPORTANTLY, LIFESTYLES WERE UNDOUBTEDLY CHANGING. CUSTOMERS WOULD COME IN LOOKING FOR DIFFERENT THINGS. YOU COULD SEE IT IN THEIR FACES. YOU DIDN'T HAVE TO TALK TO THEM. MORE WOMEN WERE COMING IN. MOST OF THEM WERE WORKING. AND THEY HAD NO TIME. WHILE IN MY FIRST BUTCHER SHOP I WAS DOING JUST ONE CHICKEN PRODUCT, BY MY FIFTH SHOP I WAS DOING MANY. THEY WERE THINGS THAT WERE SO MUCH QUICKER AND EASIER FOR CUSTOMERS TO PREPARE. IT WASN'T ROCKET SCIENCE TO WORK OUT EXACTLY WHAT THE CONSUMERS WERE DOING. MY PROBLEM WAS ACTUALLY DOING SOMETHING ABOUT IT.

'I FOUND THAT CHICKEN PRODUCTS WERE SOMETHING LIKE HALF MY SALES. MORE IMPORTANTLY, I WAS MAKING A LOT MORE MONEY OUT OF CHICKEN BECAUSE I WAS ADDING A LOT OF VALUE TO IT. IT WASN'T HARD TO REALISE THAT THAT'S WHAT THE CUSTOMERS WANTED.'

Doing something about it was the kind of challenge that ignited Poulter's passionate nature.

'I THINK A LOT OF PEOPLE KNOW THE PROBLEMS OF THEIR INDUSTRY, BUT THEY DON'T KNOW HOW TO STEP OUTSIDE THE NORMS. I THINK THE REASON IT WAS EASY FOR ME TO IDENTIFY THIS IS THAT I'VE BEEN LOOKING FOR SOMETHING BETTER ALL MY LIFE. SO FOR ME TO STEP OUTSIDE THE BUTCHER'S SHOP WASN'T HARD.'

Poulter moved to Queensland with the idea of starting an added-value chicken franchise chain of about thirty stores because he believed there were few other marketplaces that were still a little bit behind and would give him an opportunity to make a few mistakes.

'IF I'D MADE THE MISTAKES THAT I'VE MADE HERE [IN QUEENSLAND] IN MELBOURNE OR EVEN SYDNEY, I WOULDN'T BE HERE TODAY. TO GET INTO THE MARKETPLACE AS A FRANCHISOR IN MELBOURNE WOULD HAVE BEEN TOO HARD.'

Hey you'd better get back and start working on this business

One of the mistakes Poulter made in his bullish early days of learning franchising could easily have been terminal. Under-capitalised, he set about opening stores at a rapid rate with the intention of selling them to franchisees, and quickly built unplanned negative cashflow approaching half-a-million dollars.

'BEING THE NEW BOY ON THE BLOCK WITH EVERYONE BUILDING YOU UP, IT SEEMED A GREAT TIME BUT IN FACT IT WAS A VERY DANGEROUS TIME. IT WAS MY NAIVETE THAT GOT ME INTO THAT POSITION, AND THE RESULTANT SHOCK THAT SAID TO ME "HEY YOU'D BETTER GET BACK AND START WORKING ON THIS BUSINESS".'

At that time, 1989, Poulter was joined by a former McDonald's franchisee, Paul Bardwell. Both men are the major shareholders in Lenard's Pty Ltd today. Bardwell's training and experience in the McDonald's system was invaluable to the fledgling franchisor. So was Poulter's realisation that he was no longer in retailing, but in franchising. Their fellow director and shareholder, Brian Parsonage, has tirelessly driven the disciplined roll-out of stores since day one.

We believe we are ahead of any other franchise company in Australia

'OUR BUSINESS IS SERVICING OUR FRANCHISEES AND MAKING SURE THAT THEY ARE MOVING FORWARD AS A BUSINESS AND MATCHING THEIR CONSUMERS' NEEDS. THAT'S OUR JOB. AND MAKING SURE THAT OUR SYSTEM IS REFINED, OUR BUSINESS STRUCTURE IS SOUND, THAT OUR FRANCHISEES HAVE A GOOD, PROFITABLE AND SOUND FRANCHISOR TO LOOK BACK AT.'

This determination and commitment led within a few years to Lenard's being named Australian Franchisor of the Year, and doubtless to Poulter saying with conviction 'WE BELIEVE WE ARE AHEAD OF ANY OTHER FRANCHISE COMPANY IN AUSTRALIA WHEN IT COMES TO SERVICING THEIR FRANCHISEES.'

Poulter is convinced there is a much bigger game yet to be played out – quality ready-to-heat-and-eat pre-cooked meals with all the ingredients including vegetables provided – what the company has branded its 'Lenard's Easy Living' range.

Further, he believes the opportunity to reinvent and franchise butcher shops, seriously extending meal offerings into the moribund red meat industry using the now proven Lenard's brand and systems, is one of the greatest opportunities staring him in the face right now.

'FIFTEEN YEARS AGO, NINETY PER CENT OF BREAD WAS SOLD THROUGH SUPERMARKETS AND CONVENIENCE STORES. AROUND HALF THAT MARKET HAS NOW BEEN TAKEN BY HOT BREAD SHOPS LIKE BAKER'S DELIGHT. TODAY EIGHTY-SIX PER CENT OF THE MEAT MARKET IN AUSTRALIA IS CONTROLLED BY THREE SUPERMARKETS. SO THERE IS AN ENORMOUS POTENTIAL IN AUSTRALIA.'

Execution of your idea and commitment to making it work are more important than the idea itself

Poulter sums up his learnings in pioneering and shaping one of Australia's most successful franchise chains in five points:

> 1. *Make sure that your idea is not your fantasy, but what the customer wants.* Test the market constantly. Make sure they are willing to put their hands in their pockets and buy it.
>
> 2. *Execution of your idea and commitment to making it work are more important than the idea itself.* He likens a good business structure to that of a house with solid foundations, and four pillars that support everything – vision, philosophy, team and execution.
>
> 3. *Surround yourself with good people who believe in what you are trying to achieve* – making sure you communicate and share the vision so they can be motivated too.
>
> 4. *You've got to be flexible.* Be able to tack from side to side, picking changing values, and continually shaping and reshaping what you do in responding to them.
>
> 5. *Provide clear leadership, a game plan and discipline to your team as its coach or captain.* He parallels business leadership to sports leadership. In business, the leader's job is to continually make the goals and milestones as clear as they are in sport.

Paul Adler
Brad Bond

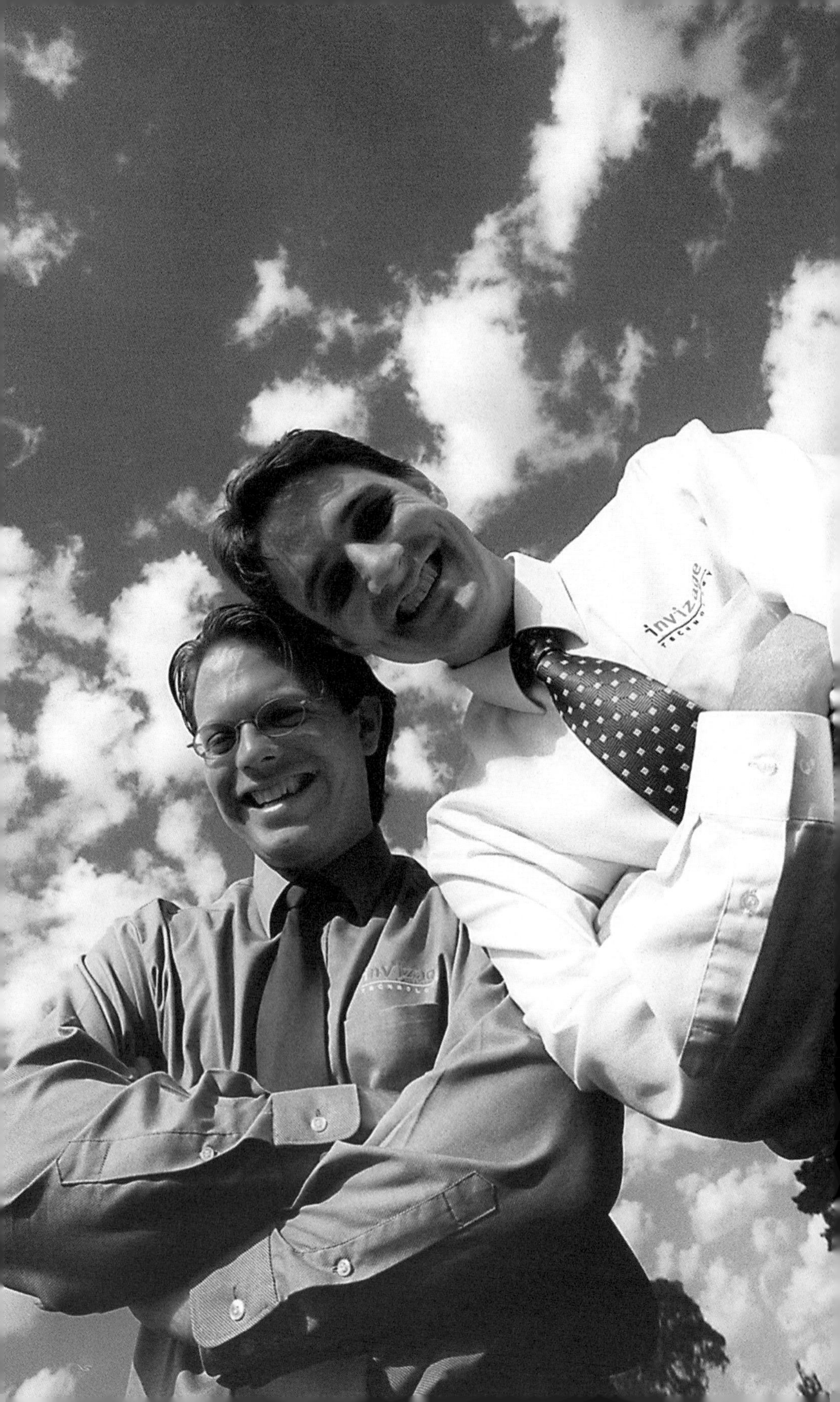

PAUL ADLER
BRAD BOND

Being proactive rather than reactive will transform our industry

Two young Melbourne entrepreneurs are well on their way to proving the concept for a substantial McDonald's-like IT support business, aimed at the large, difficult, cost-conscious and unconquered SME (small to medium enterprise) market. Paul Adler and Brad Bond, founders of Invizage Technology, reveal their battle plan.

When in 1996 as twenty-one-year-old university students, Paul Adler and Brad Bond got together to start what has become Invizage Technology, they had grand visions of building a big, sprawling empire to provide all things computer-related to all people. Invizage today is just the opposite – a tightly-focussed 'one thing' business successfully penetrating a yawning but challenging market gap – integrated IT support for SMEs.

With an investment of $250 each, used to advertise in several local newspapers to get the ball rolling, and no subsequent capital injections, the partners have already built a business which in the FY2003 expects to achieve revenue of around $8 million, and which has over fifty employees and offices in three states. The company services over 6500 different clients, supports 850 network servers and 41 000 individual computers.

Adler and Bond plan to build a substantial and sustainable company dedicated to a missionary-like cause which 'aims to improve businesses and make individuals' lives easier through technology'. The goal is to grow to around five times their present size over the next five years, and they are prepared to reinvest and live frugally in order to achieve that goal. They say the main constraint to their more rapid growth, which they believe they are well on the way to overcoming, is an even tighter system of delivery to a disparate market. Roughly ninety-five per cent of clients have less than fifty computers, and each has differing combinations of hardware, software and needs.

In 2001 Invizage Technology was ranked seventh in *Business Review Weekly's* one hundred fastest growing companies, with a compound average growth of 144 per cent per annum over the previous five years. An Australian Bureau of Statistics survey in August 2000 put Invizage in the top 1.5 per cent of IT service firms, underscoring the low barriers to entry and resultant fragmentation of such suppliers serving the SME sector. The survey shows that currently around eighty-four per cent of service is provided by operators with computer skills and a mobile phone, and between one and four people.

According to Adler, SME support expectations are changing rapidly, driven especially by clients' increasing reliance on technology as their core business enabler.

'A ONE-MAN BAND CAN PROVIDE A VERY HIGH LEVEL OF SERVICE FOR A VERY SHORT PERIOD OF TIME AND A VERY PERSONALISED SERVICE, WHICH IS WHAT CLIENTS LIKED ABOUT US IN THE FIRST PLACE. WE STARTED OFF JUST LIKE THAT AND WE SAW THAT IT'S JUST NOT POSSIBLE. YOU'VE EITHER GOT TO GO BIG OR YOU DON'T DO IT AT ALL, BECAUSE YOU JUST BURN OFF CLIENTS AS FAST AS YOU GET THEM. THE NUMBER ONE COMPLAINT WE HEAR WHEN WE GO IN TO A BUSINESS CURRENTLY SERVICED BY A ONE-MAN BAND IS "THEY CAN'T GET HERE WHEN WE NEED THEM".'

We need to continually focus on developing more systems

The decision to go big means Invizage has to perfect its delivery system, be more efficient and add value that the small operators can't. The company has overcome the 'can't get here when we need them' syndrome by dedicating a team of six to eight technicians to take their system way beyond the current largely crisis-management focus that is the industry norm. Bond emphasises: 'WE NEED TO CONTINUALLY FOCUS ON DEVELOPING MORE SYSTEMS TO MAKE IT MORE REPRODUCIBLE AND LESS RELIANT ON INDIVIDUALS' SKILLS. THAT'S DEFINITELY OUR MAJOR WORK IN PROGRESS.'

It's time to get proactive

The company's focus on greater systemisation and added value is evidenced by the launch in 2002 of a new suite of subscription-based, fixed-cost Invizage Support Plans designed to create a new category of service provision, basically *scheduled* maintenance and support, as opposed to the industry norm of crisis response. Hourly rates for customers who elect to switch to a support plan have been halved and according to the partners has put Invizage rates in the lowest quartile of the industry. In addition to covering crisis management, the new support plan fee covers replacement parts, a comprehensive scheduled maintenance program, full systems documentation, and a provision for training and ad hoc requirements. A support plan for a business with a server and five computers costs around $77 per week.

The company is blunt about its strategy which aims to deliver worry-free, cost-controlled and productive technology that its clients say they want and need. It claims:

'BUSINESSES NEED TO DECIDE WHETHER TO MANAGE IT SYSTEMS BY CRISIS, CONTINUALLY PUTTING OUT FIRES, INCURRING REGULAR BUSINESS DISRUPTION, AND ALLOWING USERS TO BECOME MORE FRUSTRATED AND WORK LESS EFFECTIVELY…OR WHETHER TO TAKE A PROACTIVE, LONG-TERM APPROACH, BY INVESTING IN A SUPPORT PLAN,'

Adler and Bond say that fifty per cent of their clients have now converted to support plans, so attractive they believe is the offer. They acknowledge that, while this initiative will not grow their support revenue with converting clients, it will give the client a fixed rather than unpredictable cost, and shift Invizage technicians out of cost-inefficient crisis response to a largely preventative and proactive service mode. The resultant efficiencies in staff scheduling and skilling, a guaranteed cash flow from subscriptions, and greater client satisfaction and loyalty are key benefits Invizage expects as its payoff.

The important 'other half' of Invizage's business is contract work, including major installations and upgrades, which the partners say is generally more profitable than support. However, it is the trust and intimate knowledge that grows from providing competent support over time that puts Invizage in the box seat to win clients' major contracts.

Support is a gateway to contracts, and the better the client's system becomes, the easier it is to provide efficient support.

The evolved Invizage business concept has some extremely useful signposts for other entrepreneurs, regardless of industry.

Elevated cause

The cause (or mission) has been elevated from "IT crisis management" to "major productivity and convenience gains through technology" for businesses who can't justify an IT department – a paradigm shift of major significance to the company and the client.

Greater value

The value delivered to stakeholders – clients, staff and the company – is potentially much greater all round: productivity, less stress, predictability, and a longer and mutually more profitable relationship.

Replicable formula

Crises can't be eliminated, but they can be minimised by better client systems, procedures and management. Using its Support Plans, Invizage, importantly, has chosen to formularise the latter in order to minimise the former.

Reputation snowball

Practically all the company's major contract work, such as new installations and major upgrades, flows from existing satisfied support relationships. In addition, over half new client business is the result of referral from existing satisfied clients. A value delivery formula that predictably creates satisfied clients, generates flow-on major contracts from them, and results in enthusiastic referral to new clients – all at practically no marketing cost – is a good example of surpetition achieved through innovative concept design.

Therese Rein

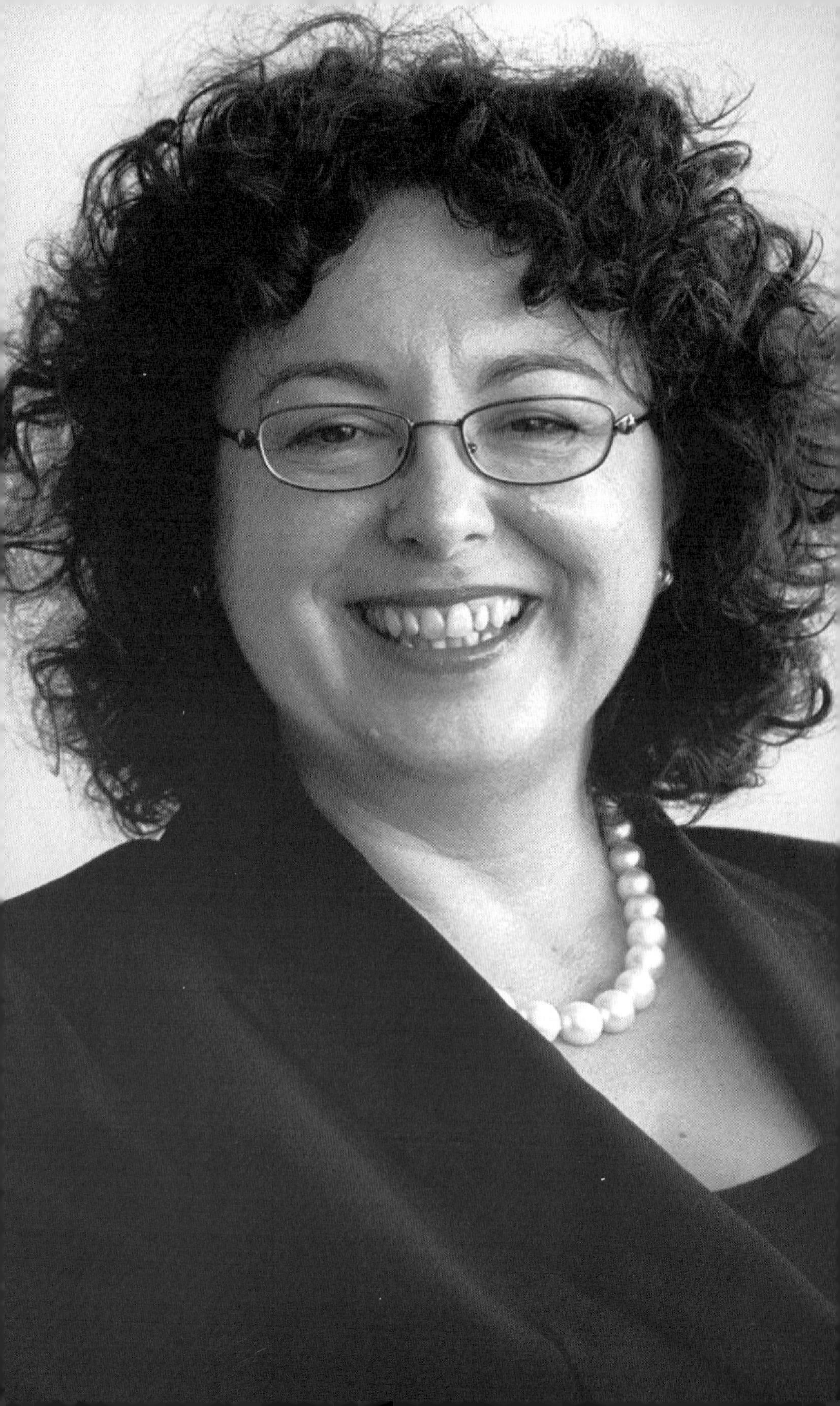

CHAPTER 4 – CREATING OUTSTANDING VALUE

THERESE REIN

We focus on what is required and just keep delivering and improving it

Therese Rein, former professional psychologist, has skilfully crafted a large business by integrating into the values of seemingly diverse stakeholders, and combining the knowledge of different professional disciplines.

In the mid 1980s, Rein was employed as a professional psychologist and counsellor to help injured workers regain productive employment and normality either in their pre-injury job or in a different role. Today, she is the major shareholder and managing director of one of Australia's largest and fastest growing integrated human resource companies, Brisbane headquartered Ingeus Ltd (formerly Work Directions Pty Ltd), which currently employs around 500 full-time staff, and a further 500 mostly full-time contractors through its labour hire subsidiary. In Australia the group has over forty offices covering four states.

In November 2002, Ingeus also commenced delivering employment services in the United Kingdom as the equal largest provider of the 'Public Sector Led New Deal'.

Rein's story is typical of an emerging breed of techno-entrepreneur – former technically-oriented professionals or academics with little or no business background who have successfully commercialised their knowledge using creative conceptual thinking, good timing and courage, usually as a substitute for money.

Work Directions started life in 1989 when Rein recognised the need and the opportunity to integrate the then disparate professional services available to injured workers, insurers and employers. She recognised that all these stakeholders have much the same objectives – to get injured people back to productive and satisfying work and a normal life at the least cost and in the fastest time possible.

The company's other major shareholder, private physiotherapist Ms Jane Edwards, believed in the opportunity and in Rein, and became a non-executive investor and director of the company from the outset.

John C Lyons and Edward de Bono — *129*

Today, Inergise Australia, an Ingeus subsidiary, integrates the diverse skills of its employed psychologists, occupational therapists, physiotherapists, rehabilitation counsellors, exercise physiologists, occupational health nurses, occupational health and safety advisers, case managers and social workers to provide problem-removal value to its stakeholders.

In the mid 1990s, having bedded-down this post-injury rehabilitation side of the business, Rein diversified into an even larger opportunity, employment and training services, basically assisting the long-term unemployed through job matching and training to obtain sustained jobs. These employment services continue to be provided under the Work Directions banner.

As a result, Ingeus Group has become a leader in 'integrated human services'. Rein says the company is now the equal third largest provider of intensive assistance services in Australia under what is the largest ever Australian Government outsourcing of human services.

About seventy-five per cent of the company's services are provided in a regulated environment, and about fifty per cent is open-tender dependent, so government policy and the ability to continually win contracts are key variables, both clearly threats and opportunities, on which management must concentrate.

Rein seems relaxed and philosophical in her approach to coping with this lumpy and typically 'public–private partnership' feature of the business.

'WE FOCUS ON WHAT IS REQUIRED, AND JUST KEEP DELIVERING AND IMPROVING IT. IN A REGULATED MARKET OR REGULATORY ENVIRONMENT, THAT'S HOW YOU HAVE TO FUNCTION, OPERATING WITHIN THE POLICY FRAMEWORK OF THE GOVERNMENT OF THE DAY.'

However, in a further diversification, and a balancing move, the thirty-year-old, Adelaide-based Clements human resource consulting business, with an established track record in largely private general recruitment, labour hire and work-focussed education and training, was acquired in March 2002. Digesting and realising the hoped-for synergies of this acquisition is a key part of Rein's work-in-progress.

Another significant expansionary and balancing move has been the establishment of a wholly owned subsidiary in the UK to provide human services in a regulatory and industrial environment which Rein says is not dissimilar to that in which the company has grown successfully in Australia.

There are *four principles* in particular that Rein has followed which are common and often defining success factors among the entrepreneurs we have researched. If followed, these principles create and communicate value which is so compelling that customers flock to them. Importantly, money is invested in creating value, not in flogging near-commodities.

A cause that is bigger than her business

'I DON'T LIKE PEOPLE BEING THROWN ON THE SCRAP HEAP. I THINK IT'S A WASTE OF HUMAN CAPITAL AND POTENTIAL. I THINK THAT PEOPLE SOMETIMES THINK THEY'RE ON THE SCRAP HEAP WHEN THEY NEED NOT BE. YOU TALK TO PEOPLE WHO ARE FIFTY AND THEY HAVE A LIFE OF EXPERIENCE AND THEY ARE BEING REJECTED BY EMPLOYERS WHEN IN FACT THEY OFFER SO MUCH – COMMONSENSE, STABILITY, COMMITMENT, CAPACITY. WHY WOULD YOU WASTE THAT? I FEEL THE SAME WAY ABOUT PEOPLE WHO HAVE BEEN INJURED. I THINK IT IS VERY EASY TO THINK THAT THIS PERSON IS DAMAGED GOODS. I THINK THAT'S A WASTE OF AUSTRALIA'S ENERGY. I THINK THAT ENABLING PEOPLE TO RECONNECT WITH THEIR COMMUNITIES, TO RECONNECT WITH INDEPENDENCE, TO RECONNECT WITH THEIR POTENTIAL – I THINK THAT MATTERS', Rein says with credible passion.

A value bundle integrated into the anticipated needs of stakeholders

'IN INJURY MANAGEMENT, IF WE CAN HELP PEOPLE RECOVER AND GET BACK TO WORK, THEY'RE HAPPY. THE EMPLOYERS AND INSURERS ARE HAPPY ALSO BECAUSE THEY WANT TO CONTAIN THEIR PREMIUMS AND COSTS. IF WE FIND A SOLUTION THAT MEETS THE NEEDS OF THE INJURED WORKER, THE EMPLOYER AND THE INSURER, THAT'S THE VALUE. LET ALONE THE IMPACT ON THEIR FAMILIES. SO THERE ARE LOTS OF WINNERS', Rein says.

'A KEY STAKEHOLDER IN EMPLOYMENT SERVICES IS THE TAXPAYER. THE TAXPAYER WANTS A HIGHLY ACCOUNTABLE, EFFECTIVE SERVICE THAT IS DELIVERED IN A HUMANITARIAN MANNER WITH RESPECT TOWARDS PEOPLE. IN THE MAJORITY OF CASES, A LONG-TERM UNEMPLOYED PERSON WANTS TO HAVE A STEADY INCOME, WANTS TO BE ABLE TO WALK WITH THEIR HEAD HELD HIGH, WANTS TO

Marketing without Money

BE PRODUCTIVE, WANTS TO BE CONTRIBUTING, WANTS MONEY TO SPEND, WANTS TO STOP TURNING UP AND PUTTING THEIR FORMS IN, WANTS TO HAVE THEIR LIFE BACK. AND IT'S GOOD FOR THE PURCHASER – THE GOVERNMENT.'

A value delivery formula that works and is replicable, though not inflexible

Rein says that Work Directions' staff deal with around 35 000 'cases' per year, people often in a stressed condition and in dispersed locations.

'I THINK THAT ROBUST COMPANIES ACHIEVE CONSISTENCY THROUGH RIGOROUSLY DOCUMENTING THEIR PROCEDURES AND SYSTEMS, SUPPORTED WITH IT IN SOME CASES, BUT ALSO HAVE METHODS OF CAPTURING, ENCOURAGING AND REWARDING INNOVATION.

'IN OUR CASE MANAGEMENT, WE ASSESS PEOPLE, WE HELP THEM DEVELOP A REALISTIC GOAL AND PLAN AND WE GET SIGN-OFF. THEN WE IMPLEMENT THE PLAN. THAT WHOLE PROCESS OF HOW WE DO THE ASSESSMENT, HOW WE WRITE THE PLAN, HOW WE DO A WORK SITE ASSESSMENT – THESE THINGS CAN BE QUITE RIGOROUSLY DOCUMENTED AND DISCIPLINED. THERE HAS TO BE DISCRETION AND CREATIVITY ON THE PART OF THE PROFESSIONAL – THEIR PROBLEM-SOLVING CAPABILITY, THEIR RESOURCING. EVERYONE IS NOT THE SAME, BUT YOU STILL HAVE TO HAVE A SIMILAR APPROACH, A FRAMEWORK IN WHICH YOU CATER FOR INDIVIDUAL DIFFERENCES.'

A reputation built more on outstanding delivery than on promotional spend

'WITH COMMONWEALTH AND OTHER GOVERNMENT DEPARTMENTS, THE PROCESS IS THAT YOU TENDER AND THAT PROCESS HAS A GREAT DEAL OF PROBITY. YOU RECEIVE THE TENDER AND TAKE A GREAT DEAL OF TIME TO UNDERSTAND IT. WE'RE TALKING ABOUT PUBLIC–PRIVATE PARTNERSHIPS. SO WHAT ARE THE KEY DELIVERABLES THAT WE ARE LOOKING FOR, HOW ARE THEY TO BE MEASURED, IS THERE CLARITY OF MEASUREMENT, WHAT ARE THE OBLIGATIONS ABSOLUTELY REQUIRED.

'THEN YOU BASICALLY CREATE A SOLUTION. YOU MIGHT DO THAT BY RESEARCHING WORLD'S BEST PRACTICE, TALKING TO PEOPLE, BEING CREATIVE, THINKING ABOUT THINGS OUTSIDE THE SQUARE. YOU FOCUS ON WHAT IS GOING TO WIN THE TENDER AND HOW TO DELIVER IT, HOW TO MAKE THE DIFFERENCE.'

Graeme Blackman

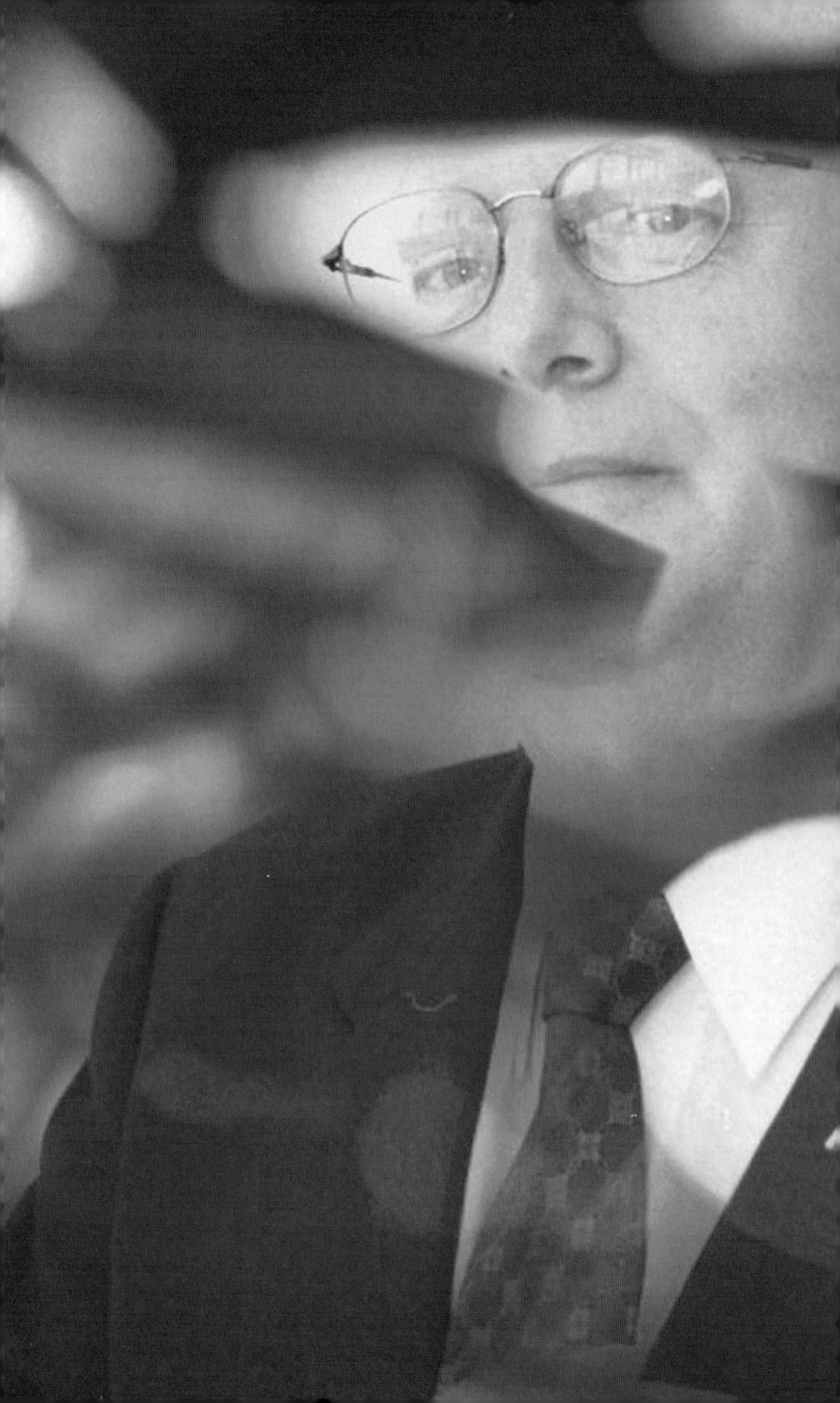

GRAEME BLACKMAN

There is nothing more motivating than having your back literally to the wall

How has a former professor of pharmaceutical chemistry managed to build a highly profitable $100 million capped company in just thirteen years, *convincing some of the world's largest pharmaceutical companies to trust his company with the development and manufacture of their 'crown jewels'?*

Dr Graeme Blackman, founder and chairman of ASX-listed Institute of Drug Technology Australia Ltd (IDT), is arguably one of the first of an emerging breed of academic turned successful entrepreneur. Blackman has created a substantial and sustainable technologically driven business from nothing, confounding the common Australian perception that once an academic, always an academic and unlikely to succeed in the real world of business.

Blackman, a Monash academic from 1979 to 1986, cut the umbilical cord to his university salary and tenure before he had made a serious sale in the new business, in the belief that there is nothing more motivating than having your back literally to the wall. He is very critical of academics who try to have a leg in both camps, retaining their university role and running a serious business, on the grounds that such people essentially have a conflict of interest in their duty to their university and to shareholders.

In 1986, Blackman led a management buyout of the assets of a university-owned not-for-profit consulting business which had been operating since 1975. He then listed the company on the then second board in 1988. For the year ended 30 June 2002 the company reported a profit after tax of $4.2 million on sales of $21.2 million. IDT's annual average growth in profit for the last seven years has exceeded thirty per cent.

The 150 strong team (average age just over thirty years) of highly qualified scientists at IDT in suburban Melbourne conduct fee-for-service research to perfect the chemistry of high-quality active pharmaceutical ingredients (API) for human drugs. Frequently, the company is then commissioned to make these active ingredients under long-term manufacturing contracts where its remuneration changes to a negotiated ex-factory price. 'THE DEVELOPMENT WE SELL BY THE HOUR; THE PRODUCT WE SELL BY THE KILOGRAM', says Blackman.

Recognition and proof of IDT's world-class credentials, especially in the very specialised area of anti-cancer drugs, has been earned from none other than the highest court in effectively world regulation of the pharmaceutical industry, the US Food and Drug Administration (FDA). In 1988 the FDA gave IDT the almost unheard of accolade of an unqualified audit of its processes.

This highest-order accreditation from the tough-by-reputation FDA has been like a secret handshake that has allowed a relatively insignificant and youthful company from down under to initiate enduring global relationships with some of the world's largest pharmaceutical companies such as Pfizer, AstraZeneca, Wyeth and Johnson and Johnson. IDT's world-leading expertise in anti-cancer API's is another qualification that according to Blackman causes otherwise heard-it-all global executives to move forward in their chairs.

The company's primary focus is on the United States and European markets where most of the huge pharmaceutical companies are headquartered. Blackman estimates that the global market in his category is about US$300 million, but that much of the obviously highly complex and sensitive work is done internally by the pharmaceutical companies. Outsourcing though is an emerging trend and one which Blackman believes will grow because 'SUCH COMPANIES ARE BEGINNING TO ACCEPT THAT THEIR CORE BUSINESS IS DRUG EFFICACY RESEARCH AND SUBSEQUENT MARKETING, NOT THE CHEMISTRY AND PROCESSES OF PRODUCTION'.

It would be easy for aspiring entrepreneurs in unrelated industries to pass off the IDT achievement as purely high-tech driven, and to miss the important lessons that can be applied to any business.

Blackman is first to acknowledge the usual struggles, mistakes and lessons that have lead the company to success, like the early loss through takeover of one of its first major customers, necessitating the retrenchment of thirty scientists, a sobering and focussing experience which caused him to radically redesign the business.

The real value to others wanting to learn from Blackman's experience lies in the now highly refined business concept which has emerged and is driving the company's success.

Surpetition, not competition

There are plenty of companies in Australia and overseas who can formulate and manufacture drugs for pharmaceutical companies, what the industry terms 'secondary' manufacture. The skill has been commoditised, margins are tight and capital investment to do it on a global scale can run into hundreds of millions of dollars. *Running in much the same race, basically being a capable competitor did not attract Blackman. He chose to start a new race in which, if successful, his company could conceivably be the winner*, what we refer to as 'surpetition', meaning to deliberately 'rise above', in order to distinguish it from 'competition' which basically means to 'run together'.

Using his knowledge of chemistry and the industry, Blackman reasoned that there could be a higher-order race which would remove him from the rat-race of competition, particularly as he could not match the capital investment of the big players anyway. He thought that pharmaceutical companies just might consider outsourcing some of their most complex and important developments, such as anti-cancer API development and manufacture, if there existed someone with deeper skills in chemistry than they could muster, and whose work and brand would be acceptable to the FDA. His hunch was right, and as a result IDT is today a leading API development and manufacturing company in the very narrow but 'crown jewel' race for drugs to conquer cancer. IDT's *active ingredient chemistry could become the 'Intel' inside these drugs.*

Integrated values, not simply product values

It is one thing to choose to start a new race, but another to grab the attention of officials, causing them to see its value as compelling.

Blackman set about investing in gaining 'preferred supplier' status, not simply with his customers, but with their god, the FDA. He knew that if he could ease and expedite the FDA approval of his clients' anti-cancer drug APIs – which, together with expedited efficacy and safety approvals, is the gateway to early market entry and first-mover advantage – his value to the pharmaceutical companies could be immense.

In conceiving and achieving this salient goal, *Blackman has gone beyond offering a valuable product to integrating his company's value into the critical and complex values of his customers.* IDT's reputation with the FDA is a value which goes way beyond its ability to develop and manufacture high quality APIs. Further, drug chemistry is now something that his pharmaceutical clients can leave off their worry-about list. They can get on with what they are good at.

In June 2002 IDT took a further innovative step towards integrating deeply with its customers' values. The company acquired CEMAX, the clinical development unit of Mayne Pharma located at the Royal Adelaide Hospital. CEMAX leases a ward from the hospital where it performs early stage clinical evaluation of potential new drug candidates. With this acquisition IDT is now able to provide an integrated resource to companies wishing to progress their research on these drug candidates from the laboratory to the clinic and ultimately to commercial manufacture.

A better formula that gains strength as it goes

The now refined IDT business concept has a real alchemy about it, even beyond the already explained creation of a surpetitive race and an iconic FDA 'preferred supplier' status.

Firstly, the primary source of IDT's output and reputation is the brainpower of its highly specialised scientists. *Blackman's academic background gives him advanced knowledge not only of that source of supply of staff, but also an empathy and collegiality with his scientists.* Like attracts like, especially in an essentially intellectual pursuit. He says staff turnover is less than five per cent pa.

Secondly, while ownership of patentable intellectual property developed by IDT is assigned to its fee-paying clients, the knowledge from cutting-edge scientific research projects, many of which according to Blackman are 'WORTHY OF A PHD', accumulates within the firm and feeds on itself adding value to subsequent projects. 'BY GETTING IN ON THE GROUND FLOOR, WE BECOME A WORLD EXPERT', he adds.

Thirdly, the 'world expert' status gained in developing and refining the chemistry of a new API feeds the next revenue stage of IDT's value extraction, the manufacture of the product it has developed. Blackman says: 'I CHOSE TO MOVE FURTHER DOWN THE VALUE CHAIN BECAUSE I COULD SEE THE SYNERGY AND THE VALUE OF GAINING PROFITABLE LONG-TERM MANUFACTURING CONTRACTS. THE DEVELOPMENT WE SELL BY THE HOUR; THE PRODUCT WE SELL BY THE KILOGRAM.'

In a very real sense, IDT *is progressively monopolising the value it creates for customers, shareholders and staff, and even to some extent the regulators of the pharmaceutical industry.* These key players would appear to be putting increasing store in the unique bundle of values that the company is designed to deliver. This of course is monopolisation by value, not by regulation, which is the essence of good business and marketing design.

Chapter 5
BUILDING A REPLICABLE FACTORY

One very clear distinguishing feature of the business concepts of leading entrepreneurs is the formula or system they have each developed to deliver value. Well-designed formulae, the basis of systems and procedures, ensure consistent and profitable delivery, and are frequently themselves a major source of surpetition. *In many instances entrepreneurs have achieved success simply by designing a formula or system to deliver in a totally replicable manner what previously was delivered only in a customised manner.*

Many professional firms such as accountants, lawyers and consultants have discovered in recent years that simply relying on the knowledge and ideas contained in the minds of their professionals is not enough and indeed becomes a threat to such firms.

Over the past decade, systems for knowledge accumulation, management and dissemination have become key success factors in large professional service firms. Brilliant professionals who will not adhere to established procedures for knowledge and service delivery are today recognised as a liability, even though their flashes of brilliance may from time to time provide considerable value.

Gerry Harvey prides himself on having been in retailing more than forty years. While he claims no monopoly on wisdom, he believes that he has evolved an extremely effective system through trial and error. What is unusual in the Harvey Norman franchise model is that franchisees are clustered in large stores which to the consumer resemble company-owned department stores. The concept, developed by Harvey, combines the discipline and scope of a large business with the motivation and personality benefits of individual ownership, all under one roof.

Entrepreneur leaders seem to have a special ability to enforce agreed procedures using enthusiasm rather than coercion. Dick Smith gives a good example:

'I MADE A RULE THAT EVERY PHONE MUST HAVE A PEN NEAR TO IT BECAUSE SO OFTEN WHEN THE PHONE RANG PEOPLE WOULD GO LOOKING FOR A PEN, AND TIME WAS WASTED AND CUSTOMERS WERE HELD UP. SOON WE DECIDED TO TIE THE PENS TO EACH TELEPHONE SINCE WE FOUND THEY ALWAYS WENT MISSING. WE THEN MADE A RULE THAT STANDING NEAR A PHONE WHICH DID NOT HAVE A PEN ATTACHED TO IT WAS GROUNDS FOR INSTANT DISMISSAL. NO ONE WAS EVER DISMISSED OF COURSE, BUT YOU NOTICE EVEN TODAY THAT PENS ARE TIED TO TELEPHONES IN MOST DICK SMITH STORES.'

Leading entrepreneurs reveal a flexible, proactive approach to the constant improvement of their value delivery formulae. Staff are encouraged and often incentivised to find better ways which, if generally agreed, are quickly adopted.

Despite its remarkable success, Gerry Harvey continues to experiment with his proven business formula. Having recently acquired the Rebel chain of sports stores, he says he has decided to leave in place "for the time being" the company-operated (rather than franchisee-operated) model which Rebel has used since inception. 'I JUST WANT TO PLAY AROUND WITH THE SYSTEM FOR A WHILE AND SEE WHAT I CAN LEARN', said Harvey.

Adrian Di Marco, founder of software and service provider Technology One Ltd, has to a similar approach to his business success formula, albeit in a totally different industry. The company has chosen to go direct to customers avoiding the normal channel of distribution, the large professional service firms used by its major competitors, thus building and retaining control of client relationships. Having identified an attractive industry sector, Technology One adopts a well-honed step-by-step formula to prospecting, product development, market development and eventual leadership within the chosen sector, initially in Australia and then in selected export markets.

A business without an effective formula for consistent and efficient value delivery cannot grow much beyond the span of day-to-day control of its founder. As it grows, it will become harder and harder to manage. It will be overly dependent on highly skilled and motivated people who are in short supply and have greater bargaining power. The stronger the formula, the more the business can grow without the day-to-day intervention of its founder. So it is clear that *one of the initial and ongoing tasks of a good entrepreneur is to design a formula by which the business delivers value.*

Building a success formula

There are three basic steps in developing a successful value delivery formula:

- Narrow the focus of what is provided.

- Simplify the delivery process.

- Recruit like-minded people to implement the formula.

Step 1 – Narrow the focus

Just as it is essential to narrow the focus in order make your value highly attractive to a particular target market, generally the same principle applies in delivering that value. The design of a formula which ensures quality and consistency in delivery of value usually demands exactly the same narrowing of focus.

There is no doubt that the success of Flight Centre is directly attributable to the founders' decision to narrow the focus from general travel to discount flights alone. A general travel agent faces huge complexity of both product choices and combinations. Furthermore, there is a need for staff to have experienced first hand the properties and places they are recommending to clients. Even if travel agency staff were not as mobile as they tend to be, moving from one employer to another, it would still be a very significant cost to the business to continuously familiarise staff with the multitude of destinations and properties; even then, this could only be achieved over an extended period of time.

Flight Centre's focus on discount flights alone removed the majority of variables which had previously been barriers to replicable value delivery. Generally speaking, the customer knows where he or she wants to go, at least to the nearest airport, so staff do not need intimate knowledge of secondary destinations and properties. Furthermore, staff are expected to have intimate knowledge only of the airline mode of travel. All the information they need can be computerised.

Another benefit of this tight focus is that a global market can be served just as efficiently as a local market. As mentioned, Flight Centre now earns a large proportion of its income and profits from its shops outside Australia. Essentially, the company can go global with the same delivery system which has enabled it so far to win approximately one quarter of all Australian-purchased airline travel sales.

In the information technology software and systems business, companies like Technology One and KAZ Group have succeeded for exactly the same reason. Instead of attempting to be many things to many people, they have focussed narrowly on markets which they believed could be penetrated with an added-value offering. This same focus has enabled the adoption of a highly disciplined product development and delivery formula.

Frequently, it is better sometimes to define what you do in terms of what you do not do, being quite harsh on your choice of markets and the products and services you deliver. Seldom is failure attributable to too narrow a focus, provided of course there is sufficient market available to allow the business to achieve satisfactory economies of scale and scope.

Step 2 – Simplify the delivery process

Narrowing the focus automatically leads to a lesser number of variables to be managed. However, there are usually many ways in which a value delivery formula can be streamlined. For example, face-to-face selling may have been required in order to sort out what the customer actually wants. However, this typically costly interaction may now be able to be handled over the telephone or the internet. Indeed, such a move may not only decrease the cost of providing service, but also increase the utility of the service for the customer.

While it may be possible to deliver eighty per cent of the service in a very economical and user-friendly way using technology, delivering the rest may be more complicated and require face-to-fact interaction. It may be practical to outsource that more difficult twenty per cent to others, or simply not offer it, rather than to complicate an otherwise replicable delivery formula. For example, the highly successful Baker's Delight bread chain has chosen to limit its product range almost entirely to dough-based formulae. It does not offer cakes, pies and the like. This means that the now more than 500 Baker's Delight franchisees have less to worry about. Staff training, especially in food preparation, is less. Raw-material range is reduced. Nonetheless, franchisees doubtless would like a dollar for every pie or cake request they have had to turn away.

The upside of being focussed is that the delivery system can be simplified and made replicable and efficient. Sometimes, there appears to be the downside of missing out on market opportunity. The same trade-off applies in making your value famous. It will be far more difficult and expensive to be famous for a diverse offering than for a focussed offering. Furthermore, the diversified business will suffer more from being attacked by specialists.

Step 3 – Recruit like-minded people to operate the system

Many of the entrepreneurs in our research deliberately avoid recruiting for perceived brilliance. As Graham Turner put it, 'IF YOUR FORMULA DEPENDS ON HAVING "BRAIN SURGEONS", THEN YOU'RE DRAWING FROM A VERY EXPENSIVE, LIMITED AND MOBILE EMPLOYMENT MARKET'. That is not to imply that you can afford to employ dummies. You nonetheless want people who are prepared to follow the system and, with the experience they gain, hopefully contribute to its improvement over time.

The Australian chairman of McDonald's, Peter Ritchie, says that you should *recruit for attitude and train for aptitude*. Like a family, the alignment of intent and outlook in a business setting is important not only for smooth operation of the business but also for the delivery of a consistent level of quality especially in customer interaction.

Another important reason for the success of businesses with like-minded people is the willingness of those people to follow their leader. By necessity, entrepreneurs in the process of building substantial businesses have to be strong-minded. Many willingly acknowledge that their success has been due to a team of people willing to put up with their arguably dictatorial approach as to how things will be done in the business.

Over the past decade, some "experts" in human resource management have promoted consensus as a way forward in preference to strong leadership. With the benefit of hindsight, consensus leadership has failed to deliver other than mediocrity. Few, if any successful entrepreneurs have relied on a consensus management style. This does not mean that people have to be compliant and add none of their personality and ideas to improve the way things are done. However, it is essential that once the best way of doing things at least for the moment is decided upon, the whole team is prepared to go forward enthusiastically using that system.

Some would argue that such compliance is a bad thing. There is, however, compelling evidence that the benefits which flow from focussing, simplifying and systemising the value delivery formula, and the resultant imperative to align staff attitude and behaviour, far outweigh any disadvantages. Of course, willingness to follow the rules does not rule out willingness to challenge and change at appropriate intervals.

Turner, McDonald and Saragossi

Graham Turner expresses a commonly held view among leading entrepreneurs that a business must be easily replicable in order to grow large. His company has grown rapidly by developing systems and procedures that govern practically everything – site selection, marketing, staff recruitment, customer retention, service delivery and financial control. *There is a constant search for alternatives, but once the "best way" has been agreed, everyone follows the procedure until an even better way is discovered and adopted by all at the same time.*

Jim McDonald (MDH) has pioneered and refined over fifty years a formula for sustainable beef production in some of Australia's most inhospitable country. MDH is designed to become not simply a large landholder and beef producer, but more importantly a sustainable business. As a drought-proofing formula, McDonald has chosen large open tracts of inexpensive land so that cattle can 'follow the storms' on each property and on adjoining properties. In addition, the property portfolio is geographically diversified so that drought is highly unlikely to affect all properties at the one time. The addition of a feedlot is yet another hedge against drought preventing the continuous finishing of cattle for market.

Joe Saragossi (G James Group) brings real meaning and practicality to the often hollow-sounding textbook term 'the learning organisation'. Further, his approach to much of that active learning being outside his industry has proven successful in enabling his company to profit from moving ahead of current industry thinking and practice through cross industry adaptation of practices, technology and ideas. Managing the risk of aggressive geographic expansion, by designing branch factories to have a fall-back position of rented warehouse, is as clever for its simplicity as much as for its effectiveness.

Graham Turner

John C Lyons and Edward de Bono

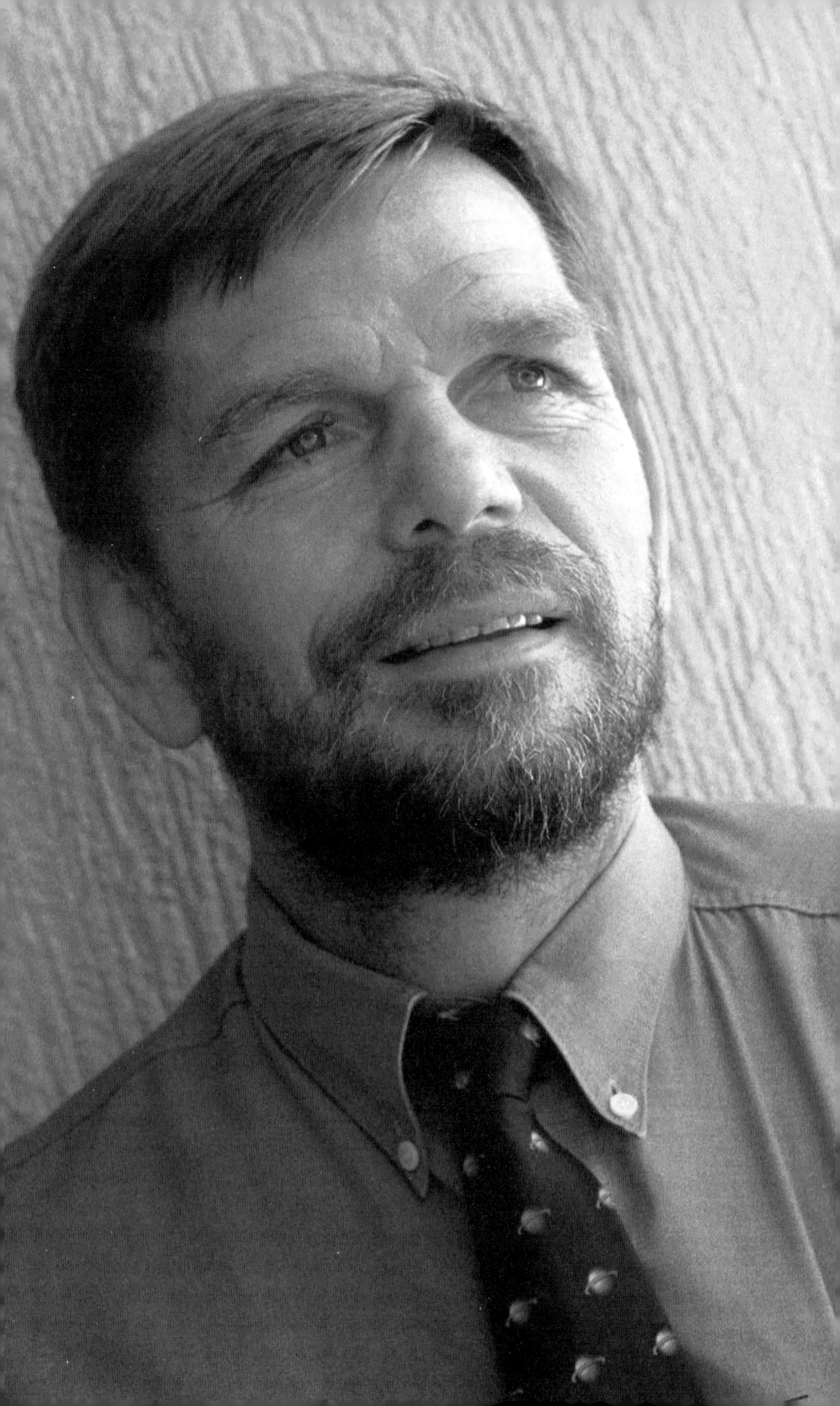

CHAPTER 5 – BUILDING A REPLICABLE FACTORY

GRAHAM TURNER

Having a business model that's replicable is vital, but I suppose that's just common sense

How has a veterinary science graduate in just sixteen years built Australia's fourth largest retailer in the mature and seemingly threatened retail travel sector, copying an idea that has been around since the 1950s, but finding a better concept to deliver it all over the world?

Graham Turner and his partners had stumbled on a good idea in the 1970s, but it was not until 1986 that they discovered the plot that would make it a huge global business. In the ensuing sixteen years, their then collection of about thirty disparately-branded general travel agencies has been transformed to become a world-leading air travel specialist with 975 shops which in FY2002 generated sales of $3.6 billion, profit after tax of $62 million, and which retain a stockmarket price–earnings ratio in the high twenties in arguably the worst aviation market environment in history.

The idea Turner had seen in London in the 1970s was called a 'bucket shop' – primarily straight airfare retail outlets which had been operating there since the late 1950s, specialising in discounted air travel. The plot he developed, starting in 1986, is probably simultaneously the simplest and most successful retail model in travel industry history. The principles that drive it are applicable to every business, regardless of industry. Ironically, Turner graduated as a veterinarian and had had no previous retailing experience.

According to Turner, Flight Centre Limited has captured an Australian market share nearing twenty-five per cent, and his goal is to take that to forty per cent. Simultaneously, he plans to make the company a global leader in the category. With one-quarter of the company's profits now made offshore, it is hard to argue that he cannot succeed. The formula is now proven beyond doubt in countries like New Zealand, South Africa, the United Kingdom, Canada and the USA.

What is the entrepreneurial creative thinking that has enabled some seemingly knock-about blokes, with little money to begin with, until they floated the company in 1995, to reshape an industry and become the "why didn't we think of that" envy of many established and well-heeled competitors?

Change the way things are done

Like many of our researched retail entrepreneurs, Graham Turner has deliberately chosen a mature market, with the usual characteristics of entrenched competition and narrowing margins, in which to make his play. There was and is no prospect that the market will expand overnight and the company will be carried on a wave of Nasdaq-like growth. Flight Centre's astronomical growth has come from market penetration, cutting deep into competition by redefining the way things are done.

Unrelenting focus

The London bucket shop focus on discount airfares was a watershed discovery for Turner. *Most travel agencies at the time were generalists – undifferentiated, famous for nothing in particular, and struggling to deliver* complex product with an ever mobile workforce.

Well-chosen timing

Prior to 1986, it was illegal to advertise discounted airfares in Australia. Turner could see that the lifting of this barrier would create an opportunity for first-mover advantage, to make Flight Centre famous as leader of the category in which he had chosen to focus, with the very proposition that had previously been unmentionable. Long after deregulation, Turner says 'MOST TRAVEL AGENTS CONTINUED TO PUT BULLSHIT IN THEIR WINDOWS, LIKE DISPLAYS WITH NICE POSTERS…AGENTS WEREN'T PREPARED TO PUT PRICES ON THEIR DESTINATIONS', adding that featuring destination prices in Flight

Centre shop windows was an enormous help in establishing the company's difference and reputation.

Simplification is key

By narrowing the product focus, Turner saw that he could turn a hotchpotch travel outlet into a well-oiled machine, simultaneously providing value to customers and making a good profit. The company's net profit margin has progressively increased from 1.57 per cent in FY1992 to 2.5 per cent in FY2002 as it has learned how to create efficiencies. In our view, one of Turner's greatest strengths is his ability to see the simplicity on the other side of complexity – a hallmark of people who have mastered their craft – and to convert that simplicity into replicable reality.

A replicable system for everything

Turner understates with his typically dry sense of humour: 'HAVING A BUSINESS MODEL THAT'S REPLICABLE IS VITAL, BUT I SUPPOSE THAT'S JUST COMMON SENSE. WE BOUGHT A FEW SMALL COMPANIES AND IT'S INTERESTING HOW UNREPLICABLE THEY ARE. YOU DON'T WANT TO HAVE A MODEL WHERE YOU HAVE A NEURO-SURGEON [KEY PERSON] AS PART OF YOUR SYSTEM, BECAUSE THEY ARE HARD TO GET HOLD OF.' Rolling out a new shop every couple of days, a hefty proportion of them offshore nowadays, has demanded that the system be unfalteringly replicable.

Rewarding people for the outcomes you want

'I THINK THE KEY IS TO BE CERTAIN TO HAVE EACH PERSON BEING REWARDED ON THE OUTCOMES YOU WANT RIGHT FROM THE START, AND TO MAKE SURE THOSE OUTCOMES ARE CLEARLY MEASURED, AND THAT YOU'VE GOT THE RIGHT PEOPLE IN THE RIGHT PLACES TO PRODUCE THOSE OUTCOMES. WE'VE PROBABLY DONE THAT PRETTY WELL', he again understates.

Pulling with human nature, not against it

Turner's well-publicised human organisation model is down-to-earth like the man himself. The company's 4500 staff work in small accountable teams of minimum three – maximum seven people (the 'Family'); shops and teams work in regions of four to ten shops (the 'Village'); Villages are grouped with their support businesses of around 120 people (the 'Tribe').

'WORK IS A PART OF PEOPLE'S SOCIAL STRUCTURE AND IF YOU WORK AGAINST THAT, IT'S A LOT HARDER. THERE'S NOTHING NEW ABOUT A LOT OF THIS STUFF…BUT IT PROBABLY HASN'T BEEN APPLIED DIRECTLY TO BUSINESS BEFORE.'

Jim McDonald

John C Lyons and Edward de Bono

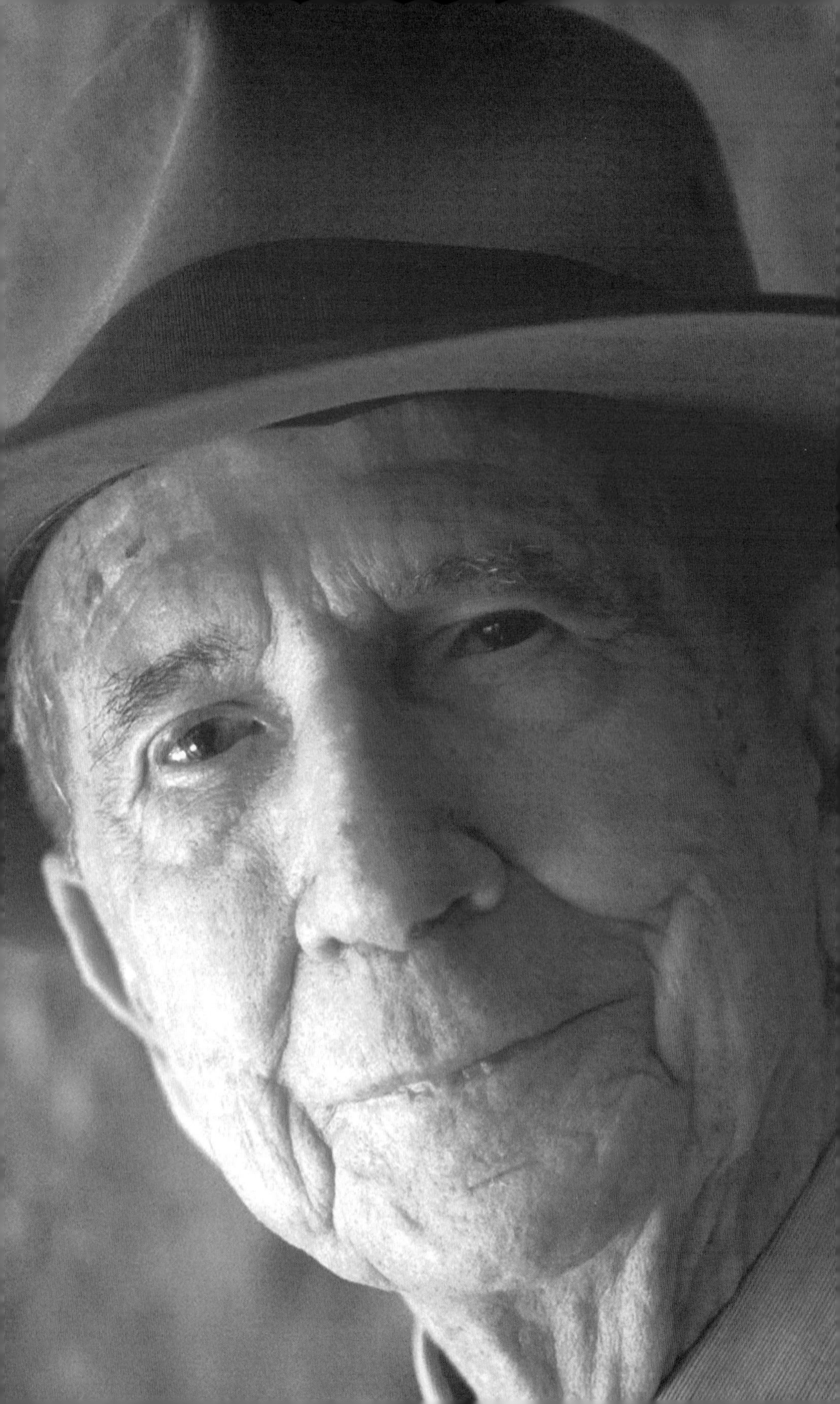

CHAPTER 5 – BUILDING A REPLICABLE FACTORY

JIM McDONALD

You've always got to be prepared to meet the market, even when it hurts

When Jim McDonald rolled his swag and headed west from Bowen in 1946, he had no plans to own properties which would make his family the tenth largest cattle producer in Australia with land holdings half the size of Tasmania.

'ONCE YOU CAN SEE THE BOUNDARY FENCES, IT'S TIME TO KNOT YOUR SWAG. CATTLE NEED ROOM, NOT FENCES. THEY NEED TO BE ABLE TO FOLLOW THE THUNDERSTORMS', says McDonald justifying his decision to move his wife and young family from an idyllic tropical living environment, on the small cattle properly he had inherited near Bowen in North Queensland, to the then remote outback near Cloncurry.

That was the first, but not the last time that his friends thought Jim McDonald had rocks in his head. It happened again in the late 1970s when prolonged drought and low cattle prices meant that cattle properties in the outback were dirt cheap. 'WE HAVE BECOME WHAT WE ARE BECAUSE WE WERE PREPARED TO SEE OPPORTUNITIES WHEN THE LAND AND CATTLE VALUES WERE LOW, AND TAKE A GAMBLE ON A FEW BIG DEALS', says McDonald.

The family company of which McDonald is chairman and his sons Don and Bob and grandson Alexander are directors, MDH Pastoral Company, now owns eleven cattle stations spread across four geographical groupings in

Queensland. About 150 000 cattle follow the storms on some 3.52 million hectares of land, producing an annual turn-off of some 40 000 head.

Like many pioneering Australian bushmen, an unpretentious McDonald would rather talk about the virtues of his cattle, the land he has tamed and made productive, and the outback characters he has met and dealt with over the years, than his business success story. *However, behind each of the parable-like stories he tells there is an important and well-honed business principle, essentially a concept.* Collectively, these concepts and a clear set of values, which he has successfully imbued in his children and grandchildren, explain much of McDonald's success.

Achieving economies of scale and scope.

'THE SECRET TO SUCCESS IN CATTLE IS AREAS AND NUMBERS', stresses McDonald. *From the outset, McDonald has worked persistently to drive down production costs, becoming one of the industry's lowest cost producers.* Ninety per cent of his company's land is leasehold, for which an annual rental is paid, thus minimising capital employed in the business. Most of the properties are located in very low rainfall areas where parasites are much less prevalent and thus stock handling is minimised. Aircraft are used extensively to lower mustering and water-checking labour costs, and as an efficient means of supervision and commuting in such vast areas.

'THE MOST EFFICIENT UNIT OF PRODUCTION IS APPROXIMATELY 10 000 HEAD OF CATTLE. WE CAN HANDLE THAT WITH ONE HEAD-STOCKMAN AND ONE MUSTERING CAMP. IF YOU ONLY HAVE ONE OF THESE UNITS HOWEVER, THEN YOU STILL HAVE TO HAVE A FULL COMPLEMENT OF OVERHEADS TO CARRY INCLUDING HOMESTEAD, FACILITIES, EQUIPMENT, COOK, HOUSEKEEPER AND COWBOY JUST FOR THAT ONE PRODUCTION UNIT. THE MORE MULTIPLES OF 10 000 YOU HAVE SHARING OVERHEADS, THE MORE EFFICIENT YOU BECOME, WITHIN REASON. SIZE IS ESSENTIAL. AND OF COURSE WITH SIZE, SOME OF THE COUNTRY IS GOING TO GET STORMS. AND YOU CAN MOVE CATTLE ABOUT.'

The properties are carefully spread throughout Queensland, from Cape York Peninsula in the north to the Channel Country in the south-west, and east to the coast near Rockhampton. Recently, the company acquired a feedlot to fatten its own cattle when necessary. However, McDonald stresses that grass is still the most efficient way to fatten. He sees the feedlot primarily as a hedge against drought preventing timely fattening, and expects more often than not it will be contracted out to other producers facing that challenge.

Picking the right assets, and getting rid of unproductive assets quickly

McDonald says that you can work very hard for very little if you don't have the right assets to start with. The company has been careful not only to buy properties at the right price, usually when the industry is in distress, but also to ensure they buy the right properties. 'YOU NEED OPEN PLACES THAT ARE EASY TO MANAGE – NOT TOO MUCH SCRUB AND NOT TOO EXPENSIVE TO FENCE UP.' On one property more recently acquired, the company is installing 300 kilometres of fencing which McDonald says will lower mustering costs very significantly.

Even though McDonald is clearly attached emotionally to the softer British cattle breeds, he is unemotional about matching the right breed with the right land-type across what is now a geographically diversified property portfolio. The company experiments with breeds property-by-property so as to maximise fertility and speed of weight gain. Cattle that don't perform are sold quickly. 'WE LOOK TO HAVE GOOD STOCK WITH A BETTER CONSTITUTION, HANDLING AND TEMPERAMENT', he says, stressing that these characteristics are fundamental given the relatively tough and open conditions under which they are raised.

People quality and hands-on personal supervision

'YOU NEED GOOD HEAD-STOCKMEN TO LEAD THE CAMPS – THE SORT OF FELLOWS WHO JUST LIVE FOR HORSES AND CATTLE. THEY NEED TO KNOW HOW TO KEEP CATTLE QUIET, KEEP THEM BRANDED, AND LOOK AFTER YOUR HORSES. ANYONE CAN BRING THE TAIL IN'.

Achieving this goal in remote and often inhospitable climatic conditions has been a challenge that McDonald has patiently pursued from the outset, often with considerable difficulty. In the early days, he learned to be very tolerant of good stockmen who were often chronic alcoholics.

Not everyone is suited to the life either. Many aspiring jackaroos and ringers were tactfully given good career advice like 'THERE ARE PLENTY OF GOOD JOBS IN THE CITY', when McDonald found that their ambitions with livestock and the land far exceeded their natural capabilities.

Before light aircraft and helicopters became indispensable tools in the outback, it would take McDonald approximately one week of quite arduous driving to check the approximately forty cattle watering points on the homestead property alone. His sons now accomplish the same task by air in about half-an-hour. However, the ingrained habit of driving around and checking things and talking to people has remained with him. He believes this hands-on personal supervision remains an essential part of effective station management.

Meeting the market and adapting to the tough environment

On the majority of the company's properties, rainfall is both low and unreliable. McDonald is philosophical in his approach to managing this key variable:

'YOU MUST KNOW YOUR COUNTRY. YOU MUSTN'T WAIT UNTIL CATTLE START TO DIE BEFORE YOU SELL THEM OR SHIP THEM SOMEWHERE ELSE. LIKE THE SONG ABOUT GAMBLING, "YOU'VE GOT TO KNOW WHEN TO HOLD THEM, KNOW WHEN TO FOLD THEM, AND KNOW WHEN TO WALK AWAY" — YOU'VE ALWAYS GOT TO BE PREPARED TO MEET THE MARKET, EVEN WHERE IT HURTS.'

Cattle stealing is another environmental condition which McDonald learned to cope with in quite creative ways. In the early days especially, when large tracts of property were unfenced, and before aircraft made supervision easier, it was not uncommon for some new settlers to stock their properties in creative ways, 'borrowing' from established graziers like McDonald.

When he drove upon one such incident catching a team of musterers red-handed on his land and branding his cattle, he simply disciplined the key offender by threatening to build a '30-mile fence' along the rugged

CHAPTER 5 – BUILDING A REPLICABLE FACTORY

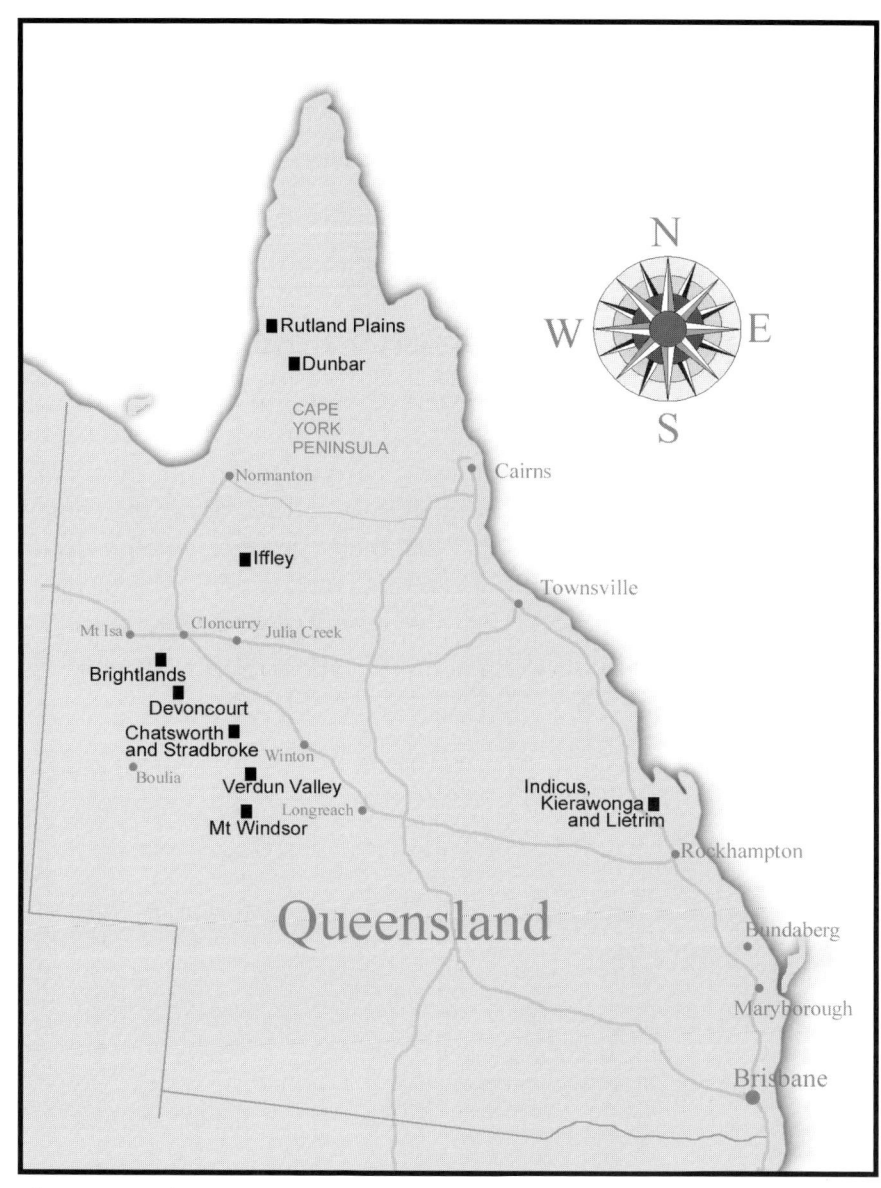

Above: map showing MDH Pastoral Company properties.

boundary with his property. Had he proceeded with the threat, the effect of having to contribute half the cost of the fence would have forced the already debt-burdened neighbour into liquidation. He says that as a result of this accommodating treatment, the offender subsequently became his best 'watchdog'. On other occasions when he found people killing his cattle for meat, his policy was to have them make a donation of equivalent value to a charitable cause.

In this way says McDonald he has been able to live with sometimes unreasonable people in reasonable harmony.

Incentivising family involvement

McDonald's grandsons are showing increasing interest and ability in continuing to grow the family business. His strategy in successfully engaging his two sons over thirty years ago was to provide them with both the challenge and the reward if they succeeded. While he remains active day-to-day, and participates in all major decisions, he has clearly passed the baton of responsibility and is very proud that it has been picked up enthusiastically and effectively by his sons. 'I'M NOT GOING TO BE THE RICHEST CORPSE IN THE CEMETERY. THEY WERE KEEN TO HAVE A GO. FOR ME PERSONALLY, IT IS STILL BETTER TO WEAR OUT THAN RUST OUT.'

Joe Saragossi

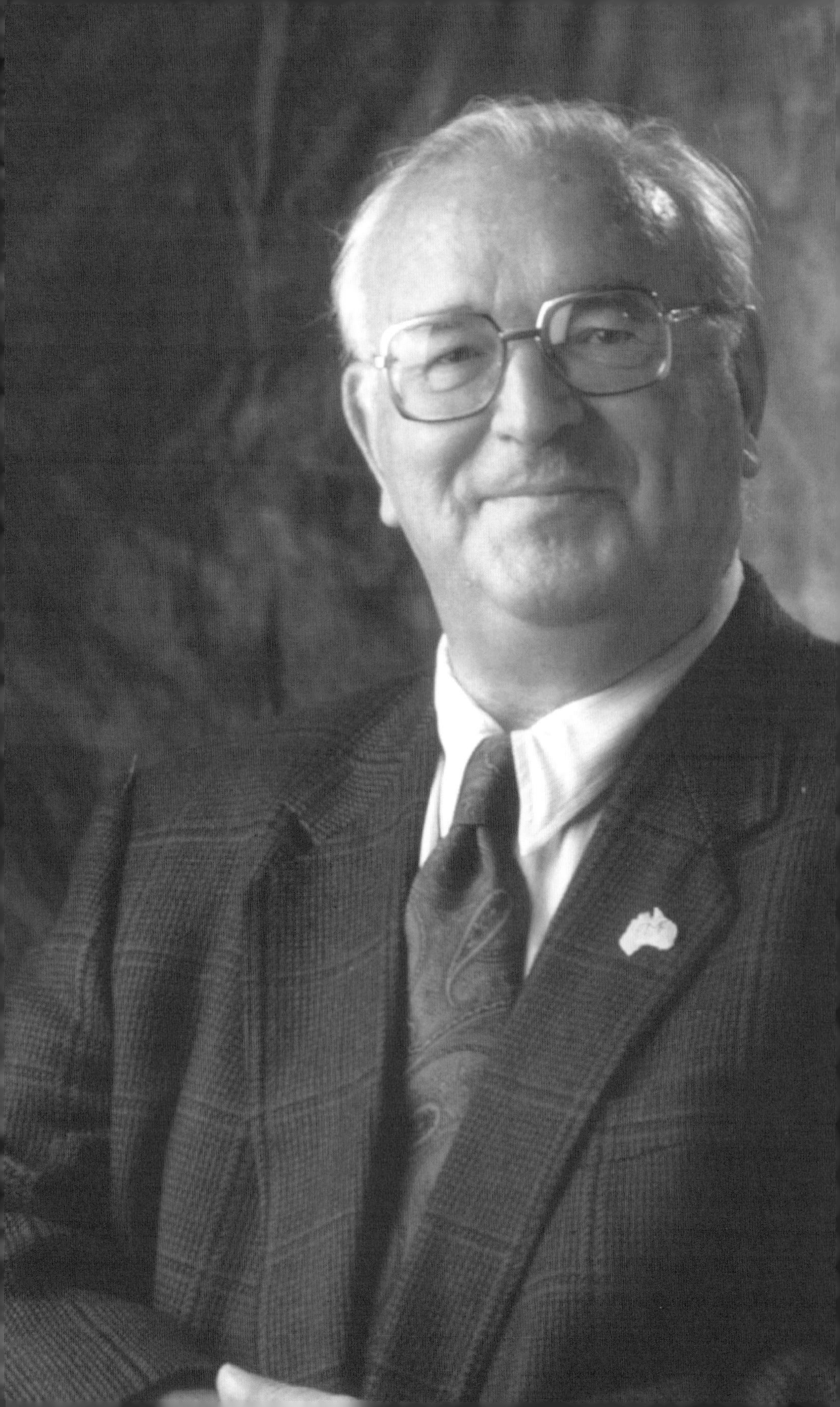

CHAPTER 5 – BUILDING A REPLICABLE FACTORY

JOE SARAGOSSI

I think if you're passionate about something, people will follow

When Joe Saragossi took over the reins at G James Glass in 1958 following the death of his father-in-law the late Mr George James, he had modest ambitions to grow the then four-person glass merchant. He says that getting to ten people proved the hardest. Now he employs 2000.

The growth of the Brisbane-based Saragossi family controlled G James Group is an impressive success story. 'WE HAVE BEEN LUCKY, BUT A LOT OF THAT IS GOOD TIMING', says Saragossi, now the company's executive chairman, aged eighty-three and with no intention of retiring from day-to-day involvement. 'REALLY YOU MAKE A LOT OF YOUR OWN LUCK, YOU STUDY AND DO THINGS AT THE RIGHT TIME. AND YOU DON'T FINANCE EXPANSION OUT OF BORROWINGS – THAT'S WHY THE ENTREPRENEURS OF THE 1980S BLEW IT. THEY HAD TO BORROW. OUR EXPANSION HAS BEEN FINANCED OUT OF CASH FLOW.'

What George James began as a glass merchandising business in 1917 has been expanded by his son-in-law into a diversified glass products manufacturing and aluminium extrusion business.

G James Group today manufactures and installs products such as windows, glass curtain walling and doors for commercial and residential buildings. Its research division develops specialised glass products for energy-saving, chemical-toughening, laminating, bullet-proofing and double-glazing applications.

G James Extrusion division reduces exposure to the building industry by turning out extruded aluminium products for a diversity of industries including transport vehicle manufacture.

Through its forty branches, some of which manufacture and others of

John C Lyons and Edward de Bono — *163*

Marketing without Money

which simply warehouse and assemble, the company serves clients and projects in all Australian states and overseas. G James has successful operations in Singapore and Malaysia which were established during a Brisbane building slump in the early 1990s.

'BRISBANE HIT A SLUMP. SO I SAID LET'S GO OUT AND DO SOMETHING IN SINGAPORE. INITIALLY, WE DIDN'T MAKE ANY MONEY. BUT WE LEARNED HOW TO DO BUSINESS IN A STRANGE COUNTRY. WE WENT THERE BEFORE WE BEGAN BUSINESS IN SYDNEY AND MELBOURNE. AND IT TAUGHT US LOGISTICS, BASICALLY HOW TO MAKE SOMETHING AND SELL IT SOMEWHERE ELSE.'

Early in the 1980s, G James made the transition from servicing customers in the small-to-medium sector of the commercial and residential markets to high-rise projects. Its first major curtain walling project was the then 'blue AMP' building in Brisbane. For Chifley Tower in Sydney, one of the company's largest projects, the curtain walling was manufactured in Brisbane and backfreighted cost advantageously to Sydney in around one thousand truckloads. Similarly iconic projects in Melbourne and Perth are handled using much the same approach. 'COMPETING FOR WORK IN SYDNEY AND MELBOURNE, IT DOESN'T MATTER THAT WE ARE LOCATED HERE. IT'S JUST A MATTER OF ORGANISING YOUR TEAMS', emphasises Saragossi.

Born in the United States, and raised in an orphanage, Saragossi first found his way to Australia in 1946 as a lieutenant (later a captain) in the US Army. Though university educated in the technical disciplines of electrical and mechanical engineering and in radio communications while he was in the Army, Saragossi appears to have gained his most influential education in the school of experience.

In the orphanage machine shop he learned to do 'anything electrical' and to make things using machines. In the US Army, his most valuable learning was army organisation and logistics.

'OFFICERS SCHOOL IMPRESSED ME. I LEARNED A LOT FROM A BUSINESS POINT OF VIEW. THE ARMY IS PROBABLY THE OLDEST ESTABLISHED ORGANISATION IN THE WORLD. I LEARNED A LOT ABOUT ARMY ORGANISATION, PARTICULARLY THE AMERICAN STYLE. YOU DON'T ASK ANYONE TO DO ANYTHING YOU CAN'T DO YOURSELF. I LEARNED LOGISTICS BECAUSE YOU'VE GOT TO TAKE EVERYTHING WITH YOU. THERE ARE NO SHOPS TO BUY THINGS. IF YOU HADN'T GOT IT WITH you, you had to make something do', he says with pride in the fact that today the company makes much of its own equipment.

Conventional business theorists and even some practitioners doubtless would argue that there are several potential flaws in some of Saragossi's quite unconventional business philosophies and concepts. The fact that the company has survived and thrived over such a long period, has never needed resuscitation from a near-death experience, and has funded its remarkable growth from profits, suggests that they might look again.

Facing reality and recognising the opportunity in timing

Saragossi says he couldn't convince his mostly window-making wooden joinery customers to start selling aluminium windows when it was obvious to him in the 1960s that the market was changing, so he began importing and then eventually fabricating them himself. This alienated his traditional customers, but put G James in as a first mover and early learner on the ground floor of massive industry change and growth, first in the trend from small casement glass panels to large-sheet glass panels, and eventually to complete curtain walling.

Concept innovation through cross-industry adaptation

'I NEVER INVENTED ANYTHING. ALL I DID WAS ADAPT THINGS TO WHATEVER WE WERE DOING. I REALISED EARLY THAT THE AUSTRALIAN GOVERNMENT DOES NOT GIVE ANY ASSISTANCE TO MANUFACTURING. SO I DIDN'T REALLY EVER GO INTO MANUFACTURING. I ALWAYS DID SERVICES.'

While G James buys its raw glass domestically and via import, Saragossi has clearly adapted and applied to the glass industry, processing and distribution concepts he extracted from other industries in which he had gained experience. The resulting value-adding and efficiency innovations have taken the company to an industry leadership position. Organisation and logistics from the US Army, electrically and mechanically facilitated materials handling from his university training, and the investment of tens of millions of dollars in extrusion machinery and product development are just a few examples of his passion for adaptive innovation.

Reinvesting in your own business and having no dividend policy

'WHEN WE FIRST MADE A GOOD PROFIT AND DISTRIBUTED IT, THE [FAMILY] SHAREHOLDERS DIDN'T REALLY KNOW WHAT TO DO WITH IT EXCEPT PUT IT IN THE BANK, OR INVEST IT IN CERTAIN THINGS. THE RETURNS WEREN'T VERY GOOD. SO I SAID IF YOU WANT TO INVEST MONEY, PUT IT BACK IN YOUR OWN BUSINESS. YOU HAVE SOME CONTROL OVER IT.'

The company does not distribute profits as dividends to its shareholders. If a shareholder has a particular financial need, then that is accommodated more-or-less by exception. Profits are re-invested to fund growth and build corporate wealth.

Reducing the risks of rapid expansion using a simple fall-back line of defense

'AS A WHOLESALER I WAS GETTING MY PANTS BEATEN OFF IN THE COUNTRY BY LOCALS. IF I BECAME LOCAL, THEN I COULD COMPETE BY HAVING DEPOTS EVERYWHERE. WE COULD GIVE A LOT OF SERVICES IF WE WERE LOCAL. BUT THE IDEA WAS TO SELL GLASS.'

He proceeded with aggressive geographic expansion, building facilities that could be rented as warehouses if they failed to become profitable in their own right. 'I ENJOY WHAT I'M DOING. IT SOUNDS STUPID, BUT I LIKE BUILDING FACTORIES. THAT'S MY HOBBY.'

Being a benevolent dictator, but recognising that the baton must be passed

While his son Lewis took over as managing director in the 1980s and has streamlined the business in many respects, Joe Saragossi unashamedly retains a strong hand on the directional tiller.

'I KNOW I'M GOING TO DIE SO I HAD TO CHOOSE SOMEONE TO SUCCEED ME. MY SON IS YOUNG AND VERY GOOD. IT'S THE FAMILY BUSINESS. I TREAT IT LIKE A FAMILY. THEY SAY I'M HARD BUT I'M FAIR. I THINK I'VE GOT A BIT OF A COMMON TOUCH. I CAN TALK TO ANYBODY ABOUT ANYTHING. I THINK IF YOU'RE PASSIONATE ABOUT SOMETHING, PEOPLE WILL FOLLOW.'

Saragossi says his job these days 'IS TO FIND THE NEXT THING TO DO, TO DECIDE HOW TO SPEND THE MONEY'. With long-serving executive directors who run the day-to-day of what is now a very diverse business, he clearly believes you don't have to worry about the detail if you've got the big picture.

Chapter 6
BECOMING A CAUSE HERO

Conventional marketing typically places an emphasis on advertising, sales promotion and personal selling as the primary means of building brand awareness, understanding and favourable perception. Some value is placed on publicity and word of mouth but these more powerful and often less expensive media of mass communication are typically treated as secondary, perhaps because there has been little successful measurement of their impact, especially on purchase decision-making.

Successful entrepreneurs frequently have a natural or acquired ability to market without the often prohibitive cost associated with conventional practices. Contrary to popular belief, this ability arises, at least initially, more from passion about their cause than innate skill. It is always difficult to ignore people with passion, particularly if they are speaking about a cause that provokes the interest and involvement of their target audience. *There is clearly a direct connection between choosing a cause about which you are passionate, and the likelihood that you'll be able to make your organisation or product famous as a logical solution to your cause.*

One of the mistakes commonly made is to focus one's passion on the attributes of the product or service. Inventors are prone to this mistake, so are large corporates. Not only does this diminish the credibility of the message, because everyone in the target audience expects you to be passionate about what you have to sell, it fails to address what the audience is really interested in. People are preoccupied with their own issues, priorities and needs. They are not interested in yours unless the two coincide closely, and are expressed that way. The masters of reputation-building through publicity and word of mouth are those who follow the *cause* route. A cause orientation has a direct effect on all communication, focussing it on what is important to the target audience, rather than on what is important to the company. If the cause is promoted, you can be sure that the company, product or service will follow.

When Dick Smith launched *Australian Geographic Magazine* in the late 1980s, he had carefully paved the way with a variety of interesting initiatives which drew market attention not only to the nature-based attributes of this country, but also to his exceptional interest and leadership in the cause. The media picked up his publicity initiatives, probably beyond his expectations. He made sure that he gave them plenty to write about. Many people thought, and still think today, that Smith was performing a national service, and in many respects he was.

When Euan Murdoch took on the entrenched Panadol brand with his practically identical Herron Paracetamol product, he realised early that the battle would not be won unless he flanked his competitor. He would be outgunned by the entrenched position and far greater resources of a global chemical giant which owns the Panadol brand. Murdoch chose what at the time seemed a real but somewhat weak issue on which to differentiate his product and to build favourable word of mouth – the fact that Herron is Australian-owned and invests its profits in Australia, hence keeping jobs for Australian employees. Murdoch chose Hazel Hawke as presenter, the very Australian former wife of a retired prime minister and a female in the same demographic as his primary target market. This choice alone created media comment and considerable word of mouth at the time.

Two subsequent events occurred to the considerable advantage of Herron Paracetamol, cementing and building the relevance of its chosen point of difference. Firstly, Dick Smith launched his new cause of fighting back for Australia against the foreign ownership of eighty-five per cent of the product in a typical Australian supermarket trolley. Concurrently, other Australian companies decided it was a good time to stand up and be counted for their Australian ownership and the fact that they were confronting heavy competition from global companies. These initiatives legitimised and strengthened the Herron stance.

Serious adversity in early 2000 subsequently turned to good fortune for Herron when an extortionist tampered with Herron Paracetamol packaging and product in supermarkets, necessitating the company's withdrawal of its product from all retail shelves and homes in Australia. The company and its product gained sustained national media coverage for months as police investigations and a product withdrawal and rectification program were in train. Both consumers and the retail trade not only became much more conscious of the company but also were impressed with its handling of a very difficult and costly exercise in consumer and retail protection.

Even though, unfortunately, Panadol was subsequently threatened in the same manner, Herron had been legitimised against the established brand. The result just three years later is that Herron's share of the category has approximately doubled. Publicity, even that which could have killed the Herron brand and perhaps destroyed the company, turned out to be a blessing in disguise because it was well handled.

Creating word of mouth

There are several fundamental steps to creating strong and sustained word of mouth which can make your cause and your product famous.

Content

The first step in creating talk-worthy content is to make it of compelling interest and relevance to the target audience. *The linkage between what you would like people to talk about and what you would like to sell them must be obvious, but the two should not be confused.* The target audience is interested in its own needs, wants and preferences, not in yours. By focussing on the cause, which is essentially a reflection of what the target audience is concerned about, not what you want to sell them, you demonstrate empathy and knowledge which establishes the kind of authority status that you would like attributed to your company, product or service. If the cause is properly 'sold', you may be sure that your solution will follow. Furthermore, there is ample evidence that the first to provide a solution to a cause, the first mover, usually retains market leadership for a very long time, all other things being equal.

Curiosity is a basic human trait. The media industry exists because people will pay handsomely to be informed and entertained. Our curiosity drives us to give priority to reading the newspaper, listening to the news and so on. We seek other people's points of view on what is on the news. Our curiosity is not limited to matters of direct relevance to us either. We are inevitably interested in people who have experienced unfortunate or happy circumstances which have no bearing on our lives whatsoever.

Provocation

A fascination with things that are different is another important human trait. If you walk down the street wearing an unusual piece of clothing or making odd movements or sounds, you can be sure that others will look at you – you have provoked them. Their minds will then try to discover why you are acting 'strangely'. For example, if you were seen wearing tails on the street in the middle of a hot summer weekday, people may start to look for a wedding or other formal function you might be going to, thinking meanwhile that this is an unusual time to have such a formal event. Not only has their attention been provoked, but also their minds are now actively trying to establish your logic. Then as you pass by they notice a sign on the back of the suit, 'Cool Tails', and an address or telephone number. Your provocation has done a superb job in conveying with impact two messages – firstly that there are tails designed with the value of coolness and secondly they are available near here.

In a commercial situation, you will find that simply being dramatically different to your competitors will draw attention. Hence, finding the difference is an important search not only to make a product or service better, but also to make it noticeable and worthy of word of mouth.

Entrepreneurs like Gerry Harvey, Dick Smith and Euan Murdoch, intuitively *provoke* attention of both the media and the consumer. They do so by pointing up often latent issues, frequently using simple analogies which most people can relate to. Harvey publicly offered to manage under contract his competitor, Coles Myer, as a timely provocation to underscore his own company's retailing ability. Smith launched 'Dickhead Matches' simply to provoke interest in his central cause – foreign domination of most Australian packaged food categories. Euan Murdoch so provoked the makers of Panadol that they took him to court over advertising claims regarding foreign ownership. Murdoch won the case and again gained a deal of sympathy and word of mouth as a result.

Challenge

When Paul Cave first came up with the idea of people climbing the Sydney Harbour Bridge, he not only provoked interest, but he set a challenge. Few of us would ever seek to climb the world's most challenging mountains. However, in our own backyard, we have been challenged by a climbing experience many would regard as well out of the ordinary.

Cave knew it was going to be hard and costly to win the exclusive right to give people "the climb of their life". From the outset, he engaged the public in his battle, which has become their challenge. Regulatory and other authorities eventually reluctantly granted permission.

Consumers are climbing in huge numbers and at considerable cost. BridgeClimb has challenged people to prove they can do it. The company has benefited from extensive publicity which in turn has created large-scale referral where a climber challenges friends and acquaintances to make the climb. Of course, Cave could not have chosen a better icon since the Harbour Bridge is not only crossed by hundreds of thousands of people every day, but also is famous internationally as one of Australia's unique symbols.

Challenge brings out the competitive spirit in all of us, whether it is a crossword puzzle or national sporting team. Challenge engages the target audience in the cause. The cause becomes the focus, not the product. The product nonetheless follows if the cause is adopted. The more enthusiastic the adoption, the more likely you will turn customers into referrers and the faster the snowball will gather snow.

Williams, Wood and Beck

RM Williams's focus on trust as the key value of his brand shows extraordinary commercial acumen, not just good personal values. 'HONESTY IS THE BEST ASSET YOU CAN HAVE IN BUSINESS. PEOPLE ARE LOOKING FOR SOMEONE WHO WILL TRADE HONESTLY WITH THEM', he says. Honesty is at the heart of his quality promise. Williams's tens of thousands of catalogue mail-order customers not only trusted and bought from him, but many also literally became word of mouth advocates and his mates as he travelled his beloved bush and the Australian rodeo circuit.

Carl Wood (Monassh IVF) had two reputation-building challenges. Firstly, he had to raise support from fellow professionals and others and the funds to pursue his cause. Secondly, he had to build the reputation of the cause with the community, which at the time was generally opposed to it. In addressing the first challenge, Wood quite remarkably engaged fellow professionals in his cause to the extent they sacrificed part of their personal income to it. This level of commitment from within helped external parties such as foundations and governments to see his cause as worthy of their financial support. Wood learned from his mistakes in addressing the second challenge. With the benefit of hindsight, he believes he should have done more in the early stages of his IVF research to spread awareness and understanding of the significance of his cause. Community buy-in was hampered not just by lack of knowledge but also by vocal and violent prejudice in some sectors which made telling a rational story much more difficult. Community opposition also made the gaining of support from foundations and government more difficult.

Max Beck (Becton) is very conscious that a company's reputation can be one of its greatest assets – the more so when stakes and risks are as high as they are with large development projects in a highly cyclical industry. Failure, for whatever reason, can destroy the value of a reputation asset overnight. Like many successful entrepreneurs, Beck has built his company's reputation primarily on sustained performance over more than a quarter-century. Consistently high project quality has become his hallmark. 'YOU HAVE TO DO MORE THAN JUST SAY IT', Beck reiterates.

RM Williams

John C Lyons and Edward de Bono

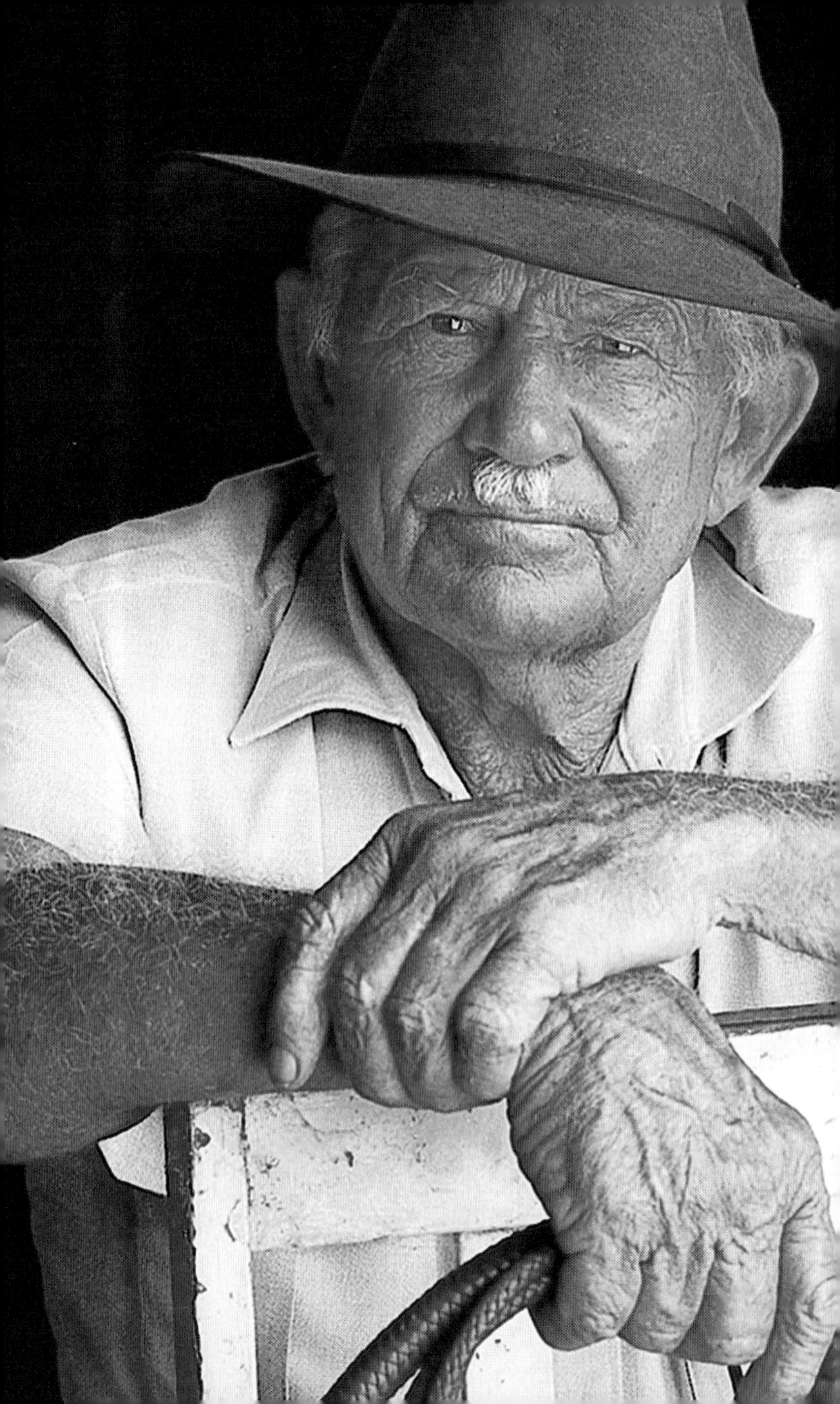

CHAPTER 6 – BECOMING A CAUSE HERO

RM WILLIAMS

I never set out to achieve anything – it just grew; I was just trying to get enough to feed the family

In the 1920s while still in his early teens, RM Williams left home in the mid-north of South Australia to take up work as a lime burner in the Mallee scrub of North-Western Victoria. He later signed on as camel boy to a two-man expedition charged with the immense task of surveying that huge tract of desert land from the Western Australian border as far as the north–south railway at Oodnadatta in South Australia. He learned to live and hunt with local Aboriginals who had barely seen White men previously.

Work followed at a number of the huge pastoral stations in central Australia and the Northern Territory. It was then that he learnt bush lore from the tough bushmen of the cattle camps and the many skills of the mounted stockman. During these formative years, Williams grew to love the bush, its people and all its moods.

It was during the Great Depression that Williams set up camp hundreds of kilometres north of Adelaide at Italowe Gorge in the remote Gammon Ranges. Barely eking out a dangerous, solitary existence sinking wells, Williams began to craft boots, bush saddlery and some of the equipment required for use on surrounding stations. It wasn't long before his work developed a reputation for craftsmanship and durability.

In 1933, the sale of a handmade packsaddle to Sir Sidney Kidman for five pounds was the beginning of a business which grew rapidly.

Williams returned to Adelaide and began selling his riding boots, clothing and other bush gear by mail order. Handcrafted, comfortable

John C Lyons and Edward de Bono — *177*

and made to last a lifetime, they were formed by a man who understood the hardship and dangers of life in the harsh Australian outback.

Soon, bushmen from all over Australia were sending 'cash with order' for his elastic-sided boots and other products. The mail-order business made him prosperous and positioned him as a household name throughout the bush.

Today, the ASX-listed company which bears his name sells unique Australian-made boots, hats, clothing and other bush products in Australia and around the world through stores in the United States, the United Kingdom, Japan, Indonesia and New Zealand.

Always restless and enterprising, Williams has never been content just to be a manufacturer. The bush is his greatest love, and throughout his life he has remained close to it in many other ways – owning and running cattle stations; trading in cattle; breeding and training horses; gold mining; publishing books, magazines and poetry; and playing a pivotal role in establishing the Stockman's Hall of Fame at Longreach. Williams is still active in several of these businesses today, his latest venture being the recently launched *RM Williams Outback* magazine.

What are the entrepreneurial learnings from a largely self-educated man who raised himself from the drought and depression-induced poverty of the 1920s and 1930s, and has experienced by any measure two business-lifetimes in one, even though he does not regard himself as a businessman?

Success is built on trust; quality; that's a matter of honesty with your customers

Parroting words like honesty, integrity and relationships is common in a business world increasingly concerned about the lack of reality. But in Williams's case such words are underpinned by substance, forming the very basis of his success in a very tangible way.

'IF YOU SOLD A PAIR OF BOOTS TO SOMEONE AND THEY WORE OUT QUICKLY, IT WOULD BE VERY COSTLY FOR THEM. THEY WERE MY FRIENDS I SOLD TO. PEOPLE ARE LOOKING FOR SOMEONE WHO WILL TRADE HONESTLY WITH THEM. HONESTY IS THE BEST ASSET YOU CAN HAVE IN BUSINESS.'

Chapter 6 – Becoming a cause hero

He sees the very hallmark of his products, quality, as an integral part of honesty. 'QUALITY. THAT'S A MATTER OF HONESTY WITH YOUR CUSTOMERS ISN'T IT?' he adds.

Trust cuts many ways. Of his first transaction with Kidman, Williams says:

'WHEN I DELIVERED THE FIRST ORDER [PACK-SADDLES AND BAGS], THE OLD MAN SAID: "WELL SON, SEND ME AN [THIRTY DAY] ACCOUNT", AND I SAID "SORRY SIR, BUT I CANNOT DEAL ON THAT BASIS. I HAVEN'T ANY MONEY TO BUY THE MATERIALS TO MAKE THE NEXT PACK AND BAGS. I WILL BE OUT OF WORK FOR THE NEXT THIRTY DAYS".' Kidman wrote him a cheque. 'I KNEW WHAT A CATTLEMAN NEEDED. KIDMAN GAVE ME THE OPPORTUNITY TO SUPPLY IT', says Williams.

He is proud that he eventually won work for all Kidman's properties – a substantial achievement when one considers that reputedly Kidman then had one-and-a-half times as many cattle as Australia's largest cattle producer today, the Stanbroke Pastoral Company.

Send money with order

'I REALISED THAT BOOTS COULD BE MADE FROM THE SCRAPS OF GREASY KIP LEFT OVER FROM CUTTING PACK-BAGS, BUT I COULDN'T AFFORD THE OTHER MATERIALS, NOR DID I HAVE THE TOOLS AND A PROPER WORK BENCH.

'IT WAS THEN I MADE THE MOST REWARDING EXPERIMENT OF MY WHOLE LIFE. I SPENT SIXPENCE ON A SMALL TWO-LINE ADVERTISEMENT IN THE *ADELAIDE CHRONICLE*. IT SAID "ELASTIC SIDE BOOTS MADE TO ORDER. TWENTY SHILLINGS. CASH WITH ORDER. 5 PERCY ST, PROSPECT". WITHIN DAYS CAME A LETTER WITH A POUND NOTE ENCLOSED AND A SIZE FOR THE BOOTS. WE COULD HARDLY WAIT FOR THE RESPONSE TO THE PARCEL THAT WE SO CAREFULLY WRAPPED. WOULD THE BOOTS FIT? WOULD THEY PLEASE THE TRUSTING BUSHMAN WHO HAD SENT HIS MONEY TO SOMEONE HE DID NOT KNOW?'

They clearly did, and the trusting bushman told his mates who told their mates, and demand grew faster than Williams could supply with his modest facilities.

Rapid expansion ensued, together with debt, staff, serious production and other responsibilities that were relatively new to the young Williams, and which he found difficult. 'I DID NOT REALISE THAT IF ONE SANK MONEY into machinery and buildings, it represented a loss of trading capital. These things I had to learn.'

Customers would literally take the shirt off my back

'It took me sixty years to build the [RM Williams] business'. He refers in particular to the time over which his products were designed and refined. His by then hundreds of thousands of catalogue mail-order customers not only trusted and bought from him, but many also literally became his mates as he travelled his beloved bush and the Australian rodeo circuit.

'I got into trousers one at a time', he says of the refinement process of customer-driven trial and error which have made RM Williams moleskins an Australian icon.

He says his customers would literally take the shirt off his back and say 'Make me one of those', and he would do it, and then gradually produce a range. He started the Australian Roughriders Association, and the now internationally famous Quilty Endurance Ride. Bush legends like Tex Morton and Tom Quilty became mates and customers, and on-your-back and word of mouth mediums for his brand.

If people have the right character, you can teach them anything

Williams's staff-selection policy is similarly clear and straightforward, and reflective of his core value with customers.

'If people have the right character, it doesn't matter much whether they are good at something. You can teach them anything. The right people means honorable people. The world hasn't enough of them. It doesn't matter whether they are smart or not smart.'

Carl Wood

John C Lyons and Edward de Bono

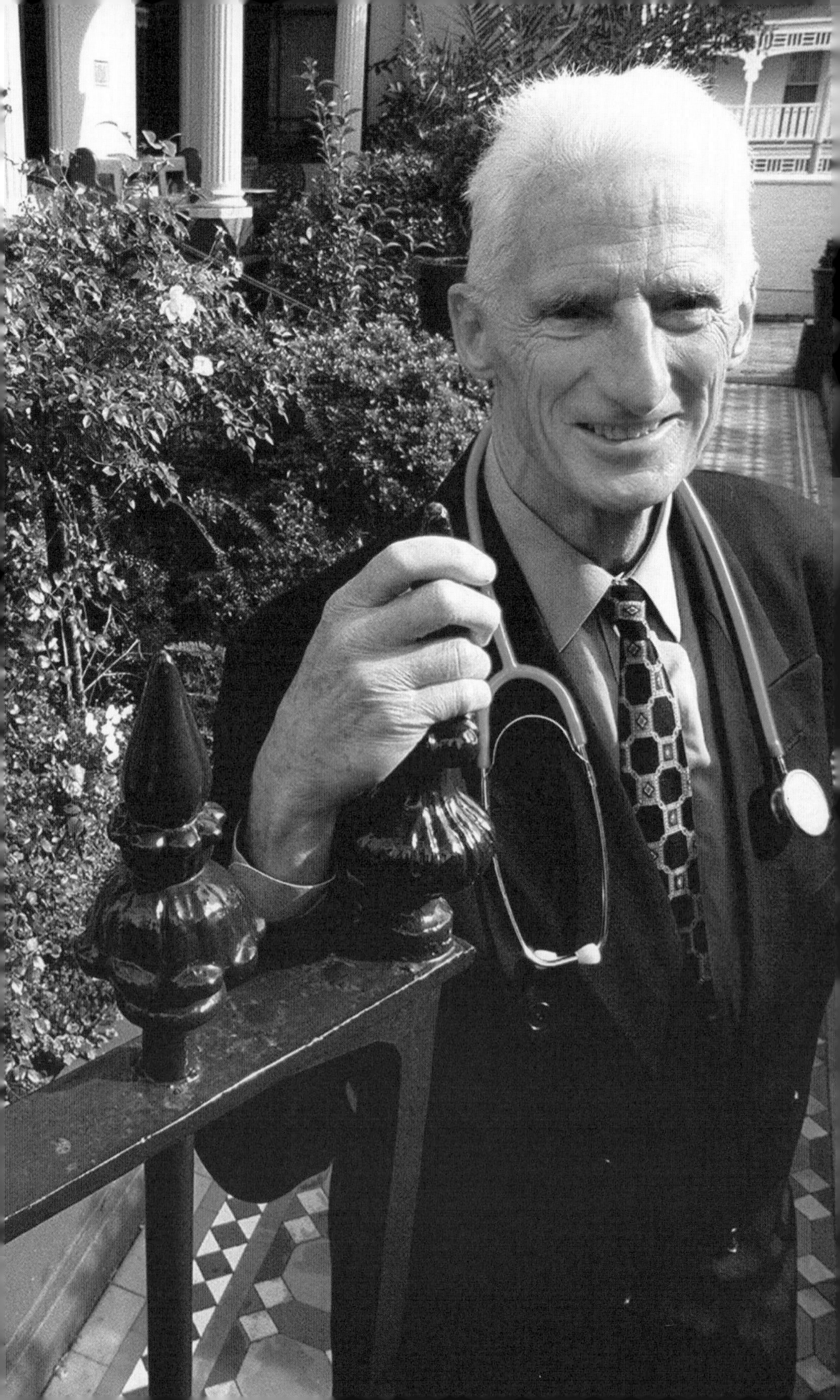

CHAPTER 6 – BECOMING A CAUSE HERO

CARL WOOD

While his science may be complicated, his cause is not

The not-for-profit entrepreneurial imagination and courage of Professor Carl Wood of Monash IVF *has changed the face of human reproductive technology worldwide against odds which would make even the most determined commercial entrepreneur cringe and possibly give up.*

In 1973, Wood led the Australian scientific team that produced the world's first IVF baby. While sadly the baby survived only two weeks, this achievement has subsequently given life to hundreds of thousands of people around the world, and unquantifiable happiness to a similar number of otherwise childless couples.

Now aged seventy-two, but with the physical appearance and mental acuity of men twenty years his junior, Wood is still passionately pursuing the development of techniques and systems to treat women's diseases. Though less controversial than his IVF achievements, which along with notoriety brought him several death threats, his current work, aimed at curing endometriosis which affects ten per cent of women and fibroids which affects forty per cent of women over the age of thirty-five, is arguably of equally great international significance.

Professionally a gynaecologist and laparoscopic surgeon, Wood has been instrumental in raising tens of millions of dollars from governments, business, foundations, and even participating medical colleagues, and has channelled this money to ever-snowballing research endeavours.

He has been a catalyst in engaging extraordinarily diverse and often controversial partners in what he describes as an 'integrated medicine' approach to preventing and curing women's diseases, particularly those related to reproductive organs. Wood has enthusiastically included massage, acupuncture and herbal treatment disciplines in his quest for better outcomes.

John C Lyons and Edward de Bono — *183*

MARKETING WITHOUT MONEY

'WE FOUND FORTY PER CENT OF THE WOMEN WITH ENDOMETRIOSIS WERE ALREADY IN ALTERNATIVE THERAPIES ANYWAY. SO WE JOINED WITH THE ALTERNATIVE THERAPIES TO HELP THE WOMEN COPE WITH THE DISEASE.'

Wood has deliberately chosen not to profit personally from the research that he has initiated and lead, even though it has resulted in the establishment of commercial IVF clinics around the world and a New York Stock Exchange listed company, IVF America. The impact on his more recent research passions, endometriosis and fibroids, is likely to be of equally great social and economic significance. Wood's community contribution has twice been acknowledged with the award of CBE in 1988 and AC in 1995.

A direct economic impact of endometriosis, a common cause of infertility and hysterectomy, is absenteeism, which in Victoria alone according to Wood is estimated to cost $15 million per annum. Commercial endometriosis clinics are now being set up around the world as a flow-on from his missionary awareness raising of the prevalence and significance of the disease affecting some 600 000 women in Australia alone.

A similar flow-on is likely to occur as a result of Wood's work with the even more prevalent disease of fibroids in the uterus, which often results in infertility and painful and heavy periods and pressure on the bowel and bladder causing dysfunction in forty per cent of women over the age of thirty-five. A multi-disciplinary team has been formed to provide less invasive surgery including laparoscopic techniques to remove fibroids instead of performing hysterectomy.

While Wood's vision, imagination and courage has created value and wealth, both monetary and non-monetary, for others, his methodology and achievement in pioneering IVF mirrors and even surpasses those of many classical for-profit entrepreneurs. One learning in particular stands out among many – the value of being passionate about a cause and a value focus, and being persistent and creatively flexible in the pursuit of the end goal.

Like most successful commercial entrepreneurs, Wood began with a focussed cause in which he successfully engaged enough people, albeit with great persistence, to fund initial research and achieve a world breakthrough in IVF. His cause is simply 'improving women's health' and his dual focus is on creating value by increasing desired fertility, and on reducing female disease associated with reproductive organs. Women he says are seven times more likely than men to suffer reproductive-organ-related disease.

Wood's work was opposed vehemently and very publicly by the Roman Catholic Church and by feminist groups, and this opposition provoked a raging debate on the morality of discarding excess fertilised embryos. Wood's initiative to avoid this issue by freezing and preserving excess embryos provoked further concern and controversy as to subsequent possible uses, and possible abuses.

Government agencies, charitable foundations and sponsoring universities who were generally privately supportive of his work, were faced with a dilemma given the hostility being expressed in influential parts of the community.

At the time, the 1970s and early 1980s, opinion polls showed that the majority of the Australian community was opposed to the idea and by implication to his research, which was of necessity conducted largely on humans, not on animals. He received death threats and was accused publicly in forums where he spoke and in graffiti of being " a murderer". A passionate young priest initiated an opposing hunger strike in Melbourne's CBD, until his superiors apparently convinced him that this was inappropriate.

Wood knew, however, that unless he persisted with explaining the importance and human significance of IVF through all mediums available, even though this meant provoking personal attack and derision, he would not achieve his goal. He had to work long and hard to reverse the tide of public opinion, and he did.

Today, community adoption of IVF is such that, in independent attitudinal surveys, ninety-three per cent of people believe it is a good thing. The tide has indeed been turned. The success of Wood's research has had many spin-offs beyond IVF, perhaps the most notable of which is world-leading research progress on stem-cell technology which Wood believes will lead to the replacement of cells that cause seriously debilitating diseases such as Alzheimer's. Even this research, however, is meeting with its share of controversy.

Wood says that, with the benefit of hindsight, he should have done more in the early stages of his IVF research to spread understanding of the significance of his work. Had he done so, adoption could have been hastened, support maximised and opposition minimised.

Max Beck

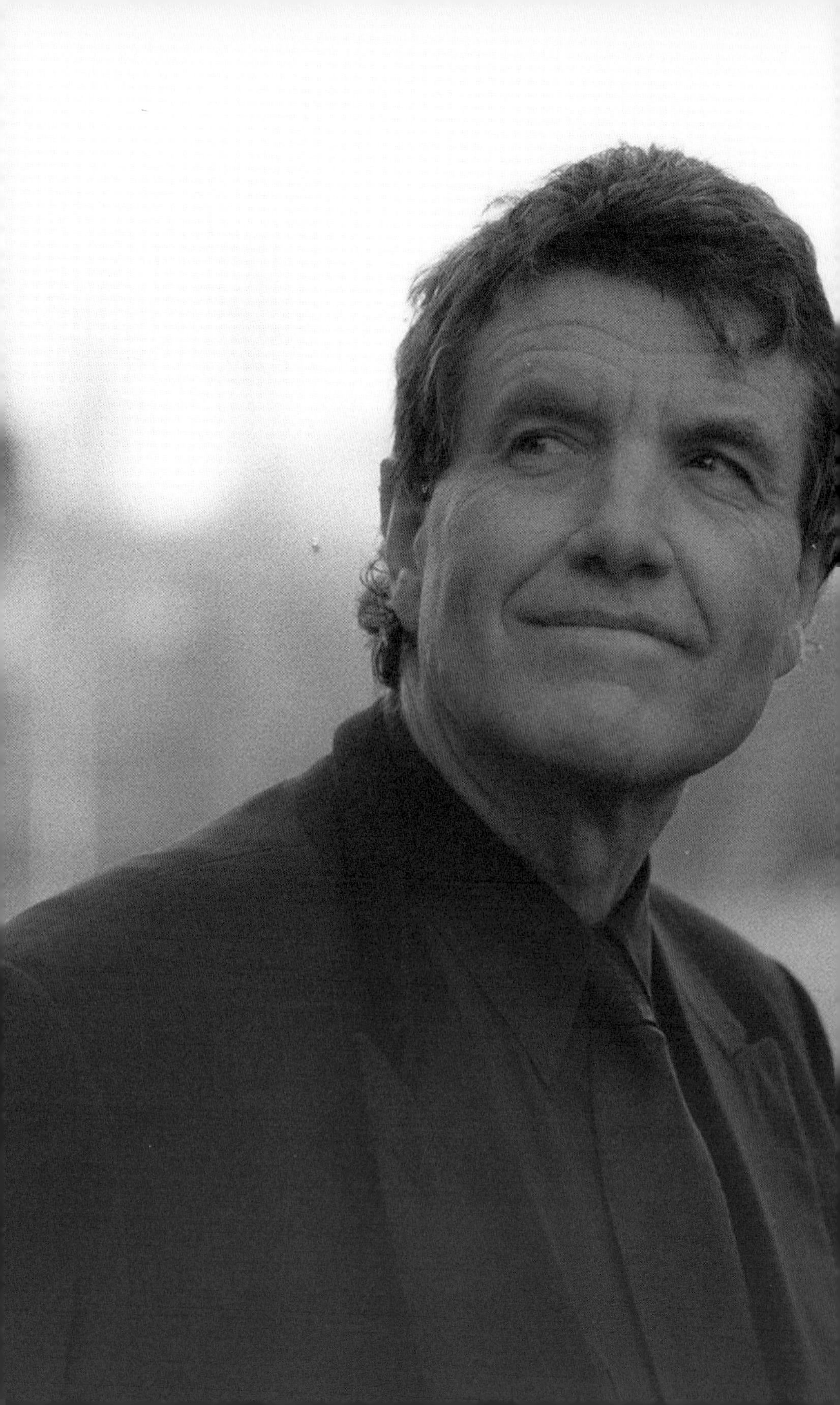

CHAPTER 6 – BECOMING A CAUSE HERO

MAX BECK

Building a reputation is vital, but you have to do more than just say it, you need to deliver

Max Beck started his career as an apprentice carpenter, doing a bit of subcontract work at weekends. By age thirty-three, though he had built a construction company employing 300 people, he lost everything except his house. Bloodied and a lot wiser, he changed direction, and today has a private company that he says this year will earn revenues of around $200 million and has a property investment portfolio that runs into hundreds of millions.

In 1973, Max Beck thought he was something of a godfather in the Melbourne building industry. His construction company had a very full order book of fixed-price contracts with what seemed to be reasonable margins. The industry was booming and the future looked rosy.

What Beck hadn't bargained on was the rampant inflation of the early Whitlam era which pushed up the cost of labour and materials dramatically overnight making his forward order book a nightmare of red ink. Unable to get out of his contracts, Beck says he lost everything except his house: 'So I WENT HOME AND SAID TO MY WIFE: "WE'D BETTER GET THE TOOLS OUT, BECAUSE WE'VE GOT TO START AGAIN".'

Max Beck Constructions Pty Ltd was forced into liquidation owing suppliers and subcontractors around one million dollars. Though concurrently there were many other much higher profile corporate collapses in Australia for much the same reason, Beck took little comfort.

John C Lyons and Edward de Bono — *189*

Marketing without Money

Losing his hard-won portfolio of several blocks of flats was not the worst of it. He says the pressure on him and his young family made the next three years the worst period of his life. His previously indestructible self-perception took a beating he would never forget. However, suppliers and subcontractors, he says, were surprisingly understanding, given they were faced with many others in the same boat.

Gathering his composure and courage, *Beck realised that the way forward for him long-term was not in the tight-margin construction business where he had little control over the variables that would determine his profitability, and perhaps even his very existence.* He looked with envy on his developer customers who typically enjoyed margins of fifteen to twenty per cent.

In 1976, Beck decided to combine his knowledge of construction with the real-estate experience of Michael Buxton, whom he had met socially some three years earlier, basically to joint venture on a development opportunity which Buxton had identified. With just $25 000 capital, Beck and Buxton formed Becton Corporation Pty Ltd, and for the next twenty years until Beck bought out Buxton, they methodically built a diversified property development and investment company. Becton built a reputation for quality and stability in an industry where these values traditionally have been in short supply.

Today the company has three major strands to its business. Firstly the development of commercial and residential projects mostly for on-sale upon completion. Secondly, the planned retention and management of some developments in what is now a significant and growing investment portfolio which includes the $140 million "Classic Residences" development at Brighton for the over fifty-five's market. More recently, Becton has added a timeshare joint venture with the Accor Group consisting of some nine properties throughout Australia.

Beck's humble beginnings as a carpenter and his sobering failure in construction in the early 1970s have left indelible marks on the man's quietly confident personality. While he is still clearly adventurous and creative, he is measured and cautious at least until he finds a clear path forward. Even then, he seeks to ensure that his company has somewhere to land if the flight forward turns out to be stormier than anticipated. 'IN ANY BUSINESS, YOU NEED A STRONG COMPASS', cautions Beck. 'I HAVE SOUGHT TO BE THAT COMPASS AT BECTON'.

He says with credibility: 'I'M JUST AN ORDINARY BLOKE. IF THERE IS ANY STRENGTH THAT I'VE GOT, IT IS PROBABLY AN ABILITY TO GET PEOPLE WHO ARE PREPARED TO FOLLOW, TO ORGANISE PEOPLE, AND I SEEM TO BE ABLE TO GET THEIR CONFIDENCE. PEOPLE SKILLS ARE RIGHT AT THE TOP OF MY LIST. YOU HAVE TO HAVE THEM.'

For those who seek to follow Beck's success, regardless of industry, he offers some deceptively simple signposts.

Choose something you know and understand which has a good margin

Beck says you must know intimately the market you are addressing. For over a decade Becton has been using formal market research to quantify markets precisely and to test and refine its project concepts. He adds 'UNLESS YOU LISTEN TO CUSTOMERS, YOU'RE GOING TO MISS.'

Beck says his company goes out of its way to meet the individual and special needs of its quite discerning clientele.

'WE HAVE MORE CUSTOMER FOCUS THAN MOST DEVELOPERS I THINK. YOU CAN ACTUALLY CUSTOMISE OUR PRODUCT. IF YOU'RE A BUYER, YOU CAN HAVE ANYTHING THAT WE CAN REASONABLY CHANGE. WE HAVE THREE PEOPLE DOING THIS WORK. THERE ARE MARGINS IN THAT, TYPICALLY ABOUT FIFTEEN PER CENT OF THE PURCHASE PRICE, SO IT'S A BUSINESS IN ITSELF.'

Employ the very best people you can afford and incentivise them heavily

Beck says:

'I THINK YOU NEED A BUSINESS WITH HIGH MARGINS SO THAT YOU CAN AFFORD TO EMPLOY THE BEST PEOPLE. BUT YOU ALSO MUST INCENTIVISE PEOPLE. BEFORE I BOUGHT OUT MICHAEL BUXTON, I WENT TO THE GUYS I WANTED TO COME IN AS PARTNERS AND SAID TO THEM "HOW MUCH [MONEY] DO YOU THINK YOU NEED?" THEY GAVE ME A FIGURE AND I SAID "WELL THAT'S THE BASE. SO YOU CAN BUY FIVE PER CENT OF THIS BUSINESS, BUT YOUR BASE IS ABSOLUTELY MINIMAL. SO IF I MAKE MONEY YOU MAKE MONEY".

'I THINK THE FURTHER YOU CAN PUSH THAT DOWN INTO ORGANISATIONS,

THE BETTER OFF THE BUSINESS IS. WE HAVE FIVE OTHER DIRECTORS AND MYSELF. THE OTHERS HAVE FIVE PER CENT OF THE BUSINESS. ALL DIRECTORS UNDERSTAND INTIMATELY. THEY LOOK AT EVERY PROJECT AS THEIR PROJECT.

'WE ROLL INCENTIVES RIGHT DOWN TO OUR SUPERVISORS. AT PROJECT MANAGEMENT LEVEL, COSTS AND TIME ARE WITHIN THEIR CONTROL, AND THEY ARE REWARDED ACCORDINGLY. BUT ALWAYS WE WILL TRY AND GET THE BASE AS LOW AS WE CAN.'

Build a brand by delivering on your promise and establishing a track record

'BUILDING A REPUTATION AND BUILDING A BRAND, YOU NEED TO DELIVER. YOU HAVE TO DO MORE THAN JUST SAY IT. WE'VE BUILT BUILDINGS THAT ARE PROBABLY BETTER THAN MOST AROUND THE PLACE, AND WE'VE HAD VERY GOOD DIVIDENDS FROM THAT. THERE ARE SOME SHOCKING EXAMPLES OF POOR DEVELOPMENT. I HAVE TRIED TO GO THE OTHER WAY. INSTITUTIONAL INVESTORS HAVE THEIR OWN CONSULTANTS AND THEY GENERALLY ARE PLEASED TO BUY A BECTON BUILDING, BECAUSE THEY HAVE BEEN DESIGNED TO HAVE A LONG LIFESPAN AND LOW MAINTENANCE.'

Always look at the downside, and make sure you have good financial controls

Beck says he learned, and has never forgotten, some very basic lessons from that hard-won experience when his construction company failed in 1973.

'FOR THE FIRST TIME IN MY LIFE I STARTED TO LOOK AT THE DOWNSIDE OF THINGS. IT'S AN AUTOMATIC QUESTION FOR ME NOW. FINANCIAL CONTROL IS ANOTHER THING I LEARNED. I HAD NO INTEREST BECAUSE I WAS A CHIPPY AND VERY GOOD AT MARKETING AND SEEING THAT THE JOBS GOT OUT ON TIME. BUT OUR CONTROLS WERE WAY BELOW STANDARD, WHICH I THINK IS PRETTY COMMON IN A LOT OF BUSINESSES PARTICULARLY IN OUR INDUSTRY, SO EVER SINCE I HAVE OVER-EMPHASISED THAT.'

Having assessed your risks, look at how you can reduce them

At the height of the Australian property boom of the late 1980s, the then quite prosperous Beck and Buxton were faced with an opportunity that had the potential to more than double their wealth. The company was in the final stages of its then biggest ever project, a landmark office tower development at 333 Collins Street, Melbourne costing $500 million. Hype was driving up price expectations just before the stockmarket crash burst the bubble. Some pundits said Becton might get close to a billion dollars for the building.

Beck's previous near-death experience paid off handsomely. He and Buxton decided to pay $11 million to the South Australian Insurance Commission for a put-option which guaranteed they could sell the building for $520 million upon completion if the market turned bad. The market turned very bad. Beck estimates that, when they handed over the keys in exchange for the Commission's cheque, the then bottom-of-the-market value of the building would have been little more than $400 million. 'THEY [THE COMMISSION] REALLY RAKED OVER THAT AGREEMENT', Beck adds.

Marketing without Money

INSPIRATION SUMMARY

Before moving on to the Education Section of the book, where we extract key learnings from our research with entrepreneurs and combine these with the principles of concept research and development, it is useful to summarise the key learnings from each entrepreneur, individually and collectively:

Paul Cave, founder and chairman, BridgeClimb, experiential tourism

- Find something different and unique – a world-first, consumerised bridge climbing experience
- Focus your offering and recognise the unique value you deliver – 'The climb of your life'
- Deliver quality every time – let nothing fall between the cracks – every climber's satisfaction measured

Les Schirato, managing director and major shareholder, Cantarella Bros, consumer products including Vittoria coffee

- Think differently and be different, even when you're successful
- Narrow the focus and manage customers for profit
- Work out who you are and what your competitive advantage is, and stick to it
- Surround yourself with a good team, not simply good individuals

Adrian Di Marco, founder and chairman, Technology One, software solutions

- Focus tightly, scope the market, and find the best access – 'What would a total solution look like for that [vertical] market?'
- Own the customer relationship and go deep – we've not imposed third parties [distributors] on our customers
- Great people need the support of great processes. 'You need to build a business that is process oriented'

Dick Smith, founder, Dick Smith Electronics, *Australian Geographic*, and Dick Smith Foods

- Copy the best ideas from around the world and bring them together under one roof
- Surround yourself with like-minded people to help duplicate your business model – 'Once I've come up with the ideas by copying the success of others, I lose interest very quickly'
- Think differently and work out how to do things better and at a lower cost

Euan Murdoch, founder, Herron Pharmaceuticals

- Develop a 'why not' approach that is not constrained by mindset – 'Financially we are not in the same league as our [huge] competitors, but intellectually we can match it with them and probably challenge them'
- Do things differently, flank rather than go head-to-head
- An unrelenting focus, and a passion for the planning process not so much the plan – 'How can we reinvent our industry and our business model?'

Peter Farrell, founder, chairman and CEO, ResMed, solutions for sleep apnoea

- Do we have a market that's accessible?
- Can we get the right people?
- Do we have the money to play the end game?
- Does the timing make sense?
- Do we really understand the technology and what the competition and potential competition is, and the intellectual property terrain?
- Are we comfortable that we have something we can manage?

Gerry Harvey, founder and chairman, Harvey Norman Holdings, retailing

- Know your business and yourself before you start your business – 'I have spent forty-three years getting experience; now if I don't exploit it over the next ten years I'm basically a failure'
- Help your people to get the most out of themselves – 'You build up a culture in the place where everyone knows you're trying to get them there all the time'
- Find the best way to do it and keep on searching – 'My ultimate aim at the moment is to take over poorly-performing public companies'

Clair Jennifer, founder and managing director, Wombat Enterprises, women's clothing

- A deep and genuine empathy with your chosen customer – fashion for the not-so-fashion-conscious woman
- A unique value proposition for 'conventional' women – 'designed to fit "real" Australian women'
- Absolutely painstaking attention to staff selection, systems and training to deliver the in-store experience

INSPIRATION SUMMARY

Jurgen Klein, founder and managing director, Jurlique International, natural remedies and therapies

- Anticipating and shaping, not following customer preferences – 'heart reading, not mind reading'
- Promoting the experience, not the product – 'customers "buy" the concept, then the product'
- Delivery concepts, not simply distribution channels – 'If the experience is not good, a long-term customer is not created'

Peter Kazacos, founder and managing director, KAZ Group, technology outsourcing and software

- Use your employment to broaden your experience and understanding of opportunities – sales, technical operations, etc.
- Look for the right type of clients – then decide the right type of space to be in
- Find a quality foundation client and leverage from their industry knowledge and credibility
- Search for what you can do for the customer; anticipate their future needs; look for opportunity
- See business as a voyage of opportunity, discovery and learning – move along the value chain

Len Poulter, founder and director, Lenard's, fresh food retailing

- Make sure that your idea is not your fantasy, but what the customer wants
- Commitment to making it work is more important than the idea itself.
- Surround yourself with good people who believe in what you are trying to achieve
- Provide clear leadership, a game plan and discipline to your team

Paul Adler and Brad Bond, co-founders and directors, Invizage, technology support to SMEs

- Elevated cause – 'to improve businesses and make individuals' lives easier through technology'
- Greater value – overcoming the 'can't get here when we need them' syndrome
- Replicable formula – scheduled maintenance and support, not the industry norm of crisis response

Therese Rein, founder and managing director, Ingeus, integrated human services

- A passionate and persistent focus on a cause that is bigger than the business – integrating people and work
- Value integrated into the anticipated needs of diverse stakeholders – workers, insurers and employers
- A value delivery formula that is replicable though not inflexible, combining many professional skills
- Reputation built more on outstanding delivery than on promotional spend

Graeme Blackman, founder and chairman, Institute of Drug Technology Australia, development and manufacture of active pharmaceutical ingredients

- Surpetition, not competition – choosing to create a higher-order race, removed from the competitive rat-race
- Integrated values, not simply product values; IDT's accreditation with the US FDA is of "outstanding" value
- A formula which gains strength – successful API development leads to long-term manufacturing contracts

INSPIRATION SUMMARY

Graham Turner, founder and managing director, Flight Centre, travel

- Unrelenting focus – most travel agents struggle to deliver complex products with ever-mobile staff
- Simplification as the key to a systems approach – rolling out a new shop every couple of days
- An easily replicated system for everything – 'You don't want neuro-surgeons as part of your system'
- Rewarding people for the outcomes you want – 'We've probably done that pretty well'
- Pulling with human nature, not against it – 'Family, Village and Tribe' organisation structure

Jim McDonald, founder and chairman, MDH Pastoral Company, beef production

- Achieving economies of scale and scope – 'The secret to success in cattle is areas and numbers'
- Picking the right assets, and getting rid of unproductive assets quickly
- People quality and hands-on personal supervision and always being prepared to meet the market
- Adapting to a tough environment and incentivising family involvement

Joe Saragossi, chairman, G James Group, glass and aluminium

- Facing reality, recognising the opportunity in timing
- Innovation through cross-industry adaptation
- Reinvesting in your own business and having no formal dividend policy
- Reducing the risks of rapid expansion by using a simple fall-back line-of-defence – factories to rented warehouses

John C Lyons and Edward de Bono

RM (Reg) Williams, bushman, grazier, businessman, founder RM Williams, Australian icon

- A business built on trust – 'People are looking for someone who will trade honestly with them'
- Send money with order – 'The most rewarding experiment of my life'
- Intimate knowledge, deep empathy and constant refinement – 'I knew what a cattleman needed'
- The right people is a matter of character – 'It doesn't matter whether they are smart'

Carl Wood, gynaecologist and laparoscopic surgeon, global "father" of IVF, not-for-profit

- Persistence in the cause – improving women's health: increasing fertility, reducing reproductive organ disease
- Engaging key players – colleagues, alternative therapists, governments, foundations, even opponents
- Spread the understanding – the key to overcoming controversy and dissent fuelled by ignorance of the value

Max Beck, founder and chairman, Becton Corporation, property development/investment

- Choose something you know and understand, and which has a good margin
- Employ the very best people you can afford and incentivise them heavily
- Build a brand by delivering on your promise and establishing a track record
- Always look at the downside, manage your risk and have good financial control

PART 2
Education

Chapter 7
BEYOND THE FUNDAMENTALS

Is there anything wrong with the fundamentals of business thinking such as efficiency, problem-solving, analysis of information, and competition?

These fundamentals were developed in the early and somewhat primitive days of business, and though they are still valid today there is a need to examine them more critically – which is what we intend to do in this section.

In the early days of business, the economic baseline was rising in developed countries and to a lesser extent in developing countries. It was only necessary to keep your place on this rising baseline and all would be well. The two things necessary to keep your place were efficiency and problem solving.

Efficiency in the use of capital, people, energy and resources could keep you on the rising baseline. If a problem arose, then you solved it and returned to the baseline.

The process is not unlike that of a family bringing up a child. There is shelter, care and nutrition. If the child falls ill you call in a problem solver, the doctor. The child is cured and goes on to grow into a healthy adult. Growth is the natural state of affairs.

Today, for a variety of reasons, the baseline is flat and may even be declining. There is a global marketplace with overproduction of goods and services – at least with regard to those who can pay for them.

Much business thinking, however, is still preoccupied only with the rules that applied in the old regime of a rising baseline, principally:

- Efficiency and problem solving
- Information and analysis
- Management and housekeeping

Efficiency and problem-solving

All the efficiency and problem-solving in the world may only keep you 'efficiently' on the declining baseline.

In short, efficiency and problem-solving are maintenance procedures. If the direction is good or if the economic baseline is rising, then maintenance is sufficient; but if the baseline is not rising and the direction is not correct, then maintenance alone can never be enough.

Businesses often feel that since they have a lot of market muscle and such a dominant position, maintenance will be enough. In recent years, however, even mighty IBM found that market domination was not enough if you fell behind on concepts. *IBM fell behind on a concept of 'connectivity' and suffered as a result. IBM also suffered from low-priced clones when the mystique of computers wore off and there was no longer a need for reassurance from the solidity of big blue.*

You may feel, therefore, that you have a secure market niche and that maintenance is enough. You may be correct in this assumption and you may not. The maintenance concept of management used to be sufficient, but in most cases is not sufficient today.

Information and analysis

A fundamental tradition of business thinking is to collect information and then make decisions by analysing and reacting to that information

There was a time when executives were very short of information. Any improvement in information, therefore, would immediately improve the quality of the decisions that had to be made. In a sense, the information itself made the decisions. Today, however, we have computers that give us much more information and the ability to handle it. If a decision only requires more information, then that decision can be made directly by the computer without the need for human intervention. The relationship between information and decision-making is suggested in Figure 7.1. At first, increasing information leads to better decisions, but after a while more and more information has less and less effect.

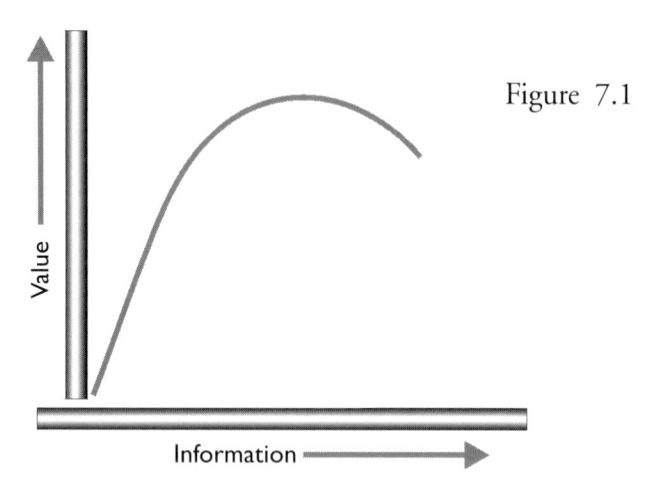

Figure 7.1

[Graph: Value (y-axis) vs Information (x-axis), showing a curve that rises, peaks, and then declines]

There even comes a time when further information makes it difficult to sort out important information from the rest. There is confusion and information overload. Yet, as most data-processing departments will confirm, executives faced with difficult decisions simply ask for more and more information in the hope that somehow the new information will do their thinking for them. In the past, information was indeed the bottleneck. Actions, decisions, and investments were held up for the lack of information or had to be merely speculative. Computers and telecommunications have opened up the information bottleneck.

Now that we have the information, what do we do with it?

You have information that your competitor is offering financial rebates on cars. What do you do? You could follow the simple knee-jerk reaction of offering rebates yourself. *The quality of your decision is not determined by the quality of the information you are getting, but by the quality of your thinking and the range of new concepts you may come up with.*

In short, getting and using information is as important as it ever was, perhaps even more important, but it is not enough. In a more complex world, the way we use information becomes even more important.

We used to think that the analysis of information would in itself produce ideas. Today we know that this is not so and that the analysis of information can only allow us to select from ideas which we already have. In order to generate new ideas, however, we have to be able to do some idea work in our minds before coming to the information. Information by itself does not make concepts.

Management and housekeeping

Any business is really an 'idea machine' as suggested in Figure 7.2. At one end of the machine are fed in the resources: capital, raw material, management, labour, machinery, and energy. *The idea machine fashions these into a product or service according to the forming idea.* What comes out at the other end is a product or service which can be sold at a good enough price to keep the machine running, to satisfy present investors, and even to entice future ones.

With the single exception of acquisitions, most of the habits of management thinking are concerned with keeping the machine running. They are concerned only with maintenance. They are concerned with providing the baseline. As suggested earlier, this kind of thinking was sufficient at one time, but is not sufficient today.

It is indeed necessary – but not sufficient. In no case have we challenged

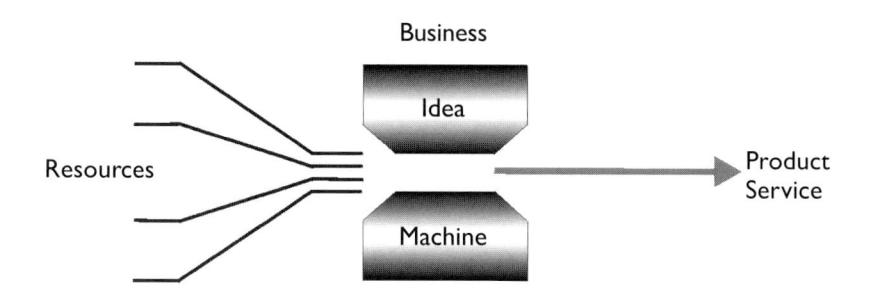

Figure 7.2

the validity of conventional thinking habits because each habit is still valid. What we do challenge, however, is the sufficiency of today's business thinking. Being content with the adequacy of our current thinking habits is a dangerous complacency.

Perhaps the very word 'management' is at fault. Imagine a stagecoach with a team of spirited horses. The driver has a hard time managing the team. The word management implies that the energy, the ideas, the resources, the people and the markets are all there – and all that is needed is someone to manage these various things. Management is like driving a car along a difficult road. Skills and guidance are called for, and if the car breaks down you repair it to keep it going. But you are not choosing the car or the road.

Management is all about housekeeping. It is assumed that the existing core ideas are valid. Energy is applied to the idea machine in order to keep it running, not to the idea itself.

At lower levels in organisations, problem-solving and housekeeping skills are most important and are what get noticed. People are indeed promoted for these types of abilities. But at senior levels there is a need for conceptual, creative and strategic thinking. Mere problem-solving can be delegated to others.

Housekeeping is very necessary, but there is also the venture aspect. This is also necessary. *What are the other values that you are selling? What are the core ideas of the idea machine?* This is where surpetition becomes so important because competition is really part of housekeeping and baseline maintenance.

There was a time when strategic planning was much in vogue. People used to plan with great formality where a company should be in the future. *Strategic planning fell into disfavour when the future refused to play the role assigned to it by planners. The sheer unpredictability of the future, the rapid rate of change, the instability and positive feedback loops in non-linear systems made a nonsense of planning.* At best, there had to be a sort of rolling strategic plan with reassessments almost every week.

So the emphasis shifted away from strategic planning to another concept. This was the concept of being fit, lean, muscular and quick on your feet. In this way, your organisation could respond effectively and profitably to any situation that arose. If market conditions changed, you could change with them. If technology offered new directions, you could be quick to jump in with a "me-too" product.

With the retreat from forward planning to corporate fitness and speed of response, the emphasis was back on housekeeping, because excellent housekeeping was what made an organisation fit.

Quality does have to come first. Quality has to be the baseline. But when others can also provide quality, innovation comes into its own.

The Japanese are great innovators. They are not very good at individual creativity, though there are clearly many exceptions, but they take the game of creativity seriously. They are, however, great innovators because they are willing to try out and put into production almost any idea they have. *In Japan, corporations blitz each other with streams of new products. Competitors immediately cover these products just in case they should turn out to be successful.* Even while they are launching one product, a company often already has in an advanced stage of product development the next generation of products and the one after that. They believe very little in market research and analysis within their own country. They prefer to get the product out into the marketplace and use the actual test of the market. People will buy the product, they believe, or it will disappear.

The main point here is that while the Japanese are much concerned with the housekeeping side of things (they provided the inspiration for quality, 'just in time', and so on) they are also deeply concerned with the venture side of innovation.

Why is conceptual creative thinking a necessity?

In practice, very few people know or accept that creativity is a logical necessity. Most dismiss the matter by asking for examples of creativity, and then show that these examples, in hindsight, are simply plain logic.

Even those who do see value in creativity believe its use should be restricted to product design, packaging, promotion, and other extraneous matters. This is a dangerous fallacy.

There is an absolute need for creativity in all thinking that involves perceptions and concepts, and there is very little thinking that does not involve perceptions and concepts. In finance, engineering and science, there is every bit as much need for creative thinking as in product design. It is one of the great failures of our education system to assume that creative thinking is confined to the arts and is not part of the hard sciences.

If we cannot use creativity, we cannot use much of the potential available in our knowledge, our experience and our assets. In fact, creativity is the cheapest and best way of getting the best return from existing assets.

There are those who recognise the importance of creativity but still believe that nothing can or needs be done about it. Such people believe that ideas will happen from time to time and that some people happen to be creative, while others are not. This is a passive attitude that is no longer tenable. We can do a lot to develop creative thinking attitudes and methods in everybody.

The human mind is a self-organising information system. Self-organising information systems set up patterns. In the mind these patterns form the basis of our perception. Incoming information is understood, processed and stored by our present perception. *Our present perception governs our thinking.*

Humour shows more directly than anything else that the human mind works as a self-organising system. Humour is the most significant behaviour of the human mind. This is a simple statement of fact and is not meant to be provocative.

Humour can only occur if a self-organising information system, which settles down in one stable state (our present perception), suddenly is reconfigured into another. The punch line of a joke creates humour only because it alters our perception of what is logical – it enables us to discover 'logic' in hindsight.

Creativity is based on the same process as humour. The time sequence of experience sets up certain patterns of perception, certain ways of looking at things. There are side patterns (as shown in Figure 7.3), but we cannot get access to them. If suddenly we do get access to the side patterns then we have either humour or creativity.

Designing ways of helping us to move across patterns of perception and thinking is the basis of lateral thinking which is discussed in a later section. The word 'lateral' is derived from moving sideways across patterns.

Every valuable creative idea must always be logical in hindsight. If it were not, we would never be able to see its value. It would simply be a crazy idea. The idea might indeed be crazy forever or until we caught up with it. Consider the following two ideas:

- If a plastic piece is not strong enough, make it thinner, and

- If you want to increase sales, raise the price

It is difficult to accept these as valuable ideas since they are not immediately logical in hindsight. With a little more thought, however, both can be seen as logical.

Because we have assumed that every valuable idea must always be logical in hindsight, we have never paid attention to creativity. We have assumed that if an idea is logical in hindsight, then better logic should have been able to reach it in the first place. We now know that in self-organising information systems, this reasoning is totally wrong.

In any self-organising system, creativity is absolutely essential. To quote Albert Einstein, 'THE SIGNIFICANT PROBLEMS WE FACE TODAY CANNOT BE SOLVED AT THE SAME LEVEL OF THINKING WE WERE AT WHEN WE CREATED THEM'.

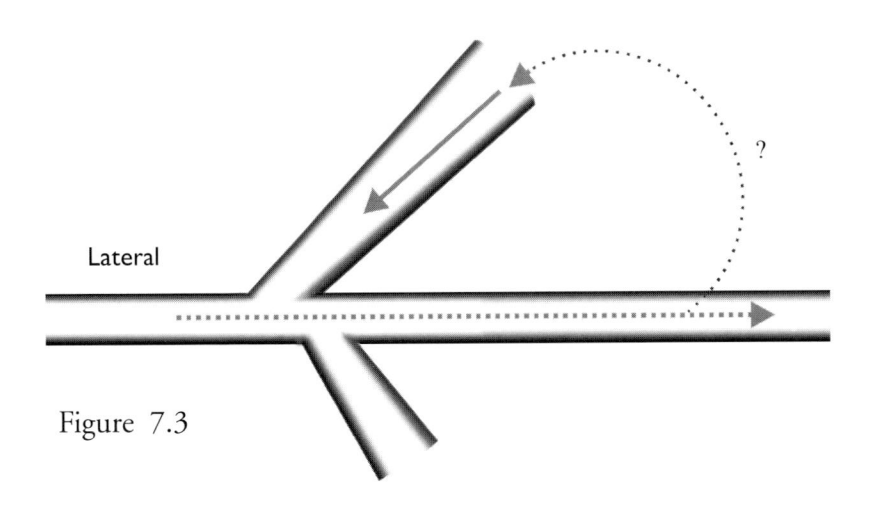

Lateral

Figure 7.3

Chapter 8
BEYOND INFORMATION TO CONCEPTS

A concept is a way of doing something that achieves a purpose and provides values. There is an important distinction between a *concept* and an *idea*. An idea is something specific that you can carry out. A concept is a more general, abstract notion that has to be carried out by means of a specific idea. For example, travelling along a road is a concept, but in practice you have to do something specific such as walk, ride a bicycle, or drive a car.

You can extract a concept from an idea by simply asking yourself the question: "This (idea) is a way of doing what?" Riding a bicycle is one way (one idea) for travelling along a road (a concept). A focus on the concept (travelling along a road) enables you to generate other alternatives, which also might include skateboarding, running, etc. The point is that identifying the concept behind an idea enables you to generate and consider the value of other alternative ideas.

Contrary to our normal thinking, concepts are often more useful when they are blurred, vague and fuzzy, because then they have more potential. If they are too detailed, they cover too little. If they are too general, they cover too much and provide little direction. In time, a creative thinker gets a feeling for when a concept is specific enough, yet general enough at the same time.

There is little distinction between a concept and a perception. When we look out at the world we never see raw data. The data we receive has already been organised into patterns by previous experience and the self-organising nature of the perception. A person born blind who suddenly becomes able to see cannot see. That person has to learn to see and to build up usable patterns. This organisation into patterns, sequences or groups we call perception. We group certain things together to obtain perceptions.

So a perception is a grouping of things realised when we look out at the world. A concept is a grouping of things realised when we look inwardly at our available experience. When we have grouped things into a perception, we often put a name on that grouping: a flower, mountain, a restaurant.

Consider a car wheel clamp. Its purpose is to discourage drivers from parking in the wrong places in cities. It prevents the use of the car until the authorities come to remove it after the parking fine has been paid.

The key concept behind the idea of a wheel clamp is inconvenience. Attempts to discourage parking by imposition of high fines do not work well, because some drivers are quite willing to pay the fine when they are caught. But the inconvenience is a much greater deterrent than the fine. So we could describe a wheel clamp as a way of using inconvenience as a deterrent to irresponsible parking. That is a broader definition of the concept.

We might then look around for specific ideas for other ways of putting this concept to work. The wheel clamp might be only one of them. It might be possible to lock something on to the exhaust outlet. In terms of design, we might try to improve the existing idea. A weakness of the clamping idea is that the offending car is left for a long time in a place that can block the flow of traffic. Perhaps raising the car into the air would be an approach to alleviate this problem.

The fundamental value drivers discussed later in this section – *convenience, quality of life, self-importance and distraction* – are the basic building blocks of concepts. For example being "clamped" not only creates inconvenience value, it also potentially embarrasses the driver in the eyes of passers-by, impacting negatively on self-importance. It may also diminish quality of life temporarily because the driver may be held up from an important appointment, thus creating stress and other potential personal downsides.

It is important to note that, while the wheel clamp is an idea for creating *negative* value for the person illegally parked by deterring such parking in the future, the clamp creates *positive* value for the community, especially other drivers.

Once we understand clearly the value concept (for example, creating inconvenience), then we can generate a practically endless list of ideas as to how that concept might be delivered. Alternatively, if we focus only on an idea (such as wheel clamping or similar) and not the concept of inconvenience, then our mind is locked into a much narrower set of alternatives, typically constrained by our experience and perception-driven pattern of thinking.

Recognising concepts

It is important to recognise concepts, look for them, design them, and use them.

The concept for a business, product or service of course goes far beyond the core idea. For example, making customer access easy and efficient (i.e. distribution) is just as amenable to creative conceptual thinking and resultant value enhancement, as are other variables such as pricing and promotion.

In recent years there has been substantial cooperation between property developers, builders and financial-services providers to expand their respective markets by making it easy for people to buy a home without the normally required deposit money. Similarly, the market for investment properties has been expanded with the introduction of such devices as rental guarantees which remove initial uncertainty regarding rental income. These ideas emanate primarily from the concept of convenience. They are ways of delivering convenience value by removing specific barriers to home and investment ownership. There is still plenty of opportunity to generate alternative ways (ideas) for adding even more convenience value. Further ideas for delivering other values – such as quality of life, self-importance and distraction – may be added to further strengthen the value bundle. For example, investment in managed resort apartments may give the investor certain priority rights of use, thus adding quality of life value and self-importance value.

When we have grouped things into an overall concept, there is often synergistic value that arises from the grouping.

The Benetton Corporation was started by two brothers and a sister in

Italy less than thirty years ago. One brother was a junior accountant, and the sister was a seamstress in a garment factory. Today, Benetton is worth billions of dollars, and this in a very crowded industry with tremendous competition. So how did it all happen? There are number of concepts that helped.

The first concept was to sell colour, not shape. Colours are easy to display, and are not as dependent on fashion as shape. Colours can be changed.

So most of the garments were made without colour. Those that were coloured were put out in shops. If red appeared to be selling well, then the garments were dyed red. If green was selling, then the garments were dyed green.

The usual pattern in the garment industry follows two lines. Either this is what has always sold, so let us stick to it; or this is what we believe people will want, so let us persuade them to buy it as this season's fashion.

The Benetton concept was both reactive and flexible. This sort of immediate reactivity is common in the mail-order business, but was new in the garment industry. Flexibility, as everyone knows, is now one of the key trends in business anywhere.

Another concept was to start with jumpers, sweaters, pullovers, cardigans, and other semi-premium, high-margin items. Such items would best show colour. They were also very traditional items without much innovation. Later, Benetton opened up a wider range of products.

In addition, instead of having to go through store buyers (what would buyers have bought, anyway?), Benetton opened up its own stores with very simple layout and design. Today there are thousands of stores worldwide. *This allows direct access to the public and instant feedback.*

Finally, there is a high degree of automation and computer control. For example, a warehouse handling about half a million items a day had just six people involved. All these concepts put together led to a success in a very difficult field.

The Body Shop has also been a successful retailing concept. Since people were becoming health- and environmentally conscious, The Body Shop focussed on natural products. Putting together body-treatment products separately from the usual drug and pharmaceutical context also had a positive effect. Finally there was a great deal of skill in carrying through the concept with design, colours, and sound organisation. This is a good example of the 'integrated value' aspect that we will consider later. *Any successful concept always consists of two parts: the concept and its implementation.*

The Wright brothers were the first to fly because they changed the base concept. They did not start off with any superior technology. All those working on flying machines knew that curved wings would provide lift, and they all had access to gasoline engines that would drive propellers. *But most designers were seeking to design a stable plane.* They had experimented with hand-launched models that had to maintain their balance as they flew through the air, so "stability" became the design objective, and designers tried harder and harder in that direction. *The contribution of the Wright brothers changed this direction; they became interested in 'unstable' flying machines.* This meant that sooner or later one wing would dip down. Unless they could bring that wing up, the plane would crash. So they now focussed their attention and experimentation on how to bring up the dipped wing. They found that by twisting and warping the wing, they could increase lift on one side and decrease it on another. They developed controls. They became the first to fly. Much later on, inherently stable planes were developed. Today, fighter planes have to be made deliberately unstable, otherwise they are too slow to manoeuvre.

The great civilisations of Egypt, Greece and Rome were unable to measure time effectively. They had the technology – water clocks, hourglasses and other instruments – but they did not have the concept. They were trying to divide the day into twelve equal hours and the night, quite separately into twelve equal hours. Since the day and night varied in length throughout the year, trying to divide varying quantities into equal amounts was not easy. It was not until the thirteenth century that an Arabian mathematician, Abu L'Hassan, came up with the idea of measuring the day from the sun's peak (midday) on one day to its peak on the next day, and then dividing this into twenty-four hours.

Concepts are extremely important, but often difficult to generate. *In hindsight, of course, almost all successful concepts seem easy and obvious.*

CHAPTER 8 – BEYOND INFORMATION TO CONCEPTS

In his seminars, Edward de Bono often puts a heavy steel ball on the surface of the overhead projector and then asks the audience to think of a practical barrier that could be used on the projector to stop a ball from rolling forward. The use of hands is disallowed, and a barrier must be practical and available in the room.

Three broad types of suggestions usually emerge:

- The concept of *heaviness*: some barrier that would be heavy enough to absorb the energy of the ball, such as books, a briefcase, or shoes.

- The concept of *fixity*: a barrier could be taped down on the surface of the projector and so resist the motion of the ball. The barrier need not be heavy.

- The concept of *resistance*: some sticky stuff or double-sided tape could be used to increase the rolling resistance and bring the ball to a halt.

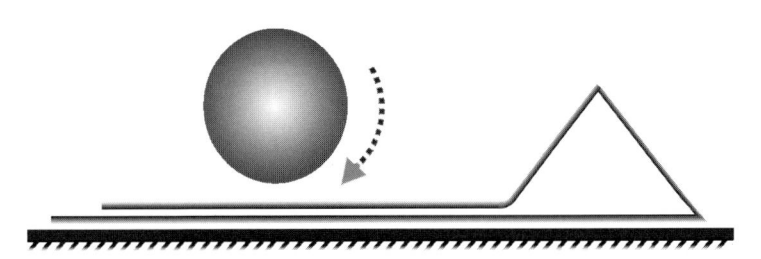

Figure 8.1

A different concept of a barrier is then shown. This is a piece of folded paper as shown in Figure 8.1. This barrier is so light that it can be blown away with a puff of breath. Yet it serves to halt the ball. Rolling onto the paper, the weight of the ball itself creates a barrier. This barrier is not necessarily any better than the ones previously suggested, but it is a different concept – that of getting the ball to stop itself.

Concepts come from our ability to imagine possibilities and test whether they are logical in hindsight. The analysis of information does not provide new concepts though it may contribute to identifying the need for a new concept. For example, we may look at some retail sales figures and find that people over sixty are not spending much money. What does that mean? Does it mean that we should be avoiding building retail outlets in areas with ageing populations? Does it mean that older people do not have money to spend? Does it mean that they are unwilling to spend money? Or, could it mean that at the moment there is nothing for them to spend their money on? Perhaps there is a lack of attractive goods designed for the seniors market. Perhaps people have money, but are uncertain of their future medical requirements. So there might be an opportunity for different types of insurance. There might also be an opportunity for reverse mortgages which unlock the capital of residences so that the money can be used during a person's lifetime. So we see that a simple piece of information can give rise to many concepts. But the concepts come from our own minds.

Children's books often contain a simple puzzle in which there are many fishermen and a tangle of lines. On one of the lines, a fish is hooked. The child is asked to find out which fisherman has caught the fish. If you start off with the fishermen, the task is quite hard, because you have no way of telling which line leads to the fish. *If you start off with the fish then all you have to do is to follow the line back to the fisherman.* What could be easier?

It is the same with concepts. They are obvious in hindsight, so logical and so related to existing information that we believe that we could easily have achieved them by analysing the information.

Concept and context

What is the significance of the colour red?

- In terms of traffic lights, it means stop

- In a political sense, red means Communist

- As purely a colour, red is one of the primary ones

⊃   In the context a wine, red is the one that has tannin

⊃   It all depends on the context

Data only becomes information when it is put into or viewed in a context. The context may be a set of circumstances or the context may be a concept.

In many supermarkets, eighty per cent of purchases are said to be on impulse. In considering ways of increasing impulse buying, you could look at traffic flow, eye levels, where people pause, whether customers can go straight to the shelves they want, and a variety of other factors. Things which are not significant in one context can become very significant in another.

Sometimes an anomaly or a blip in the data can arouse suspicion and even trigger a concept. Then we are able to look at the data through that concept.

The important point, which we keep repeating, is the need to do conceptual work in our head and not just wait for information to provide us with concepts – because it will not.

Concept design

A good architect does not usually begin a residential design project simply by putting some possible shapes and other ideas on paper for a prospective client.

The first step is to define what values the building is intended to provide.

What are the *quality of life* values sought by the client? For example, is the house for relaxation or a more formal lifestyle? What about initial affordability and subsequent operating cost? How important are privacy and security, leisure and work precincts, etc. What about *convenience* values such as ease of cleaning, maintenance, refurbishment, resale, etc.? *Self-importance* values are another consideration. Who will see the house and what impression does the owner want it to give? How can *distraction* (peace and stimulation) value be maximised – the enjoyment of views which relax or stimulate the mind, peaceful settings, activity areas, meeting places, interesting design features and so on?

Having determined the broad values to be included, the architect would typically present alternative concepts and ideas as to how the design could deliver the values sought.

Creative thinking tools are a practical means of generating alternative concepts and ideas for the delivery of values. For example, a home that is specifically designed to be flexible (a concept) by being easily altered internally or extended externally (an idea), potentially delivers important value in coping with initial affordability and changing family composition, and even the needs of later owners (resale value).

In designing or improving a business, product or service, which after all is simply a concept for delivering value to customers, staff, shareholders and others, the steps of scoping the values to be provided and the alternative concepts and ideas for delivery are essential.

How Dick Smith uses concepts

Dick Smith is clearly an *intuitive* conceptual thinker. He intuitively knows how to create outstanding value and make it famous. Though Smith is an accomplished conceptual thinker, and highly creative, his skills are so intuitive that he is not necessarily aware of the processes his mind is going through in order to arrive at his concepts and ideas. His focus and passion take him exactly where he wants to go in much the same way as a great artist is usually *naturally* gifted. Importantly though, others can learn a lot from Smith by observing and extracting the concepts that lie behind his ideas. Further, once Smith has a *purpose focus*, he provokes his creative thinking by searching for and adapting to his own purpose the successful ideas others have developed.

◐ Elevated cause

Smith seamlessly elevates his product into a cause with which many Australians become emotionally engaged. His proven ability to think differently about how to provide a solution to that cause has created exceptional wealth for him and others, and has significantly helped Australian charities and the aviation industry.

◑ Outstanding value

Smith's iteration of successes carries a clearly identifiable hallmark of value creation. In Dick Smith Electronics, he simplified electronics for ordinary consumers by introducing consumer catalogues, consumerised merchandising, price ticketing, excitement and helpful assistance to a previously complex and largely industrial category. *Australian Geographic Magazine*, an idea he copied from other in-country geographic magazines, helped to focus this nation on the virtues of our own natural wonders. Dick Smith Foods offers a painless solution to our natural desire to fight for the retention of Australian jobs and businesses. Each of Smith's businesses has been passed on to others who generally continue to provide those values.

Smith is an outstanding example of the general principle that money flows towards great concepts and ideas which create outstanding value for others.

◕ Replicable formula

Smith not only religiously sticks to his stated four-step formula, but importantly applies creative thinking every step of the way in:

- ➲ Bringing together the best ideas from around the world
- ➲ Designing a replicable business with systems and processes
- ➲ Surrounding himself with enough like-minded people to duplicate his system
- ➲ Striving continuously to do things better and at a lower cost

◗ Hero reputation

Smith publicises his causes and products by prodding, provoking, challenging and stirring people from their lethargy in a multitude of ways. He makes people think. He confronts people, including and especially competitors. He is not afraid to start a fight, and relishes its continuance because it provokes attention, media coverage and word of mouth.

Love him or hate him, the media clearly finds Smith interesting material. Importantly though, Smith's cause focus coupled with his predilection for generating empathy and controversy, traits shared by other outstanding reputation builders such as Sir Richard Branson of Virgin, is in effect driven by creative conceptual thinking – a skill anyone can learn.

How Les Schirato uses concepts

Les Schirato is clearly a *conscious* conceptual thinker. He works tirelessly at the process. He developed the concept of introducing pure coffee to Australians by first giving them a good coffee experience in cafés, one where they would recognise and hopefully remember his brand. From this concept came the idea of training café operators to make and decorate good coffee, and the idea of providing Vittoria-branded café fit-out items such as cups, umbrellas, etc.

◖ Elevated cause

Schirato knew, based on overseas consumption patterns, that Australians would eventually develop a widespread liking for pure coffee. However, supermarkets vehemently opposed stocking the product saying,

'Australians will never drink strong coffee…'

Schirato became a missionary for the cause of introducing Australians to pure coffee. He has been a prime catalyst in taking Australian in-home pure coffee consumption from zero to fifteen per cent of the overall market, of which his company's pure coffee brands represent every third cup.

Outstanding value

Customers often don't know what they want until they know what's possible. Schirato established The Vittoria Coffee College in Sydney in 1996 amid growing demand from industry chefs and hosts for a resource dedicated to teaching the fine 'art and science' of coffee-making in Australia.

Cantarella's mission statement 'Building brands – In step together with customers for greater profits' proactively positions the company as a cooperative brand builder, not simply a supplier.

'The perfect cup of coffee' has become part of Australian vernacular. Schirato set out to show the Australian café trade what 'perfect' means and how they can achieve it, providing greater value to their customers.

Replicable formula

Schirato used cafes as the vehicle not only to introduce people to his coffee, but by branding café umbrellas, cups and other highly visible items, he made sure they would get to know and be reminded regularly of his brands.

The decision, taken under great financial stress, to carefully choose long-term customers and manage them for profit using good systems to capture all costs and a good set of KPIs, has proven seminal to the company's success.

Hero reputation

Few consumer packaged goods marketed through supermarkets can claim the sustained high level of visibility and trial which café umbrellas and café consumption have afforded Schirato's Vittoria brand. With this entrenched exposure, it is little wonder that sales leadership through supermarkets has followed.

Schirato's penchant for guerilla tactics and being deliberately different to his multinational competitors, well exemplified by his April Fool's day white coffee bean advertising provocation, has enabled him to build valuable consumer brands without the financial resources normally regarded as a prerequisite to large scale consumer brand building.

How Len Poulter uses concepts

Len Poulter's conceptual thinking skills are outstanding. He recognised early the then emerging desire of consumers for fresh, convenient and added-value meals, and continues to develop and refine concepts of stores, products and delivery with that cause in focus. Lenard's sustained success in a ferociously competitive Australian food retailing environment is almost certainly due to innovative concepts, well implemented. Indeed, Poulter's formal title in the company says it all: 'Director – Concepts'.

◕ Elevated cause

Poulter's mind is challenged by reforming the way things are done in an industry he knows well, and where he has already been a very significant catalyst of fundamental change. His cause is the constant search for outstanding value and streamlining the concepts with which to provide it.

He does not confine this search to the meat industry. His cause embraces the total meals business. His ambitions go beyond in-home meals to food service. His ambition to include red meat and vegetables reflects his desire to integrate deeply into the complex values of his customers.

◖ Outstanding value

Poulter's business concept is designed to provide outstanding value to Lenard's franchisees which they cannot obtain economically or easily by themselves or elsewhere.

His value bundle to Lenard's franchisees means ensuring that:

- They (the franchisees) are moving forward as a business
- They are matching their consumers' needs
- They have a good, profitable franchisor on which they can depend
- The Lenard's system is constantly being refined and improved
- The Lenard's business structure is sound

◣ Replicable formula

Poulter is very conscious of the opportunities and threats presented by the massive swings and roundabouts in, for example, meat, bread, and fruit and vegetable retailing. His concept, however, is not to grab market share in conventional commoditisable categories, but to combine them into a value bundle that enhances the lifestyle of consumers, and is monopolisable. This greenfield approach has its obvious risks, demanding:

- Flexibility and constant alignment with reality and timing
- Creativity in implementation, not just in the original idea
- A team with a shared vision of breaking convention
- Strong leadership as coach and captain
- Absolute discipline in implementation right through to the customer

◗ Hero reputation

Poulter's reputation building is mostly based on capturing customer trial and provoking repeat custom and favourable word of mouth. He has learned through necessity how to grow the business without plentiful advertising funds.

Lenard's stores are mostly located in or near to major traffic generators. Though principally in major shopping malls, Poulter sees a bright future for stores in retail convenience centres and strips as a means of facilitating trial and customer convenience, and lowering rentals.

Word of mouth at consumer level is driven by constant product innovation, and franchisees who are trained to proactively help the customer's decision-making with meal suggestions.

Word of mouth at industry level is driven by frequent award winning and by public speaking and publishing.

Chapter 9
BEYOND COMPETITION TO SURPETITION

Designing concepts and ideas to deliver value and to underpin your business is fundamental. But how do you avoid being reduced to competing on price once what you have created is copied and there is little perceived difference between you and your competitors? If the new value you manage to create is easily matched, then you have gained little except maybe a short-term advantage.

Your goal should be to not only create outstanding value but to protect it from being imitated easily – to create a value monopoly, to monopolise your value.

Competition is the key ingredient in free-market economics. It prevents monopoly pricing and ensures that consumers get the best deal. Competition ensures that producers make every effort to be efficient and to provide quality. If not, they risk being driven out of business by a producer who offers better prices or better quality.

The purpose of competition is to benefit the consumer by keeping prices down and quality up. Competition also benefits the economy as a whole by ensuring the most efficient use of resources and by encouraging enterprise. Newcomers with better ideas, prices or quality can enter the field and compete against those already in it. There is, then, a great deal to be said for competition. But competition is designed for the benefit of the economy as a whole and for the consumer. Only part of the benefit of competition is for producers. To be sure, producers are driven to greater productivity and efficiency, but the benefits of this are not reflected in greater profits, only in survival.

If two people are tugging at either end of a rope, a huge amount of effort on both sides does not mean that the rope will move. *Organisations may put a lot of effort into competing with one another, but the end result may be merely the same existing market share for each.* It is true, however, that competition allows the more efficient producer to increase market share at the expense of the less efficient producer. Sales volumes may go up, but margins and profits may not.

In short, competition puts pressure on producers. You have to be competitive in order to survive. Just as labour costs and environmental concerns are pressures on business, so also is competition. Competition is necessary for maintenance and to ensure survival.

Surpetition, on the other hand, is concerned with how you move upwards from the baseline. Physical monopolies are illegal in many countries, but value monopolies, market dominance that arises from value that is in a class of its own, are not. *Value monopolies are for the benefit of producers, and are also in the interests of consumers.* Value economics means that consumers can choose what value means most for them. You do not need a video cassette player in order to survive. You choose a particular one because that is the value you want. You can choose to spend $5000 on a Rolex watch because you value something about it. From a survival point of view, you could get just as good timekeeping from a Timex.

In today's value economics, surpetition and value monopolies are very much in the general economic interest. *Without value monopolies, all would be commodity economics.* There would be nowhere to spend money and no point in earning it. That is precisely what went wrong in the Soviet Union; people had money but nowhere to spend it, except on low-priced commodities. Value economics is concerned with creating opportunities for spending money as you wish.

So value economics, surpetition, and value monopolies are good for the economy, for consumers, and for producers. This is in contrast to competition,

CHAPTER 9 – BEYOND COMPETITION TO SURPETITION

which mainly benefits the economy and consumers. Classic competition certainly needs to be there, otherwise the benefits of value economics will quickly disappear. But once classic competition is in place, it is no longer sufficient. *We need surpetition in order to make value economics work.*

Surpetition goes far beyond housekeeping. Getting things right within the organisation (cost control, quality, etc.) is certainly essential but this merely gets the baseline right. Surpetition is not so much concerned with differentiating changes in the product being offered as it is with the sustainable uniqueness of the value being provided. So when we are firmly focussed on surpetition, how are we going to make this happen?

It is difficult to be certain about the real story of the origin of the Sony Walkman because hindsight changes most stories, but we suspect it was quite simple. There was probably a suggestion that the tape recorder should be made much smaller – perhaps the size of a book. We doubt very much indeed, however, that there was any concept of the Walkman as such. It is simply a very natural tendency for the Japanese to want to make things smaller. They live in a crowded country, often in very small apartments. Everything has to be miniaturised. Added to this is the Japanese propensity for things to be delicate and exquisite – as in the serving of a Japanese meal. So there was simply a tendency to make a smaller tape recorder, as there is with all products today. That was all.

Suddenly it became obvious that the small tape recorder was now small enough to be carried around. However, this was not an obvious value in Japan. Why should anyone want to carry a tape recorder around? But the portable tape recorder then snapped into the powerful 'integrated values' of the United States.

A generation brought up on watching television thirty hours a week was in need of constant stimulation. Habits of internal stimulation, such as thinking, had never been developed. Without external stimulation, the brain was inactive. Thus the portable tape recorder provided the ideal means of providing stimulation wherever you went.

In this way, the great success of the Sony Walkman came about. The name itself was even a particular success, although if you examine it closely, there is no indication whatever of either music or its function. The real contribution of Sony was not in devising the Walkman, which we believe came about unintentionally, but rather in recognising its potential success and running with it. Further, *Sony did not sit back and relish its success. It started producing model after model.* Today, Sony is still leader in the field.

The way Sony handled its success is a real lesson. Too many Western companies with an initial success like the Walkman would not have known how to follow up. For example, Philips invented the VCR and made absolutely nothing out of it. Western companies would have been pleased with the success and determined to make the most of it before competitors jumped in and destroyed the value monopoly. That is precisely why many companies have been disillusioned with innovation. They claim that they put in the development costs and open up the market, and then the "me-too" operators jump in and take all the profits. This is indeed what happens if you sit back. Once it got started on the Walkman, Sony did not sit back, but rushed to get out second and third-generation models even while the first model was still profitable.

Sony established surpetition with the Walkman by a combination of initial concept and vigorous follow-through. Sony created its own race — which is what surpetition is all about.

Surpetition versus competition

We are reasonably certain that the gurus of competition will insist that surpetition is really part of traditional competition, and that it is something they have been advocating all along. We would agree that there have been numerous examples of surpetition and that the approach of some people to competition is very close to surpetition. But we also believe that it is very important to make the distinction between competition and surpetition; otherwise, we cannot give surpetition the full attention that it deserves. Otherwise we can so easily get the sequence: 'it is just part of competition' and 'we have been advocating competition for years' and 'therefore we need not do anything about it'.

There is a well-known story of two boys who are walking through a national park. They encounter a bear that seems about to attack them. One boy suggests they should start to run away. The other boy calmly sits down on the ground and starts to put on his running shoes. The first boy looks at him in amazement: 'you don't think you're going to outrun the bear, do you?' he says. The boy on the ground looks up. '*No. But I don't have to outrun the bear. All I have to do is outrun you.*'

This story is often put forward as the essence of competition. We agree, it does illustrate the essence of competition. The behaviour of the boy putting on the running shoes is entirely dictated by the behaviour of his companion. It is enough to outrun the other boy. That is precisely the limitation of classic competition. It is often designed to beat the other fellow – on price or quality.

There is good sense in this. If you do not beat the other fellow, the bear eats you, or in business terms, you go out of business. So we are as much in favour of classic competition as anyone else. Competition is necessary for survival. Competition, as we maintained earlier, is part of housekeeping, part of maintenance, part of ensuring the baseline.

Competition is necessary for survival. Surpetition is needed for success. That is why we need to distinguish between the two.

There is a very simple test to illustrate the difference between competition and surpetition. *Can there be competition when there are no competitors?* The answer must be that there cannot, because competition is based on comparison with others. Can there be surpetition when there are no competitors? The answer is that there can because you are trying to provide even better value. You try to exceed the value that you provided before. *Surpetition is value driven. You strive to surpass yourself.*

Value monopolies

There are a number of traditional ways in which value monopolies have been established in the past. Some of them are still as important as they ever were, while others have become less important.

PHYSICAL UNIQUENESS

There is only one Mona Lisa. There is only one Van Gogh 'Irises'. There are three things that are important in building a hotel: location, location, and location. There are prime sites, and if you have a prime site you have a value monopoly. Prime sites can and do change in value; for example, many grand old hotels were built near railway stations, hardly a prime site today.

The art and antiques business is built on physical uniqueness. The value of art works tends to fluctuate because they get overblown at times and then collapse in order to start the cycle all over again, to the benefit of dealers who can never thrive in a static market.

TECHNOLOGICAL UNIQUENESS

Most people know of the $600 million settlement that Polaroid obtained against Kodak for infringement of their patents on instant film. Patents are an obvious example of value monopoly. The emphasis of courts in developed countries has swung recently much more in favour of patent holders. At one time, the mood was that patent holders were extortionists obstructing free competition. But along with the rise of some eastern economies, there arose a realisation that intellectual property is important and should be protected. There was, for instance, successful pressure on Singapore to clean up the video copying industry that used to thrive there.

The pharmaceutical industry is perhaps the most favoured by patent protection and technological uniqueness. The industry spends an amount approaching twenty per cent of sales on research. It is in everyone's interest that new drugs be developed, so it is only appropriate that this huge investment in research be rewarded. Countries like Italy, which do not allow drug patents, consequently never develop new drugs. There are approximately twenty years of patent life for every drug. The US Food and Drug Administration uses the first eight–ten years in trials and testing. That leaves ten–twelve profitable years for a company to recoup its investment and to pay for future research. In even this short period, many pharmaceutical companies reap huge rewards.

Outside the pharmaceutical field, surpetition through technology is much less assured. At best there is only a six month to one-year lead available through technology. State of the art scientific development will soon make technology available to everyone.

NAME RECOGNITION

There is a whole industry in Agatha Christie films and videos. The designer industry is based on individuals with moderate good taste, slick marketing, and image-hungry consumers. Whether it is Reebok, Gucci or Calvin Klein, there are people and names. Books by popular authors or films with well-known stars are all in the people uniqueness area of surpetition.

Hollywood and the music industry are special examples of American surpetition. The large home market and American hype have created stars who are saleable throughout the world. Overseas sales now account for around half of Hollywood studio income.

DOMINANCE

Occasionally a corporation gets into a position that is so dominant that it provides surpetition by virtue of the position alone. This is certainly true in the case of Boeing which dominates the aircraft industry. A succession of sound models, and in particular the very successful 747, has given Boeing this position. There is growing competition, but they have a long way to go. Down the road, there may well emerge a powerful competitor based on USSR aviation technology supplemented by German and Japanese advanced technology.

Microsoft gained a dominant position by virtue of its development and ownership of Windows at a time when standards in the computer industry were in their infancy. Windows has become the standard language by which the majority of computers communicate. Maintenance of this dominant position, though a challenge for Microsoft in the courts, feeds on itself. The more widely Windows is used, the more people see it as their only logical choice, and hence the more the computer hardware and software industry designs new products that run on Windows. Microsoft has achieved surpetition via a dominant position that is based as much on customers' risk aversion values as it is on intrinsic values.

A dominant position is a good base for surpetition but needs to be used and maintained. In fact, a dominant position is always much more valuable than it looks. Maintenance of a dominant position demands constant attention to outdoing yourself. Most likely the once-upon-a-time saying 'No one was ever sacked for buying an IBM' is now a case of surpetition lost.

COST OF ENTRY

Where the cost of entry to a market is high and requires continuous injections of development funds, there is protection from newcomers. There has to be existing cash flow, however, to cover these development costs.

Once something is established, the cost of displacing it may be huge. For example, the QWERTY keyboard was designed to slow down typing so that the mechanical keys of the early typewriters did not jam. The continuance of that layout of keys meant that more and more typists learned on it, so makers produced that kind of keyboard. *Today we could design a much more efficient keyboard, but the cost of introducing it would be huge.*

BRAND IMAGE

The most traditional way of getting some sort of value monopoly is through brand image. McDonald's does very well in spite of its many competitors. Heinz tomato sauce continues to be a favourite. Familiarity, availability, dependability and general image are important when other values are similar. Brand images are always threatened by private labels from retailers, by the way in which retailers in many countries squeeze margins, and by the insistence of retailers on doing their own advertising. Advertisers will find it increasingly difficult to suggest real value differences among many competing products.

Although brand images are a useful way of getting surpetition, and although there probably is an even greater need for them in the future, we suspect that it will become increasingly difficult and expensive to sustain them as quality improves all around and consumers become more and more conscious of real values.

Harvard Business School is a good example of the circularity of brand image. A lot of very bright people come out of Harvard Business School and enhance its reputation. This means that the value of getting there increases, so more people apply. This gives the school a greater range of selection, allowing it to take only the very best. This both enhances its reputation and ensures that its products are of good value. The actual teaching methods there are as irrelevant as an archway through which a number of highly intelligent people walk. If intelligent people enter the archway, it is no surprise that equally intelligent people emerge.

SEGMENTATION

While there is over-capacity in retailing and companies are shedding or closing stores, Clair Jennifer of Wombat is rapidly opening more stores. The secret is that she is focussing on fashion followers who place a high value on convenience – which people are prepared to buy because it is also less susceptible to fashion and therefore longer lasting.

Very specific niches, segmentations, and market focus have always been a way of achieving surpetition. At the very least they give the company a good starting position. Even when others enter the same area, there is still an initial advantage, provided that management can keep up the quality. The very successful Marks and Spencer retail chain in the United Kingdom was originally known for selling middle-income underwear. It then established a position in good-quality, mid-priced clothing. It used this base to get into food retailing with its own label products. Today it is as successful as ever, making more money from food than from clothing.

Protection or plus

We have considered above some of the more traditional methods of getting value monopolies. Some of them are forms of protection, like patents and cost of entry. A few are based on unassailable uniqueness, like special geography or individuals. *The rest have to be based on some sort of 'plus'.* Brand image, for example, is a traditional way of promising a plus, and in the past this was a real value in terms of product quality or consistency.

The real plus factors are going to come from careful attention to integrated values. Perrier is a good example of integrated values. Perrier introduced the concept of "designer" water and kept up the pressure to remain the market leader. People were becoming more health conscious. Drink-driving laws were impacting on the consumption of alcoholic drinks at lunch. So what was the sophisticated person going to drink for lunch? You could not ask for a Coke, because that was for teenagers, and beer was not sophisticated enough. Water may make you seem very cheap and often tasted awful. *So consumers were crying out for the most expensive possible way of drinking water. Perrier satisfied that need.* All at once water became not only socially acceptable, but even a mark of sophistication.

As before we need to recognise the initial concept and also the successful follow-through.

The source of surpetition

Surpetition goes far beyond housekeeping. Getting things right within your organisation (cost-control, quality) is certainly essential, but this merely gets the baseline right. Classic competition is really part of housekeeping, though it is also concerned with getting the baseline right. Quality and prices have to be right. There is indeed a slight overlap between product differentiation and surpetition but the overlap is not large.

So when we have distinguished between housekeeping and surpetition, how are we going to make it happen?

Some of the abovementioned traditional approaches to value monopoly will still hold their importance. Some of them can be improved and polished up. *But what other sources are there, particularly for the plus aspect of surpetition?*

There are three broad sources.

1. Integrated values. At several points in this section and also in preceding sections we have emphasised the growing importance of integrated values as distinct from product values. The whole area of integrated values is considered in much more detail in a later section.

2. Serious creativity. Surpetition is based directly on concepts and ideas. However much information, experience, and decision-making ability we may have, there is still going to be a huge need for new ideas. Such ideas are not going to be created by analysis or computer sorting of information. They are going to be generated by human creativity. We have to move beyond the crazy view of creativity to focus on serious creativity and how we can use it. It is not enough to hope that the creative people in your advertising agency will provide the ideas you need. This sort of reliance has been largely ineffectual. Serious creativity is also considered in a later section.

3. Concept R&D. Organisations spend millions and billions of dollars on technical research and development. They know that they have to do

CHAPTER 9 – BEYOND COMPETITION TO SURPETITION

this in order to survive. In the future, wise organisations are going to learn that they need to treat concept development every bit as seriously as they now treat technical development. Indeed, technology is becoming a commodity, while profits and surpetition are going to come from application concepts.

So the overall message is that creative and conceptual thinking is going to become ever more important. *Every successful organisation is going to have a three-part strategy:*

1. Get the housekeeping right.
2. Develop the concepts for surpetition.
3. Have an energetic follow-through.

We want to end this section by emphasising the need for energetic follow-through. The best concept in the world has only a limited value (certainly in time) unless there is energetic follow-through.

How Paul Cave achieved surpetition

Achieving surpetition by harnessing and monopolising the Sydney Harbour Bridge as an *entertainment asset* is not a really a first for Paul Cave. Earlier in his career, Cave capitalised on the value in disused service-station sites, with a location monopoly, as outlets for his Amber Tiles stores. Nonetheless, his creation of BridgeClimb is about as good as it gets as an example of integrated value, serious creativity and concept development leading to a sustainable surpetitive position, and his bottom line shows it.

John C Lyons and Edward de Bono — 235

◕ Elevated cause

Cave persisted for eight years to secure for consumers and his company climbing rights to arguably Australia's most internationally recognisable built icon, the Sydney Harbour Bridge.

◔ Outstanding value

The *tangible* asset, likely to cost up to a billion dollars to reproduce, already existed, unexploited as an adventure. Cave's creative conceptual thinking identified another value the asset could provide, a value divergent from its original purpose.

Of even greater value, the Bridge was already famous to hundreds of millions of people around the world – an *intangible* asset arguably likely to cost many billions of dollars to reproduce.

◕ Replicable formula

There is only one Sydney Harbour Bridge in the world. The uniqueness of Cave's location choice has effectively monopolised his value at least for the tenure of BridgeClimb's lease.

Cave recognised that the climbing experience could be positioned as "The climb of your life". The value to the customer potentially exceeded scaling any replicable built structure in Australia. BridgeClimb's stringent qualifying and preparatory procedures for each climber are designed to make a mandatory safety process into a value-enhancing part of the adventure.

◕ Hero reputation

Sydney is Australia's most populous and most tourist-visited city. The Bridge is at its heart, highly visible and architecturally engaging. The city of Sydney is Cave's primary traffic generator, free of charge.

BridgeClimb's uniqueness provides the company with millions of dollars worth of free advertising each year. It is inevitably featured by governments and many others wanting to attract customers to the city, because it is an integral and unique part of the attraction.

Cave has designed rigorous systems and procedures to ensure that customers and others who experience BridgeClimb, now over one million people from around the world, have become word of mouth advocates.

How Graeme Blackman achieved surpetition

Graeme Blackman's highly intellectual background has been a help, not a hindrance, in the achievement of surpetition. At the supply end (highly qualified researchers) and the demand end (focussed, accredited, specialised API research and manufacture) he has created a value monopoly which will be extremely difficult for others to match.

◐ Elevated cause

Outsourcing is an emerging trend and one that Blackman believes will grow because pharmaceutical companies are beginning to accept that their core business is drug efficacy research and subsequent marketing, not the chemistry and processes of production.

◐ Outstanding value

Blackman knew that if he could ease and expedite FDA approval of his clients' anti-cancer drug API's – which together with expedited efficacy and safety approvals, is the gateway to early market entry and first-mover-advantage – his value to the pharmaceutical companies could be immense.

◐ Replicable formula

In a very real sense, the IDT business concept is progressively monopolising the value it creates for customers, shareholders and staff, and even to some extent for the regulators of the pharmaceutical industry.

➲ Firstly, the primary source of IDT's output and reputation is the brainpower of its highly specialised scientists. Staff turnover is less than five per cent per annum.

➲ Secondly, the knowledge from cutting-edge scientific research projects accumulates within the firm and feeds on itself adding value to subsequent projects.

➲ Thirdly, the 'world expert' status gained in developing and refining the chemistry of a new API feeds the next revenue stage of IDT's value extraction, the manufacture of the product it has developed.

◗ Hero reputation

It is a tough call for a relatively tiny company from down-under to be taken seriously in the heady and risk-averse international pharmaceutical industry, even more to become a partner in some of the most sensitive and value-creating work companies are doing there. IDT's unqualified FDA audit has proven the masterstroke of its reputation building and entry into this market.

Reputation and experience built with a client during the research phase of an API is a powerful surpetitive advantage in subsequently winning long-term manufacturing contracts.

How RM Williams achieved surpetition

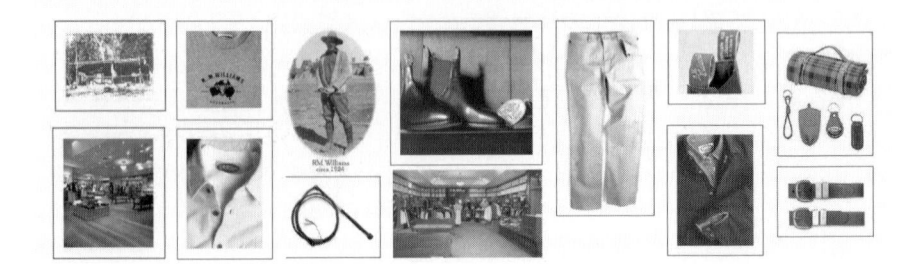

RM Williams achieved surpetition by monopolising trust in his category. Trust is the essential ingredient that enabled successful catalogue marketing and payment up front in those early days in the bush. It still is. From the concept of trust, ideas such a quality, durability, fitness for purpose, and even the *dependable style* of the clothing have emerged.

◔ Elevated cause

At the outset, Williams was not passionate about building a business, rather it was survival and the achievement of a cause, and even today he does not regard himself as a businessman.

The fact that "it just grew" reflects however his passion for the cause of applying his interests and skills to improve the lives of people in the bush.

Central to Williams's cause was giving his customers, whom he regards as his friends, a company and a product they could trust. 'IF YOU SOLD A PAIR OF BOOTS TO SOMEONE AND THEY WORE OUT QUICKLY, IT WOULD BE VERY COSTLY FOR THEM.'

◔ Outstanding value

Williams sees the very hallmark value of his products, *quality*, as an integral part of honesty. 'QUALITY. THAT'S A MATTER OF HONESTY WITH YOUR CUSTOMERS ISN'T IT?'

Handcrafted, comfortable and made to last a lifetime, the values in Williams's boots were formed by a man who understands the hardship and dangers of life in the harsh Australian outback. The integrity of Williams's value bundle was driven by passion. 'WE COULD HARDLY WAIT FOR THE RESPONSE TO THE PARCEL [HIS FIRST MAIL ORDER DISPATCH] THAT WE SO CAREFULLY WRAPPED. WOULD THE BOOTS FIT? WOULD THEY PLEASE THE TRUSTING BUSHMAN WHO'D SENT MONEY TO SOMEONE HE DIDN'T KNOW?'

◔ Replicable formula

Williams learned the value of a foundation client when he made a pack-saddle for the then iconic Kidman organisation seventy years ago, and went on to win all its business. 'I KNEW WHAT A CATTLEMAN NEEDED. KIDMAN GAVE ME THE OPPORTUNITY TO SUPPLY IT.'

The early days' necessity of having clients finance the production of their orders, taught Williams an important 'marketing without money' habit which remained with him – that customers would pay up front if they trusted you.

When Williams experimented with what became a huge mail-order business – 'THE MOST REWARDING EXPERIMENT OF MY WHOLE LIFE' – the principle of money-with-order was a major innovation and one of the central platforms of his success.

'IT TOOK ME SIXTY YEARS TO BUILD THE [RM WILLIAMS] BUSINESS.' Williams refers in particular to the time over which his products and processes were designed and constantly refined.

Williams's staff-selection policy represents simplicity distilled from today's human resource management complexity. 'IF PEOPLE HAVE THE RIGHT CHARACTER, IT DOESN'T MATTER MUCH WHETHER THEY ARE GOOD AT SOMETHING. YOU CAN TEACH THEM ANYTHING. THE *RIGHT* PEOPLE MEANS HONORABLE PEOPLE.'

Product and production development have gone hand in hand. 'I GOT INTO TROUSERS ONE AT A TIME', he says of the process of customer-driven product initiation, trial and improvement which have made products like RM Williams moleskins an Australian icon.

◗ Hero reputation

Williams's focus on trust as the key value of his brand shows extraordinary commercial acumen, not just good personal values. 'HONESTY IS THE BEST ASSET YOU CAN HAVE IN BUSINESS. PEOPLE ARE LOOKING FOR SOMEONE WHO WILL TRADE HONESTLY WITH THEM.' Honesty is at the heart of his quality promise.

Starting the Australian Roughriders Association, the international Quilty Endurance Ride and the Australian Stockman's Hall of Fame, while not undertaken for a commercial motive, has become a major factor in institutionalising the RM Williams brand, and Williams himself, as Australian icons.

Bush legends like Tex Morton and Tom Quilty became mates and customers, and free endorsers of his brand. In much the same way today, sporting goods manufacturers now use famous sports people, except they pay millions for the privilege.

Williams's tens of thousands of catalogue mail-order customers not only trusted and bought from him, but many also literally became word-of-mouth advocates and his mates as he travelled his beloved bush and the Australian rodeo circuit.

How Max Beck achieved surpetition

Max Beck has no ambition to become Australia's largest developer, so surpetition through industry dominance is not his goal. But in the context of his served market, there is ample evidence that Becton is definitely not perceived as a "me-too" competitor. Not unlike the RM Williams example, surpetition has been achieved through a high level of trust in a context where that value is scarce and highly prized by certain market segments.

◔ Elevated cause

One word sums up Beck's cause – *performance*. Having failed dramatically early in life, he is passionate that his company performs for its customers, that his people are performance driven through ownership and incentive, and that each and every project the company chooses should perform to the company's profitability benchmarks.

◕ Outstanding value

All value creation is contextual. In the context of an industry that is plagued with questionable quality, and where institutional investors are risk averse and consider deeply the lifespan and maintenance cost of their assets, Beck has concentrated on 'going the other way', designing his buildings to be outstanding in quality and durability.

◑ Replicable formula

On choosing what you do: Beck's early inexperience and the competitiveness of the building industry taught him to 'CHOOSE

SOMETHING YOU KNOW AND UNDERSTAND, AND WHICH HAS A GOOD MARGIN'.

On people: like most of our researched entrepreneurs, Beck puts the opportunity and the challenge presented by people skills at the top of his list.

On ownership and incentive: 'I THINK THE FURTHER YOU CAN PUSH THAT DOWN INTO ORGANISATIONS, THE BETTER OFF THE BUSINESS IS.'

On managing risk: failure is perhaps the greatest of teachers, because it puts the student under pressure. Always assessing the downside and actively managing for it are now Beck's clear success factors in a failure-prone industry.

● Hero reputation

Beck is very conscious that a company's reputation can be one of its greatest assets – the more so when stakes and risks are as high as they are with large development projects in a highly cyclical industry. Failure, for whatever reason, can destroy the value of a reputation asset overnight.

Like many successful entrepreneurs, Beck has built his company's reputation primarily on sustained performance over more than a quarter-century. Consistently high project quality has become his hallmark. 'YOU HAVE TO DO MORE THAN JUST SAY IT.'

Chapter 10
BEYOND PRODUCT VALUES TO INTEGRATED VALUES

In order to understand how to create surpetition, it is important to realise that there are three basic modes of thinking in business. These could be likened to three phases or technologies of business. Each of them covers a type of thinking and action, and a view of what should be done.

- *Product values*: thinking and action driven by a largely product focus.

- *Competitive values*: driven by the desire to be competitive because an increasing number of people are now providing much the same goods and services.

- *Integrated values*: the focus of thinking and action is on integrating products and services into the complex lives and values of customers and other stakeholders.

The stage of *product* values

In the early days of business it was enough to produce a car or to offer banking and insurance services. So long as these functioned moderately well, there was a market for them. The market was also growing, so there was even room for new entrants into the market. Thinking certainly went into getting the product produced. Thought was given to price, but not in a competitive sense. The purpose of a low price was to increase the product's market size. Henry Ford, with his famous Model T, wanted to offer a sound vehicle that was available to millions of people. The market was big enough to absorb all that could be produced. Smaller companies were driven out of business or forced to join together, not by competitive pressures, but by the need for a critical size to sustain large overheads.

The stage of product values is not set at one moment in time, but occurs over and over again when there is a totally new product or service line, or when a new market opens up. Countries such as Russia, Eastern Europe, India and China provide these new markets today. The hunger for previously unavailable or unaffordable products and services outstrips demand.

The stage of *competitive* values

In time, businesses become established and profitable. Existing businesses start to expand and newcomers are lured into what they see as lucrative markets. *The simple hunger for goods becomes more or less saturated. There is still a need for goods, but now it becomes a matter of offering better quality and of persuading people to buy.*

So began the technology of competition. There was a choice of things to buy. Why should you buy one thing rather than another? Values were no longer simple product ones, but comparative competitive values: this car is cheaper than the other, goes faster than the other, or has more inside room than the other.

Production was still important, but it was now aimed at competitive values. Could the product be made at a lower price than the competitor's product, or, at least, could it be made at a similar price? Classic competition soon settled down into a matter of competing on price, quality or product differentiation. There were those who set out to be low-cost producers and to sell volume to a mass market. Price, with tolerable quality, was the aim. There were others who aimed for premium quality and sold to buyers who could afford to pay for that quality. Product differentiation had very little real substance, but was heavily pushed by the advertising industry, which was given the task of showing why one brand was different from competing brands.

In time, product differentiation became more real. For example, the Japanese car industry gained entry to the United States when US dealers told their suppliers that they did not like smaller fuel-efficient cars. After the second OPEC oil-price rise in 1973, the Japanese were able to provide the smaller fuel-efficient cars that the US makers were reluctant to produce. The Japanese also realised that price and quality were not as mutually exclusive as some marketers had assumed. The Japanese offered low-price cars with good quality, and with the many extras that American car-makers had thrown out in order to reduce costs.

In the stage of competition, which is the predominant stage even today, values are determined very largely by what one's competitors are doing.

The switch from the first stage to the second stage is simply the switch from an empty market to a crowded one.

The stage of *integrated* values

Integrated values are not simple product values or competitive values, they are *values that integrate into the complex values of a customer*. Nor is it just a matter of asking a customer what he or she wants. Customers may not know what they want until it has been suggested that it might be available.

A classic example of integrated values is the very successful French Club Méditerranée. The French do not like travelling abroad, partly because they do not speak foreign languages and partly because they believe that they have a better standard of cooking than almost anyone else in the world. The concept of Club Méditerranée integrated directly into these values. *The French could now go abroad, but they could take a piece of France with them.* A French person could be abroad, but he or she could speak French and enjoy French cooking.

The provision of *integrated values may lead to surpetition, but this is not its original purpose.* The purpose of the original thinking is rather to achieve surpetition through the creation of a value monopoly. Integrated values do not always lead to surpetition, but surpetition is always based on value monopolies. The initiative of Domino's Pizza offering home delivery may have been surpetition for a while, but then it fell back to being mere competition when Pizza Hut set up its own home-delivery system.

The three stages of business can be summarised as follows:

- In the first stage, attention is on the product and on production. Getting the product out there is all-important.

- In the second stage, attention is on the competition. How can we do better or at least keep up?

- In the third stage, attention is on integrating into the complex values of the customer and seeking to achieve surpetition through concept design.

Very few organisations have consciously moved into the third stage of business – integrated values. Strong examples of integrated values have certainly occurred in the past, just as they are occurring in the present. But these have happened more by chance than through deliberate strategic effort.

Examples

We can now look at a number of different examples and try to trace these three stages.

In the *automobile industry,* competition is heating up because of over-capacity and the penetration of Japanese and Korean cars into the market. Astonishingly, however, the motor industry has not yet moved into the phase of integrated values. New products are by and large still focussed primarily on competitive values. While there is some dawning of the realisation that when people own cars they also own lots of other problems and opportunities related to car ownership, the industry is generally slow in reshaping its thinking around integrated values. The focus is still largely on engineering and fashion values.

CHAPTER 10 – BEYOND PRODUCT VALUES TO INTEGRATED VALUES

In the *airline industry*, the stage of integrated values has not yet arrived. Booking seats over the internet and being able to telephone from the air are minor matters. The whole business of air travel remains clumsy, cumbersome, and highly inconvenient. Perhaps further steps await the technical development of vertical take-off aircraft that can operate from city centres.

In the *computer industry*, the stage of integrated values is taking place more rapidly than in many other industries. The emphasis now is on connectivity and networks. Individuals use their own desktop computers, often working at home and on the move with laptops. Microcomputers are being integrated into different appliances. Fuzzy logic in smart washing machines can tell the size of the load and decide what to do about it – without human help.

Traditionally, Western manufacturers have regarded their suppliers as being on the other side of the fence – almost as enemies. There is always pressure on the suppliers to keep quality up and prices down. There is always the threat of switching to another supplier if the price or quality is not good enough. The standards of Marks and Spencer in England are so high, for example, that they insist that a single suit of clothing should be capable of being made from two pieces of cloth one mile apart on the roll.

Over the past decade, there has been a surprising change of attitude towards suppliers. This has followed the traditional Japanese attitude. In Japan, manufacturers regard suppliers as partners, and they work jointly with suppliers to improve quality. They share technical know-how instead of giving the skimpiest of specifications. All this is also beginning to happen in Australia. There is an increasing integration of the manufacturers' values up the value chain.

A good deal of integration also has been happening down the value chain over the last five years. It is not just a matter of making a quick sale and then moving on to the next sale. Magazine publishers, for example, have long known that it costs four times as much to get a new subscriber as it does to retain an old one. Banks are beginning to learn that lesson. Customers are valuable.

Integrated values take the process a very significant step beyond competitive values. *By designing and offering integrated values, the producer integrates not just with the customer, but with all the complex values of a customer's lifestyle.* We all live in a complex world with many values. Millions more people would buy pets if there was a good way of boarding them when leaving town.

The Swiss watch industry invented the quartz movement, but did not use the invention because it felt that it would kill the existing market. Anyone could use the quartz movement, whereas only the Swiss had the skills to make little cog wheels and balance springs. They were right in their thinking, as it turned out, but wrong in their strategy. *Watchmakers in Japan and Hong Kong eagerly grabbed the quartz movement, and in one year the sale of Swiss watches dropped by twenty-five per cent.* What rescued the Swiss watch industry was the very unSwiss concept of the Swatch. The Swatch provided two things. First, it provided a bulk market for the quartz movement so that prices could be brought down. More important, *the Swatch signalled that telling the time was no longer the most important thing in a watch.* A $5 watch tells time every bit as well as a $30 000 watch. The Swatch was not selling time so much as fun and costume jewellery.

The Swiss watch industry recovered as soon as it realised that it was not selling watches, but jewellery. Indeed, wearing an expensive watch is sometimes the only legitimate way a man can wear, enjoy, and flaunt jewellery. And that has become the nature of the watch business today.

You only have to open an in-flight magazine to find that fully thirty per cent of its advertising is for very expensive watches. Telling time is only the gateway value to selling jewellery to men. This is a very clear example of integrated value, though it is an example of surpetition only insofar as the Swiss have a reputation for watchmaking.

When Mars launched the first twin candy bar there were no great expectations for this slightly different format. To their surprise, sales soared. Other makers copied with different tastes, names, and prices, and all of them did well. What was going on? At that time, people were beginning to become conscious of weight and diet. If you have a single bar and eat it, that is one unit of guilt. But with a twin bar, you only intend to eat one of them. You have no intention of eating the other one right away. So that it is only half a unit of guilt. Later on, somehow, you do get around to eating the remaining twin, but that is also half a unit of guilt.

Chapter 10 – Beyond product values to integrated values

And as everyone knows in the mathematics of guilt, two halves do not add up to one whole.

The same concept was taken, consciously or unconsciously, by Cadbury's and used in a very successful product called Flake, which is chocolate full of air – for which you more or less pay normal chocolate prices. But people are very happy to pay chocolate prices for air, because the integrated value is that they can eat chocolate but not feel guilty about it.

In the highly competitive fruit juice area, the introduction of briquette packaging was a huge success. This was just a package of a certain size. However, the handy size and the attached straw turned fruit juice into an instant drink. This contrasted with normal bulky packages of juice, which were bought as part of basic household shopping, taken home, and put in the refrigerator. In this case, *a simple packaging change opened up new values.*

Finding integrated values is somewhat similar to looking at the spaces in a painting. You look at the customer and the relationship (or space) surrounding that customer. The customer is already integrated into the world. With integrated values we seek to integrate into existing values, taking us beyond traditional product and competitive values.

Efficiency and integration

Efficiency and integrated values sometimes seem to go in opposite directions. You can work out the most efficient number of people to serve at a counter. To do this, you have to measure the actual flow of customers and estimate the degree of impatience that would lead them to go elsewhere. The most efficient outcome would be the need to stand in line for a moderate amount of time. *Unfortunately 'average' impatience means absolutely nothing.* Some people are going to get very impatient very soon. From the efficiency point of view, you could point out that to cope with these very impatient people would require an expensive number of serving staff.

An integrated value solution would be to have one serving position with a sign indicating that there is an extra charge for high speed service at this point. *Demand for this service could be regulated by price.* Of course, this principle already operates in small stores which charge a premium for convenience. Exactly the same principle could be applied to many other situations where people are forced to line up for service.

Whenever we deal with average behaviour or average consumers, we are hiding a large number of variations in personal values. For example, in retailing, there are several types of shoppers and different shopping occasions. The chore shopper wants to take the car to a mall on the weekend and stock up on the week's shopping. Telephone shopping, standing orders, and delivery service would suit this shopper. Then there are pleasure shoppers, for whom shopping is the best excuse to be out of the house and to meet friends. Then there are those who enjoy window-shopping and are willing to expose themselves to impulse buying. All these may not necessarily be different people, for the same person may, at different times, have different attitudes.

Market segmentation and psychographics help in getting at individual values, but we need to use them within the framework of integrated values. Ordinary market segmentation may show that young marrieds buy one type of car and yuppies buy another. Integrated values might seek to design a way of giving the young marrieds occasional access to yuppie type cars and of giving the yuppie greater carrying capacity in a young marrieds type of car on the occasions when it is needed. Integrated values might work on a trade-in scheme so that the family car can be smoothly changed when the family changes.

Surpetition

Integrated values do not always result in surpetition. *Sometimes it is quite easy for others to copy the integrated values so that there is no value monopoly.* Integrated values can, however, give an initial advantage which may then be maintained permanently by good follow-through.

This was the case with the Sony Walkman, but not the case with the Sony Betamax videotape system which was pushed out of the market by the VHS.

Kit Kat chocolate biscuits and Avis rental cars are both good and rare examples of the sort of surpetition created by advertising. The positioning of Kit Kat as the snack you have when you're having a break creates a unique market niche and is a mild form of integrated value. The Avis slogan is powerful because it is durable. There is no element of integrated value, except perhaps the suggestion of politeness and service.

In conclusion, not all surpetition arises from integrated values but not all integrated values lead to surpetition. However, it is likely in the future that *surpetition will depend heavily on the design of integrated values, rather than on pure product quality or image building.*

We are sure that most people in marketing will quickly claim that the concept of integrated values is the same as product differentiation and that they have been doing it all along. We fully agree that there have been many instances of integrated values – some intentional and some accidental. We are also sure that some people in marketing do think this way. But we are equally sure that we need, very deliberately, to separate integrated values from normal marketing and product values.

With integrated values, we seek to integrate a product into the complex value systems of the buyer. *Integrated values are neither product- nor customer-based. The values are based on the relationship between the customer, the product and, most importantly, the world around them.*

Successful entrepreneurs generally speaking have been outstanding in integrating their offerings with the broader values of their customers and others. In most instances, these entrepreneurs have sensed some of the missing values and have designed new or improved business concepts to provide them. They actively look for unexpressed needs and values – they are focussed on what certain types and groups of people will discover they need tomorrow when it is available, seldom on today's expressed needs which determine today's rules of competition.

How Clair Jennifer integrates her value

Clair Jennifer has entered a seemingly mature and ferociously competitive category by integrating deeply into the previously unmet values of her chosen market segment. Not only that, a key reason she successfully operates company-owned stores is that her concept also integrates well into the lives of the mostly part-time, mature-age staff she hires.

◐ Elevated cause

Jennifer is passionate about the cause of her customer – the 'real Australian women' – who do not have a model figure and who put function ahead of fashion, though by no means ignoring the latter.

◐ Outstanding value

Like Gerry Harvey, Jennifer is faced with the reality that giving people a valuable in-store experience is probably the biggest challenge in a retail business, yet is probably the single most important factor in making a sale on the day, and in creating repeat and enthusiastic referral. Mastering that challenge means mastering the people issue.

Beyond product and merchandising, important factors the added value of which she can directly control, Jennifer has harnessed the right staff to provide the other major component of value – how the customer feels.

◐ Replicable formula

Jennifer's basic value delivery formula, refined by her business and retailing experience and sharpened by her passionate empathy for the customer's cause, is an inspiration for others:

- An almost counter-intuitive focus on fashion-followers, not fashion leaders, who place function ahead of fashion.

- Catering proactively and in a very practical way for the figure and lifestyle reality of her chosen customer, and Australianising her unique offering.

- Hiring her customers as staff, supporting them with precise systems and processes, training them to proactively empathise and give confidence and a special experience to her customers, and appraising and rewarding them against accountabilities.

◗ Hero reputation

It is quite extraordinary that a highly successful retail business of Wombat's size, and in the heartland of the fiercely competitive fashion retail category, has been built and continues to grow rapidly without media advertising and has a chief executive who "does not believe in advertising". Jennifer has proven beyond reasonable doubt that a value bundle consisting of the right product, good merchandising and exceptional personal assistance, aided by a significant traffic generator (such as a shopping centre) is a more-than-adequate reputation builder.

How Carl Wood integrates his value

Carl Wood clearly looks at the big picture, integrating into the broad and complex health values of his served market. His cause goes way beyond the traditional medical focus of solutions to *hygiene* health problems, to embrace women's overall physical (and by implication, psychological) *wellbeing*. His creative conceptual thinking not only integrates deeply into women's values, but even beyond this he chooses to integrate his work with that of *natural* health disciplines. Furthermore, he sees the spin-offs of his research being integrated into other urgent areas of human need such as stem-cell research. In addition, he is concerned with the mass delivery of the scientific advances he helps discover, through the growth of distribution mechanisms such a IVF centres.

◖ Elevated cause

Like most successful entrepreneurs, Wood began with a focussed cause in which he successfully engaged enough people, albeit with great persistence, to fund initial research and achieve a world breakthrough in IVF. Today, his cause is simply 'improving women's health' by increasing desired fertility and reducing female disease associated with reproductive organs. There are now thousands of centres in the developed world where Wood's value is delivered at the coalface. These are yet to be replicated in many third-world countries where the need is obvious but infrastructure does not yet exist.

◗ Outstanding value

Women are seven times more likely than men to suffer reproductive-organ-related disease.

In human value terms, Wood's entrepreneurial IVF research has given life to hundreds of thousands of people around the world, and unquantifiable happiness to a similar number of otherwise childless couples. This value, of course, continues to grow with time. Further, its extension into stem-cell research, if successful, will create further immense human and economic value.

◗ Replicable formula

Wood's early experience with IVF has refined his formula for 'IMPROVING WOMENS' HEALTH'.

He has chosen need areas which will have a significant value impact on society, now having progressed to endometriosis (affecting 600 000 Australian women) and fibroids (forty per cent of women over the age of thirty-five).

Since struggling with community acceptance of IVF, he devotes more time and other resources to raising the profile of each new cause, promoting greater understanding of the significance of the diseases and their real impact on peoples' lives.

He has become a catalyst in engaging extraordinarily diverse and often controversial partners in what he describes as an 'integrated medicine' approach to preventing and curing women's diseases, often including massage, acupuncture and herbal treatments.

He goes with the flow. 'WE FOUND FORTY PER CENT OF THE WOMEN WITH THAT DISEASE [ENDOMETRIOSIS] WERE ALREADY IN ALTERNATIVE THERAPIES ANYWAY.'

Wood has helped see to it that his value reaches the masses, though he has not sought to profit personally from the flow-on. From a commercial perspective, there are now thousands of clinics around the world where Wood's value is delivered at the coalface.

◗ Hero Reputation

In the case of IVF, Wood had two reputation-building challenges. Firstly, he had to raise support from fellow professionals and others, and the funds to pursue his cause. Secondly, he had to build the reputation of the cause with the community, which at the time was generally opposed to it.

In addressing the first challenge, Wood quite remarkably engaged fellow professionals in his cause to the extent that they sacrificed part of their personal income to it. This level of commitment from within helped external parties such as foundations and governments see his cause as worthy of their financial and moral support.

Wood learned from his mistakes in addressing the second challenge. With the benefit of hindsight, he believes he should have done more in the early stages of his IVF research to spread awareness and understanding of the significance of his cause. Community buy-in was hampered not just by lack of knowledge but also by vocal and violent prejudice in some sectors which made telling a rational story much more difficult. Community opposition also made the achievement of support from foundations and governments more difficult

History is repeating itself today with the recent successful, but somewhat tentative approval and support by government for stem-cell research, much of the technology for which was learned in the IVF program.

How Adrian Di Marco integrates his value

Much of Technology One's success results from Adrian Di Marco's focus on integrating his company's value into the complex values of his vertical-market customers and those of his industry partners. Di Marco saw that many organisations were struggling with the *integration* of software to drive their core business processes, not the availability of seemingly appropriate individual software components. His concept of integrating deeply into selected vertical market customer segments demanded that he also integrate into the values of potential partner companies with relationships and mission-critical software already established in those segments. Importantly too, he sees the use of intermediaries as an impediment to close integration with customers.

◕ Elevated cause

Di Marco has deliberately limited the scope of his company to several specific vertical markets, such as local government, retail, higher education, etc., which he judges have opportunity and scope for penetration and growth.

He is a missionary for the cause of totally integrated solutions to each of these segments – streamlining their businesses in ways they may not have dreamed possible.

◕ Outstanding value

While the backbone of Di Marco's solution is a world-class financial management accounting system, this is simply a baseline requirement – an entry ticket to the game.

The real value-add lies in his company's absolute focus on providing a fully integrated business solution to each vertical market – one which embraces existing specific mission-critical software and caters for the way participants will increasingly want to do business, not simply the way they do business today.

◗ Replicable formula

Rebelling against the industry norm of distributing through intermediaries such as large professional service firms, Di Marco decided to directly couple his company with its customers and their respective industries.

The vertical-specific needs of customers drive his company's product development, sales, implementation, support and alliances. That way, customer feedback, negative or positive, is instant. No time is lost in rectifying problems or developing better ways to add value.

Di Marco's conviction that great staff need the support of great processes, drives a tight manufacturing system for his complex product. He uses a formal marketing process to simplify concepts and ideas gleaned from customers so that his development team is better able to make it happen responsively and efficiently.

◗ Hero reputation

In much the same way as Microsoft's Windows achieved surpetition by becoming the industry standard or language across a very broad market, thus becoming the natural product of choice for most participants, Di Marco's business formula aims to achieve surpetition in each of his much narrower chosen vertical markets.

Forming partnerships with providers already well-positioned in each vertical, and giving them value and performance incentives, is a key plank not only in providing a total solution but equally importantly in leveraging off their established relationships and reputations.

How Therese Rein integrates her value

Ingeus exists because Therese Rein's concept for the business simultaneously met a crying need for more deeply integrated values in at least three primary customer groups – workers, employers and insurers. In order to achieve her value monopoly, her challenge was also to integrate internally the different professional disciplines required to deliver deeply integrated customer value.

◖ Elevated cause

Rein, like many successful entrepreneurs, believes that every successful business should have a cause(s) bigger than the business itself – something which expands the mind and engenders passion in people.

From an *economic* perspective, Rein's cause could be summed up as making the best possible use of human capital, efficiently.

From a *human* perspective, Rein's cause is very well captured in her words 'I THINK THAT ENABLING PEOPLE TO RECONNECT WITH THEIR COMMUNITIES, TO RECONNECT WITH INDEPENDENCE, TO RECONNECT WITH THEIR POTENTIAL – I THINK THAT MATTERS.'

◖ Outstanding value

Rein provides a value bundle which is carefully integrated into the anticipated needs of seemingly disparate stakeholders. 'IF WE FIND A SOLUTION THAT MEETS THE NEEDS OF THE INJURED WORKER, THE EMPLOYER AND THE INSURER, THAT'S THE VALUE. LET ALONE THE IMPACT ON THEIR FAMILIES. SO THERE ARE LOTS OF WINNERS.'

◖ Replicable formula

On sticking to procedures and systems: 'I THINK THAT ROBUST COMPANIES ACHIEVE CONSISTENCY THROUGH RIGOROUSLY DOCUMENTING THEIR PROCEDURES AND SYSTEMS, SUPPORTED WITH IT IN SOME CASES, BUT ALSO BY HAVING METHODS OF CAPTURING, ENCOURAGING AND REWARDING INNOVATION.'

On discretion and creativity: 'IN OUR CASE MANAGEMENT, WE ASSESS PEOPLE, WE HELP THEM DEVELOP A REALISTIC GOAL AND PLAN AND WE GET sign-off. Then we implement the plan. That whole process of how we do the assessment, how we write the plan, how we do a work-site assessment — these things can be quite rigorously documented and disciplined. There has to be discretion and creativity on the part of the professional — their problem-solving capability, their resourcing. Everyone is not the same, but you still have to have a similar approach, a framework in which you cater for individual differences.'

◗ Hero reputation

On enhancing reputation to win tenders: 'You basically create a solution. You might do that by researching world's best practice, talking to people, being creative, thinking about things outside the square. You focus on what is going to win the tender, how to deliver it, and make the difference.'

On reputation-building on the job: 'We focus on what is required, and just keep delivering and improving it. In a regulated market or regulatory environment, that's how you have to function, operating within the policy framework of the government of the day.'

Chapter 11

BEYOND MAKING PRODUCTS TO MAKING VALUE

The building blocks of outstanding value are the carefully anticipated needs and preferences of customers responded to creatively. The word 'outstanding' is key because there is no (profitable) point in offering customers only the value they are already being offered at much the same price.

The base materials available for building a house are standard – earth, stone, timber, metal and so on. These raw materials are value-added to form a second level of still fairly standardised base materials including bricks, concrete, beams, roofing, cladding, glass, fasteners and the like. A third level of value adding is where shape, texture, colour, strength, packaging, ease of use, maintenance and other variables are introduced. The fourth and final level is where these materials are designed into a unique "bundle" to provide tailored value to the end users – the builder and the eventual occupant or the investor.

What makes the difference, and has the potential to create outstanding value, is how the combination of materials is designed, or bundled, to be more functional and pleasing, and to enable the home to be built faster and more economically.

CHAPTER 11 – BEYOND MAKING PRODUCTS TO MAKING VALUE

Much the same happens with the process of value formation for other products and services. In this section we consider:

- People and values – how values are determined
- Fundamental value drivers – the values which drive our decision-making
- Types of values – our differing perceptions of values
- Nature of values – multiple, focussed and by-product value

People and values

Human beings are always the recipients of value regardless of the perception that in many instances an "organisation" may appear to be making the purchase decision. It is also worth remembering that in the end all decisions are emotional. Such is the power of emotion that even choices that appear to be evaluated against highly rational and objectively measurable criteria, are frequently emotional decisions rationalised in hindsight. These emotional influences reflect our true values and are often quite difficult to define

In our view, the best way to assemble the components of a new or improved business, product or service is to think in terms of a bundle of values designed to serve the human being(s) who will be affected most. There is no such thing as a value unless there are people involved. *A value is something that provides benefit or opens up the possibility of benefit for someone.* Values do not hang like clouds in the air – they have to be attached to people. Value creation requires a constant asking of questions:

- Who is going to be affected by this?
- Who is going to benefit? (Positive values)
- Who is going to be inconvenienced? (Negative values)
- What will the perceptions be?
- What are the immediate effects, both short and long term?
- Will this value be noticed; will people talk about it?

- Are there any special circumstances where the value will be different?
- Are there special people for whom this could be a value?

In this process there is a need to de-average people, to look beyond the average person. An average is only an assortment of different people with different circumstances, tastes, and needs. Every teacher knows – or should know – that there is no "average" student in the class. If there are characteristics of intelligence, discipline, laziness, energy, troublemaking, boredom, troubles at home, and so on, then a teacher knows that every possible combination of these factors will be exhibited in an individual.

The trick is to recognise this individuality as a source of value, but not to end up with a market that is so small that it is of little or no commercial interest.

The great thing about the value bundling approach is that most humans want the same values, albeit in differing combinations, basically depending on context. Just as the house is built ultimately from very few basic materials, so human needs and wants are also quite basic. Remember however, as Abraham Maslow discovered, *when one need is satisfied, another appears in its place.* So knowing where people are at and where they are trying to go, and anticipating and shaping their emerging priorities, is the key to designing an outstanding value bundle. It is the way we shape and combine the basic materials that will spell our success or failure both short and long term.

'Valufacture' – *the creation of value* – is a term invented by Edward de Bono to describe this process of designing and assembling the components of value which will provide an outstanding value bundle to carefully targeted customers and other stakeholders.

As in the house-building analogy there is nothing really new in the basic raw materials. Maslow too has demonstrated that human needs are similarly basic. *What makes the valuable difference is how these materials are designed and combined or bundled to create outstanding value in a particular context.*

The creation of value has been going on for a long time before the invention of the word valufacture, but the word helps refocus attention on the deliberate creation of outstanding value.

CHAPTER 11 – BEYOND MAKING PRODUCTS TO MAKING VALUE

Creating new, outstanding and hard-to-imitate value bundles is the very basis of surpetition. However, businesses are generally quite astonishingly bad at predicting what will be of value in the future. This is because they are trained only in analysis and looking backwards. The key to surpetitive value creation is creativity and looking forward.

- The typewriter, for example, was seen only as an aid for blind people because everyone else could use copperplate handwriting.
- The market for ballpoint pens was assumed to be limited to high-flying aviators who could not use fountain pens because of the drop in air pressure.
- The first market calculations showed that the world demand for computers would be limited to eight machines.
- The Xerox process, which gave rise to the world office copier industry, was seen only as an aid to printing and at one time was offered to IBM, who turned it down.
- Western Electric rejected the patents of Alexander Graham Bell which were offered to them, because the telephone was seen only as an electronic toy.

Fundamental value drivers

A highly effective first step to the process of valufacture is to consider how the four fundamental value drivers apply in a given context. These fundamental value drivers, introduced briefly earlier, provide the building blocks for making and strengthening value bundles. Examined in more detail below, they are the keys to the value economics that has replaced survival economics in developed nations and markets.

1. Convenience value
2. Quality of life value
3. Self-importance value
4. Distraction value

MARKETING WITHOUT MONEY

PURPOSE

CREATING VALUE MONOPOLY

DRIVERS

CONVENIENCE	QUALITY OF LIFE	SELF-IMPORTANCE	DISTRACTION

VALUES

CONVENIENCE	QUALITY OF LIFE	SELF-IMPORTANCE	DISTRACTION
FASTER SIMPLER EASIER PROBLEM REMOVAL	HEALTH EXERCISE ENVIRONMENT LIFESTYLE FAMILY LIFE WORKING HABITS LEISURE TIME	SELF-ESTEEM OTHERS' ESTEEM RECOGNITION EXCLUSIVITY	PEACE STIMULATION COMFORT ENJOYMENT

EXAMPLES

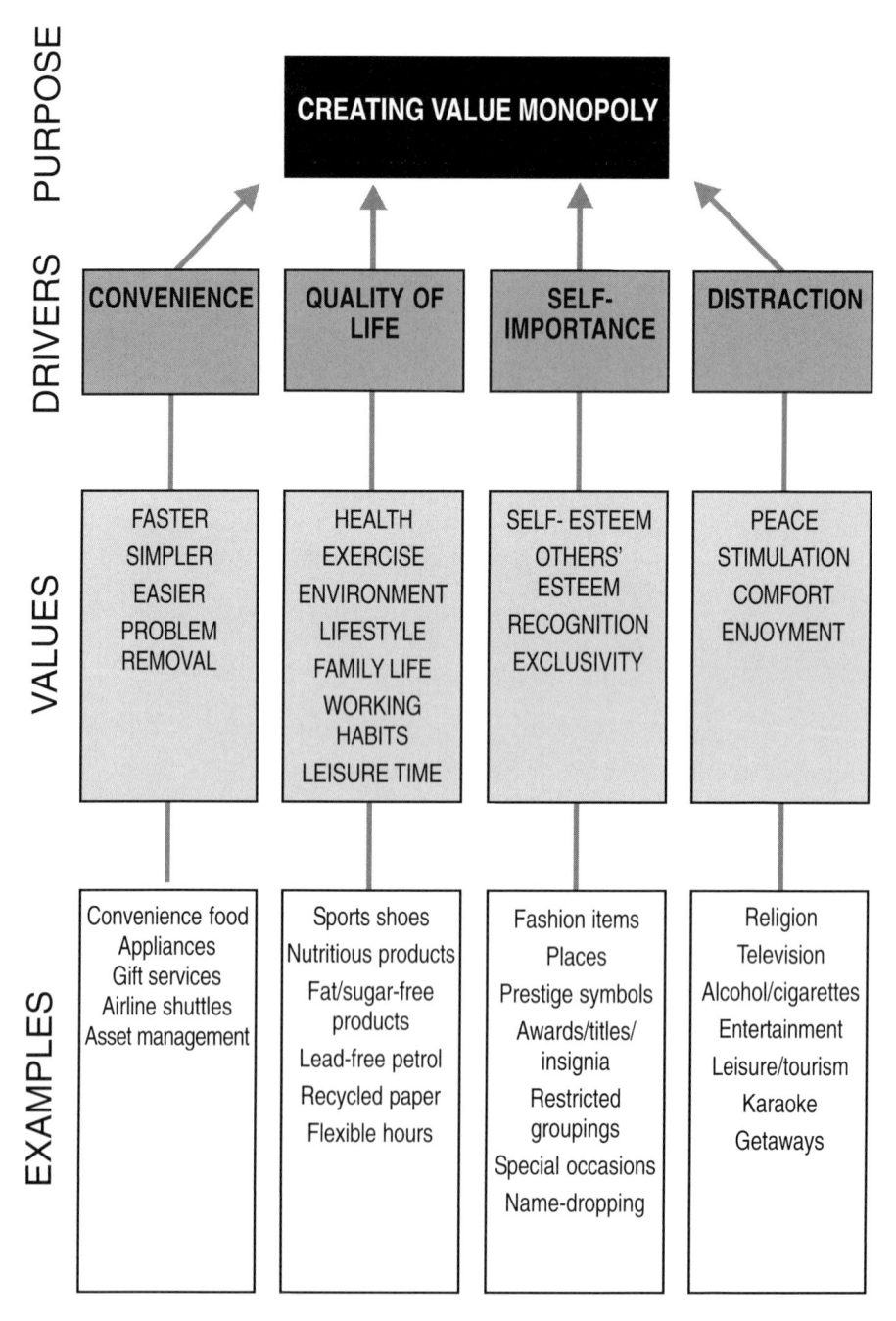

Convenience food Appliances Gift services Airline shuttles Asset management	Sports shoes Nutritious products Fat/sugar-free products Lead-free petrol Recycled paper Flexible hours	Fashion items Places Prestige symbols Awards/titles/insignia Restricted groupings Special occasions Name-dropping	Religion Television Alcohol/cigarettes Entertainment Leisure/tourism Karaoke Getaways

Figure 11.1 – Fundamental value drivers

Driver 1 – Convenience value

You only have to look at convenience food to know that convenience has been around a long time. It will become more and more significant. Appliances will be chosen directly for their simplicity of operation. The fuzzy logic approach of the Japanese to household appliances may take hold – but only so long as it is totally reliable.

As life gets more complex and opportunities are provided by technology, there is a thirst for simplicity and low-hassle living. The well-established idea of the airline shuttle service, as for instance from New York to Washington, is a clear convenience value (no booking, no uncertainty). Things like car rentals and normal airline ticketing are still far too complicated.

A phone service at airports that allows you to send gifts directly is a high convenience. In Japan, there is a phone service that will apologise to other people for you. In the United States, there is a similar service that will insult people for you. There is no end to services that offer convenience.

Finally, the concept of 'asset management' is a move towards convenience. Instead of trying to follow the markets and make the right decisions, let someone else do it.

Driver 2 – Quality of life value

Quality of life covers concerns with health, exercise, environment, lifestyle, family, and working habits. In the health and nutrition area, for example, quality of life values have made a huge impact. The success of sports shoes (Reebok, Nike, LA Gear) and health equipment is only part of this. The food industry is busy churning out nutritious products for both adults and children, and developing sugar-free sweeteners and fat-free smoothers.

On the environment side, there is much concern and political action, but it is rather difficult to get individuals involved. Lead-free petrol and recycled paper are examples. Individuals are apt to be for environmental issues in the abstract, but few make individual choices on this basis if the inconvenience or price is high.

When workers in Europe were asked if they would like more money or more leisure time, the Germans and Swedes both opted for more time, while the British still wanted more money. The tax rates in Sweden are so high that more money means virtually nothing. The Germans, however, are (generally) prosperous and can buy all the material things they want, so a higher value to them is more time. Shorter and more flexible working hours, and part-time and cafeteria-style working will all become more popular in the near future. People will want to work in pleasant surroundings. This has already translated into ways of people working at home using the internet and other technology.

Driver 3 – Self-importance value

The 'me-generation' has been around for almost four decades now. Self-importance and self-image are powerful value drivers, as the auto industry knows very well. The designer industry and the luxury industry both know that *people with money are more willing to spend it on self-image than on anything else.* If a charity ball in London is going to be attended by the Prince of Wales, a thousand tickets are sold without difficulty at £2000 each.

New production methods allow much shorter runs. In Japan, the concept of limited-edition cars (perhaps only 10 000 made of the type) is already in action. Further customisation could mean hand-painted cars. People will come to employ exterior designers for their cars, just as they now employ interior designers for their apartments.

Napoleon was probably one of the first to realise that giving people medals and honours was much cheaper and more effective than giving them more money. This is a perfect example of value which is closely integrated into the customer's values. The British honour system is a continuation of that habit. People like to feel important.

You can often feel important in small groups, because you are a member of the group and others are not. This is clearly the reason for gangs in Los Angeles and elsewhere. If society does not feel you are important, then you set up a mechanism in which to feel important.

Interestingly, the growing success of cruise lines illustrates all of the drivers listed here. There is the high convenience of everything being arranged for you: hotel, meals, travel, entertainment, and so forth. Quality of life is provided by the high quality surroundings. Self-importance is achieved by your choice of cruise line and by the social grouping you quickly achieve on board the cruise ship. The distraction element is also obvious in the entertainment.

Driver 4 – Distraction value

If Karl Marx were alive today, he would say that television is the opiate of the people. Marx thought that religion was the opiate, because it soothed people's pain and suffering and prevented them from rising in rebellion. Television and similar entertainments are even more of an opiate because of their addictive tendencies. If you are used to having your stimulation come in from outside, your mind never develops its own habits of thinking and reflecting. Everything is based on reacting. The more stimulation you have, the more you need to have it. The social implications of this are considerable. The commercial implications, however, mean that the entertainment and leisure industries will continue to grow.

A possible new direction for distraction is the way in which people can become entertainment for each other. The karaoke concept in Japan is extraordinary for two reasons. The first is that it seems so unlikely in Japan, where people are shy and inhibited (actually, inhibited people often welcome a formal way of shedding inhibitions). The second reason is the simplicity of the concept in which customers pay to entertain themselves by singing at a microphone and to listen to other customers.

Types of values

*An important **second step** in the valufacture process is to consider the types of values associated with the above four fundamental value drivers.* Human values are extraordinarily complex and overlapping, so, just like the finishing textures and colours of a house, there is a risk of oversimplification if we focus solely on the fundamental drivers or base materials used in valufacture.

What are the values of the house that you are thinking of buying?

- There is the actual cost.
- There is the possibility of it rising in value so that you can resell at a profit. If you buy on a rising market, you hope that it will rise forever. If you buy on a fallen market, you hope you are buying at the bottom.

- There is the location, which itself has several values: convenience to shopping malls and schools; convenience for getting to work; potential for impressing others with a classy neighbourhood.

- There is the external appearance of the house, which is the image you hold in your mind – even though it matters very little when you are actually living in the house.

- There is the space and layout within the house: work space, storage space, space for the children or guests, and so on.

- There is the cost of running the house: heating, repairs, painting, and the rest.

- There is the hassle of getting a mortgage, insurance, survey, and so forth.

- There is the problem of selling the house when you want to move on.

- There is the inconvenience of moving in and moving out.

It is a wonder that anyone can ever decide which house to buy. In the end the appeal value of a house probably wins if the financial value is acceptable.

We have listed some *types* of values below. This is by no means an exhaustive list and some of the types overlap. Other people may slice types of value up in a totally different way. What is important is to have a rich sense of potential values as a basis for deliberate valufacture.

Perceived

The perception of values is the most important value of all, because it is the main driver. Most advertising, in fact, is about building the perception of values. We believe that wide-eyed blondes are sweet and innocent, when they are no more so than other people. In the end, most of our thinking and behaviour is based on perception.

The Japanese motor industry realises that if an automobile looks as if it might be a snazzy sports car, then it will be bought as such by many people. Similarly, if it looks like a macho country vehicle, people buy it for precisely that image or perception.

There are perceived values that frequently have no real substance, since it is the perception that is being sold.

There is perceived value that reflects a true value, but one that is irrelevant to the purchaser.

Many watches are sold as being waterproof down to 100 metres. This is a real value and it is perceived as being a significant value. Yet the number of buyers who are going to be wearing a watch at 100 metres under the surface of the sea is rather small. Similarly, the excellence of expensive claret is usually wasted on the drinker, but the perceived value is there.

Real

Reality in values means very little unless they are also perceived. If you have occasion to use something for a length of time, you can discover its real values. Word of mouth can also spread this, but the process is slow. Even a real value reduction in price is often perceived as not being real value at all. Why, if the product is so good, is it being reduced at all?

The mother who urges her child to eat spinach rather than junk food may know something about nutrition, but the child's perceived values are different.

In the world of technical specifications, reality in values, of course, becomes more important – but it still has to be relevant. A computer may do a lot of wonderful things. But if you are not going to need those wonderful things, what does it matter? In this respect, the demise of the word processor is interesting. Many people use their computers only for word processing, so you would think that a dedicated word processor would make sense. What went wrong? It is true that any computer today can use a software package that turns it into a word processor. Many people felt that since the prices were similar, they might as well have the whole computer. It is also possible that the quality of the programming on word processors fell far behind.

Gateway

Timekeeping in a watch is only a gateway to selling jewellery to men. Men will often not wear jewellery unless there is the excuse of telling time with it.

At boarding school, the common practice of boys taking turns at dividing up food at the table, and having the person doing the dividing take the last portion, is a gateway to delivering the values of highly accurate apportionment and perhaps a penalty for miscalculation.

Context

An English-speaking person in Brazil can set up as a language teacher. There is little or no such value if that person is living in Australia or England.

Water can be sold at a high value to thirsty people. In countries where contamination of local water is suspect, uncontaminated water can be highly priced.

All values are contextual. Indeed, market segmentation should be treated as a means of identifying potentially valuable contexts. Providing values in certain contexts can be extremely profitable. Obviously, however, context values overlap with rarity values. A painting by an obscure Dutch old master might be of little value to the owner, but of high value to the art auctioneer who knows the market.

A beautiful face is of far more value on a catwalk in a Paris fashion house than in a nightclub.

Synergy

All the builders of conglomerates and the energisers of takeovers talk about synergy values. The whole is greater than the sum of its parts. It is always easier to make up a story and then believe it, than to show synergy after all the parts have been brought together.

Is the synergy value based on cost saving, secure supply or real combined value? Real combined values are much more rare than many believe.

Security

Fear of uncertainty, fear of the unknown, and fear of risk are the basis for the whole insurance business. If the price is right, security has a high value. But if the price threshold is exceeded, people suddenly become fatalistic and decide they can do without insurance.

Wherever security values can be attached to the used-car market, there is success. Wherever security values can be attached to builders or plumbers, there is again success. *Whenever the real values of what you are buying are uncertain, then some guarantee makes a huge difference.* Imagine the success of an organisation that could give some security guarantee on marriage?

Appeal

Appeal values overlap greatly with perceived values. Perceived values can, however, usually be defined, but appeal values may be vague and undefinable. The object just has "appeal". It may be the colour, the design, or something else. There is a totality of appeal. There are appliances which sell better than rival appliances simply because they have appeal. *It may be irrational and far from real or perceived values, but it works.*

A window-shopper might say 'I LIKE THAT BASKET VERY MUCH – I WONDER WHAT I COULD USE IT FOR?' *The appeal is there, and there is a search for use.* Even important functional objects like cameras may be bought simply on visual appeal and "feel". Designers have known this for a long time, but not too many manufacturers have been listening. The danger has been that new designs may appeal to some people, but not to others, whereas selling what has always been sold carries no surprises.

Fashion

Fashion values involve the artificial values of excitement and change. How do you get people to be more interested in clothes and to buy more than they need on a direct-wear basis?

The true value of gambling is not winning or losing, but paying for the enjoyment of anticipation. *In the same way the true value of fashion is to make more interesting what would otherwise be very dull.* Centuries ago, men were just as interested in clothing fashions as women, but today men's fashion seems dull.

There are fashions in investment as well: things to read about, talk about, and in which to be interested.

Fashion values are really interest values, but they merge into self-image values. How do I look to myself? How do I look to others? If religion does not give you reassurance, your self-image has to – but it is usually much less reliable than religion.

Function

Computers have to work. Mobile phones have to work. Cars have to work. In the end, there are function values. The difficulty is that they quickly become baseline. *You expect your computer to work, so you buy it for its size appeal.* You expect your mobile phone to work, so you buy it because it seems handy. You expect your car to work, so you buy it for its low price. *Function values quickly become commodity values.*

In the old days when you used a computer, you had to go through the whole rigmarole of booting up, selecting from basic menus and so on every time you switched the machine on. Today, we take it for granted that you come back to the exact place you were when you switched off.

New function values are powerful for a time. Then they are copied, become state of the art, and become commodity values. At the same time, new function values are high risk, because if they go wrong, they can really turn a consumer off the product. Many people have gone back from totally automatic cameras to manual ones. Others would not know how to handle a manual camera, because automatic functions have become a standard expectation.

Nature of values

Some values are intended. Others just happen. When customers were asked if they would use a cash dispensing machine instead of a smiling human teller, most of the surveys showed that they hated the idea. Once the ATMs were in place, many found that they preferred to use the ATM even when there were no queues at the tellers.

We need to be quick to recognise and pick up on values or bundles of value which were not intended, but which simply have arisen.

Value bundles may be focussed, multiple or by-product.

1. Focussed values

A small restaurant down by the wharf has built its reputation on just one dish. You go there to have chilli crab. The dish is superb. Many go there specifically for this dish, but the ambience is very ordinary.

Another restaurant, with moderate food and a moderate ambience, gains a reputation for just one thing: the owner is a very outspoken character and can be very rude to the customers. In a masochistic way, some people like this, because it makes them feel important.

A cafe is known to be open all night. So if you need a meal after all other places are closed, you know where to go.

All of these examples reveal focussed values that are successful.

2. Multiple values

Your restaurant has a beautiful view of the valley. The food is superbly cooked. Food writers have written up the restaurant in glowing terms. It is fashionable to be there. You see and are seen by important people. A famous television star lives nearby and occasionally comes for dinner. These are multiple values. All of them are a plus but there is also a danger. The expectations of customers are so high that any fall-off in standards, such as a dirty restaurant, could lead to instant disappointment.

3. By-product values

A restaurant is much frequented by financial journalists who go there to talk to each other and to pick up the current gossip. You may want to know if there is anything more to the rumour you have heard. You may even want to check out whether anyone else knows about the scoop which you think you have. Another restaurant has a view of the entrance to a large toy store, and you want to do research, observing what sort of people go into the store at lunchtime.

These examples reveal by-product values that may or may not make your restaurant a success.

Should you design for one strong value and leave it at that or should you try to build up as many parallel values as possible? The answer is not easy, because it depends very much on the field and on whether you are offering a new product or service. Certainly a multitude of weak values never adds up to much. Probably the best strategy is to design for the strong values and then add other values later – as long as they do not weaken the core value.

Valufacture is no different from any other design process. There is a need to get to know the materials, the methods, and the clients.

How Peter Kazacos makes value

For Peter Kazacos, foundation clients are a *gateway* to yet unexplored territory in which he can learn and discover *contexts* and *synergies* in which technology can provide outstanding value. Much of the company's growth has been driven by providing *convenience* and *quality of life* values to its customers, especially in outsourcing to KAZ their critical repetitive processes, which can be enhanced and made more cost efficient using intelligent technology. Kazacos segments his market after he has discovered whether it has value-adding potential, not as usually beforehand. Interestingly to, he partners with customers to discover *mutual* value opportunities.

◖ Elevated cause

Kazacos' cause could be described as one of discovering what value he can add to a client's business which, if successfully added, he can share proportionately with the client.

He seeks out clients who are not only receptive to this cause, but become engaged in it themselves. They become explorers together, and the exploration is not limited to the project at hand.

◖ Outstanding value

Kazacos is open and opportunistic as to where his company should participate in an industry value chain, and at what time it should expand up or down from its present location, or even exit parts.

In common with many entrepreneurs studied, he is constantly in search of opportunities to harness emerging technology to do things better and at a lower cost. His is another good example of customers not knowing what they want until they know what is possible. What is possible can in some instances reinvent his client's business formula.

🍂 Replicable formula

Contrary to the normal textbook approach which suggests segmentation should come first, Kazacos prefers to choose the customer before settling on the market segment(s) or the final product offering. Getting a foothold with a foundation customer enables learning, exploration and leverage.

He lets his company's joint learning with the foundation customer determine the shape of the final product offering to the broader market. It also determines the choice of like clients and specific market segments to which the product should eventually be offered.

A well-chosen foundation client provides not only technical knowledge in how to add value, but the client's credibility makes further market access a lot easier.

🍂 Hero reputation

For the most part, the company's reputation is built on the job. Mutual trust builds as value opportunities are discovered and exploited.

Kazacos uses his foundation client's corporate reputation and his company's track record with them to leapfrog, rather than walk, to attractive and synergistic new clients and segments.

How Jurgen Klein makes value

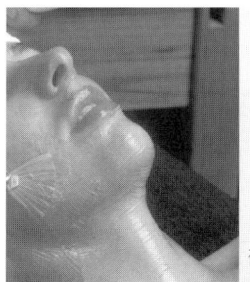

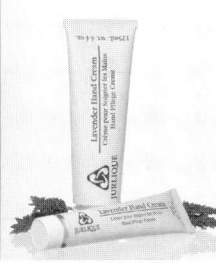

The initial Jurlique retail experience is a *gateway* to outstanding *perceived* value, and ultimately to referral, by customers. Jurgen Klein is succeeding despite the challenges that his business concept brings at this gateway point. Klein's elevation of the cause from simply maintaining health, to enhancing overall *quality of life* (making the best of what you've got), is an important and timely value creator – and will become more so as baby boomers and the stress generation exert their considerable purchasing power.

◖ Elevated cause

Klein is a missionary for the cause of improving the quality of peoples' lives using scientifically based natural remedies and beauty treatments.

His focus is on people who consider they are suffering from an over-urbanised and stressed lifestyle – a cause he believed would emerge when he and his wife set out on this life and business mission some thirty years ago. He almost had to be right, but he knew the big risk was in getting the timing right.

◖ Outstanding value

Klein's value bundle aims to go well beyond the basics for people who see their health and wellbeing as a means of preventing illness, and thus minimising the need for cure. More than that, he recognises that most people want to *enhance* the health and beauty they already have.

Despite the credible heritage of natural remedies, particularly evident in Chinese medicine from which he has drawn significant inspiration, Klein has had to fight the negative value of the "quackery" label commonly associated with broad-brush perceptions of his category. Trust has had to be built.

◖ Replicable formula

The formula for delivering Klein's value promise is almost certainly the most difficult part of his trail-blazing business concept.

The ultimate goal is to create long-term customers who are also enthusiastic referrers. Media advertising has little impact in this respect. Klein is selling a concept, not just a product. The customer must first savour the experience in order to gain trust and knowledge and be converted to belief in the concept – a complex task compared with most retail challenges.

The really difficult-to-manage variable in Klein's business formula is the quality of the critical introductory experience delivered by staff and franchisees in Jurlique retail outlets, "day spas" and "wellness sanctuaries". Despite quite scientific experimentation, Klein still struggles with making this a reliably replicable process.

Provided the skilled, resource-intensive introductory experience achieves conversion, then servicing the customer thereafter by mail, telephone or internet is highly efficient.

◗ Hero reputation

Reputation building is more complex for Jurlique than for Wombat or Harvey Norman. Jurlique is creating a new category of value, one which the prospective customer may not previously even have thought about. Success depends heavily on very personal and professional one-to-one interaction in the first instance.

While Klein is still honing and even examining ways to totally reinvent the combined reputation-building and value-delivery process, much can be gleaned from what has been achieved.

How Euan Murdoch makes value

Euan Murdoch's challenge was to make and sustain tangible value from the largely intangible. Herron Paracetamol labelling must declare the core product's active ingredient – proof there is no technical advantage to offset the perceived *negative security value* of a small company in typically a large company field. In this situation, where otherwise small differences have the potential to sway customers, Murdoch used non-core values with great effect at both consumer and trade levels.

◕ Elevated cause

Grabbing substantial market share from a large entrenched competitor who has the resources to outspend you ten-to-one in advertising, with a product that is effectively identical, demands deliberately different thinking.

Murdoch, not unlike Dick Smith, is fired by the cause and the challenge to do his part in not selling off Australian-owned production and brand assets. Like Smith, his commercial interests are of course one driver. However, his belief that 'AUSTRALIA EITHER MAKES IT OWN FUTURE OR IS DRIVEN TO IT' underpins a broader conviction. His decision to sell Herron to an Australian company, when most potential acquirers are overseas companies, is proof of that conviction.

◔ Outstanding value

Having no discernible advantage or positive difference in his flagship product, and a dominant competitor to challenge, demanded Murdoch think differently to provide value.

Offering a price advantage or an Australian-owned advantage over a technically identical product was of little use unless the consumer and the trade accepted direct comparability of the products.

Murdoch used creativity and circumstance to close the negative value gap, and turn it into a positive.

◓ Replicable formula

The highly regulated pharmaceutical industry environment demands a manufacturing business is rigorously driven by systems and processes to ensure quality, consistency and consumer safety and confidence. Replicability of product and the ability to upscale production are a prerequisite to growth.

Chapter 11 – Beyond making products to making value

Shortening product life cycles and barriers to market entry arguably posed Murdoch with his greatest threats and opportunities. Murdoch's ever evolving creative formula proved his principal weapon:

- Cultivating a "why not" mindset in his management team
- Deliberate pursuit of industry-divergent thinking and doing
- Flanking with creative guerilla tactics, pitted against financial muscle

Hero reputation

Murdoch's reputation building focussed on two key audiences in particular – the consumer and the retail trade.

The retail trade always wanted a *credible* strong alternative supplier to balance the bargaining power of Panadol. Murdoch however had to build the required credibility. He extracted from the dark grey cloud of extortion, which could easily have wrecked his business, a silver lining of credible performance under threat.

While leveraging from the relevant credibility and reputation of Hazel Hawke as a presenter in advertising, which has given Herron's reputation a considerable lift with consumers, capable handling of the extortion publicity probably legitimised the brand more than any other factor.

Chapter 12
FROM BRAINSTORMING TO SERIOUS CREATIVITY

There can be no doubt that creativity is the most important human resource of all. *Without creativity, there would be no progress, and we would be forever repeating the same patterns.*

If creativity is so important – and almost every corporation claims to be creative – why do we not treat it more seriously? There are several powerful reasons.

- Every valuable creative idea must always seem logical in hindsight – *otherwise, there is no way in which we could recognise its value. So we assume that better logic would have been sufficient to get to the idea in the first place. This is totally wrong in a self-organising, pattern-making information system like the human mind.* Since less than 0.1 per cent of thinkers or educators have any idea of the nature and function of self-organising information systems, most people still assume that logic must be sufficient.

- We accept that new ideas do happen from time to time as a result of change or through an unusual coming together of circumstances. We

CHAPTER 12 – FROM BRAINSTORMING TO SERIOUS CREATIVITY

feel that it will always be a chance process and that there is nothing we can do except wait for it to happen.

⇨   We accept that some people seem to be creative, while the rest of us are not. We believe that there is a mysterious talent for creativity which you either have or do not have, like perfect pitch in music. There is nothing a business can do except try to find and employ such creative people.

⇨   We have not begun to understand creativity. We haven't got a handle on it. Attempts to understand creativity by analysing the process by which people have come to ideas are pretty useless, since they tell us nothing about the mechanism.

⇨   There has been a dangerously mistaken notion that the best you can do to unlock creativity is to remove inhibitions and let people be creative. This was the basis of such weak traditional methods as brainstorming. Such methods have done great damage to the development of creativity by making it seem crazy and peripheral.

⇨   We have believed that creativity was fine for artists, advertisers, designers, packagers, and product developers, but that serious matters like engineering and finance require only analysis.

———— ** ————

For all these reasons we have not treated creativity seriously. What has changed? A very great deal. We can now look at creativity in a totally new way.

⇨   *For the first time in human history, we have begun to understand the difference between traditional passive-information systems, in which information is moved about by a processor, and self-organising, active information systems, in which information organises itself into sequences and patterns.* There is nothing mysterious about this. Once we understand the way in which self-organising systems create asymmetric patterns, we can then understand why every valuable creative idea must always be logical in hindsight. We can also start to design the powerful tools of creativity that we must use to move laterally across patterns. Creativity is a logical process, but it is the logic of self-organising systems, not the traditional logic of passive systems.

- By reference to the behaviour of self-organising systems, we can now understand why new ideas have been stimulated by chance, mistake or accident. And we can now do something. We can set about using the process deliberately, instead of just waiting for it to happen.

- If we do nothing about creativity, it must remain a matter of natural talent – that is obvious. Now that we have begun to understand creativity and to design specific tools, we can do something about it. We can develop creative thinking as a skill. For those who do not have a natural talent (motivation, curiosity, speculation), the deliberate tools will enhance their natural skill. The paradox is that those who are good at playing the games that are put before them will become good at the game of creativity once it has been laid out. In fact, they might become even better than the traditional rebels who have achieved creativity in the past by refusing to play the accepted games. This is why the Japanese are becoming better at creativity.

- Instead of merely analysing the behaviour of creative people, we can now look at the fundamentals of the information system of the brain and design creative tools on that basis.

- *The human brain is not designed to be creative. The brain is designed to allow incoming information to organise itself into patterns and then to use these patterns. So the traditional notion that it is enough to release inhibitions is inadequate.* Releasing inhibitions will produce a mild sort of creativity. *To produce serious creativity, we have to go further and use methods which are not natural, which go against the way the brain likes to handle information. Such methods as Provocation (discussed later in this section) are not at all natural.* The traditional process of brainstorming is a little better than nothing, but it is far too weak.

⊃   We know that if you have to do anything at all – even about the most technical matters – *there is an absolute need for new concepts. The brain can only see what it is prepared to see.* The analysis of information will not yield new ideas unless we have already started them in our brain through the process of creativity. It is creativity that produces the hypotheses and speculations that allow us to see things differently.

It is for all these reasons that we use the term 'serious creativity'. This is to distinguish creativity based on an understanding of self-organising information systems, from creativity based on inspiration and messing around in the vague hope that something will happen. Serious creativity is concerned with laying out the logic and the game of creativity so that it is no longer a mystery. At first sight, the use of the term "serious" will seem a contradiction, because we have always thought of creativity as wacky, crazy and off-the-wall. That approach has held back the development of deliberate creativity.

The application of creativity in an organisation

Serious creativity within an organisation needs to be used in two ways:

1. *As an essential part of the general thinking skill of everyone in the organisation.* At a shop-floor level serious creativity is needed to make more effective such processes as quality circles, work improvement and cost-cutting suggestions. Creativity not only provides tangible ideas, but also is a great motivator because *it gets people to think about what they are doing.*

In total quality management, for example, analysis can only take you so far. There is an absolute need for alternatives and for new ideas. Problem-solvers have a great need for creativity, especially when the cause of the problem cannot be removed and the way forward has to be designed. Improvement depends heavily on creativity, especially the improvement of small successive steps.

Senior management, including chief executives, must get involved in creativity. It is not enough to delegate it to others. Creativity is simply part of thinking, and you cannot put one part aside and say it is someone else's business.

2. *Focussed creativity is also needed in special areas, including strategy, research, product design, marketing, labour relations, finance, and production methods. In these areas there is a constant need for new ideas in order to solve problems or to open up opportunities.* To rely solely on experience, information, and analysis is like relying on a car with only three wheels. Sometimes people in specialised departments that need a lot of creativity are very complacent and even arrogant. They feel they know it all and are very talented. Such arrogance is usually misplaced. Being busy is not the same as having good ideas.

Serious creativity requires four things:

- Motivation
- Attitudes
- Focus
- Techniques

Everyone knows that the implementation of a new idea is even more important than the idea itself. At this point, we are dealing with serious creativity, and assume that an organisation has a need for new ideas and is willing to implement them.

1. Motivation

The main difference between people who are creative and people who are not is motivation. Call it curiosity if you like. The motivated person is willing to pause and look for alternatives. The motivated person is willing to look for alternatives beyond the obvious ones that are offered. The motivated person stops to focus on things which other people take for granted. The motivated person enjoys creative thinking almost for its own sake.

Other people need to see the need, logic and value of creativity before they can become motivated. They also need to feel that they, themselves, can do what needs to be done.

There has to be a belief in the possibilities of creativity. Thinkers whose horizons are limited only to fixing things, often do not have the vision to imagine better or different ideas. Executives who see management as no more than maintenance regard creativity as extra hassle.

Motivation can be changed through culture changes in your organisation (endorsed by senior management), through exposure to the logic of serious creativity, through training, and through structural changes that set up channels of responsibility and stimulation.

2. Attitudes

Attitudes arise partly from motivation and partly from the practice of lateral-thinking techniques.

There is the attitude of *Challenge*:

- How did this come to be done this way?
- Why do we do this?
- Let's look at this. Do we really need to do it?

There is the attitude of *Possibility*:

- Are there any alternatives here?
- What other possibilities are there?
- What other explanation could there be?

There is the attitude of *Provocation*:

- This may seem a crazy idea, but let us look at it.
- There are some interesting points in that idea.
- I don't like the idea, but it is a good provocation.

There is the attitude of *Focus*:

- Let's focus on this.
- What are we really trying to do here?
- We have never looked at this before, so let's look now.

All these attitudes are based on the belief that creativity and further thinking can make a difference. They are also based on the belief that things are not necessarily being done in the best way, but only in one particular way that has evolved over time – and it could be changed.

A key part of the attitude of creativity is the willingness to make an effort. *Creative effort is what really matters.* If effort is made, then results will follow – not necessarily on this occasion or on every occasion, but from time to time. *The object is to try, to make an effort, to put in some thinking time.*

Attitudes to creativity are very much set by the corporate culture. If the chief executive shows an interest in creativity, then much will happen. If creativity is regarded as a rather peripheral activity to be confined to the research and marketing departments, then nothing much happens.

So there are really two attitudes:

- The attitude towards creativity on the part of senior management, other management, and individuals.
- The creative attitude towards possibilities, work, problems, and other people.

3. Focus

If you ask a room full of executives to put down their problems, they have no difficulty in putting down five, ten or as many as requested. A problem does not need seeking out. A problem usually announces itself. It is there and must be dealt with. *Many problems do need creative thinking. But there are also other creative-need areas that are not problems.* These are other areas which have never been looked at (because they are not problems), but the change in idea can lead to savings or greater effectiveness.

We strongly recommend a Creative Hit-list as a way of making tangible the need for creativity. The Creative Hit-list is a formal list of creative-need areas. No more than half of the areas may be problems. The list is printed in in-house publications, put up on bulletin boards, and printed on postcards for people to keep in their pockets.

The Creative Hit-list can be put together from suggestions submitted by individuals and then condensed into a master list. Or a small team may be set up specifically to put together a Creative Hit-List, which is done by asking around. There may be Hit-Lists for groups, departments or the whole organisation.

The points on the Hit-List should be reasonably specific, and should not be general ones such as how do we make a profit. *There can be three types of points on the list:*

- *A specific problem*: how do we get the paint to dry more quickly?
- *A direction for improvement:* can we speed up delivery of the sales information?
- *A general area need:* let's have some new ideas in the area of packaging.

Points in the Hit-list might get replaced by better points. Other items may be there for years without any ideas being produced. Still other items may be dropped off the list when there are enough good ideas to be followed up.

Individuals can use their creative thinking on items on the Hit-list.

Groups that are thinking about other matters may devote a few minutes from time to time to consider an item on the Hit-list.

Creativity may be introduced into a department by asking the head of that department to put together a Creative Hit-list. If that person is unable to do so, then help may be offered in putting together a Creative Hit-list. Once the Hit-list is set up, inquiries can be made from time to time as to what has been happening. What sort of efforts have been made? It is at this point that specific training in lateral thinking can be offered. *The need for creative thinking comes first, and that need is defined by the Creative Hit-list.*

Although the Creative Hit-list may seem very simple, there is a high value in simply finding focus areas and defining them. Some people call this "problem-finding", but that term is misleading and only useful to contrast with solving problems that present themselves.

Once the Creative Hit-list is set up, it becomes both a challenge and an opportunity. People who want to be creative now have specified focuses. They can show their skills.

4. Lateral thinking techniques

So now we are motivated to be creative. We have the right creative attitude. We have also defined a specific creative need area. We need some new ideas right here and right now. So what do we do about it?

Let's say we are talking to the Xerox Group. The focus is on the "general area" type: we want some new ideas in the general area of convenience of copy use.

We use the random-word technique. This is the simplest of all possible creative techniques.

A glance at the wristwatch indicates a second-hand reading of seventeen seconds. This number selects word seventeen from a list (frequently changed) of sixty words. The word is *nose*.

Clearly the random word *nose* has nothing whatever to do with copiers and was not selected to have any relevance. This is what provocation is all about.

Nose suggests smell. What does smell have to do with copiers? Nothing – yet. Smell is only an indicator.

Suddenly there is an idea. If the copier is not working, instead of checking lights and dials all you have to do is sniff. If, for example, you smell lavender, then the copier is out of paper. If you smell camphor, the copier is out of toner. Technically this is easy enough. Cartridges could have the different scents in small containers. When a particular circuit is activated, then the appropriate scent could be heated up and released. You could now smell what the trouble was.

The added advantage of smell as a diagnostic read-out is that you do not have to be standing at the copier. If you are working at your desk and smell lavender, then you put in more paper. The idea might even be more important for fax machines, which often run out of paper. The smell could be released as the paper is coming to an end.

The general concept is that of using smell as an indicator system. Perhaps we could use it in cars. If the car does not start, you could start sniffing!

On another occasion, the general area subject is cigarettes. The random words are *traffic light*. Within ten seconds comes the idea of printing a red band on the cigarette paper at selected distances from the end. A smoker would only smoke up to the red band, so smoking would be less

Chapter 12 – From brainstorming to serious creativity

harmful. Smokers could select cigarettes with the band placed where they want it to be. With hindsight, it is fairly obvious how "traffic light" (signal, danger, stop) lead to the cigarette band idea.

The random word technique is now widely used by people ranging from product designers to rock groups seeking inspiration for a new song.

Why does it work? Logically, it is totally absurd. If the word is truly random, then it has no obvious connection whatsoever with the focus subject. True. Therefore, any word will do for any subject. Also true. This must be nonsense. While it is nonsense in a passive-information system, it is perfectly logical in a self-organising patterning system.

Figure 12.1 shows that when you leave home, you take the usual, most-familiar road away from it. If however, you are given a lift and dropped on the periphery of the town, then you find your way home by using a road you would never have used when starting from home. Technically the pattern access is different from the periphery than it is from the centre. There is no mystery about that.

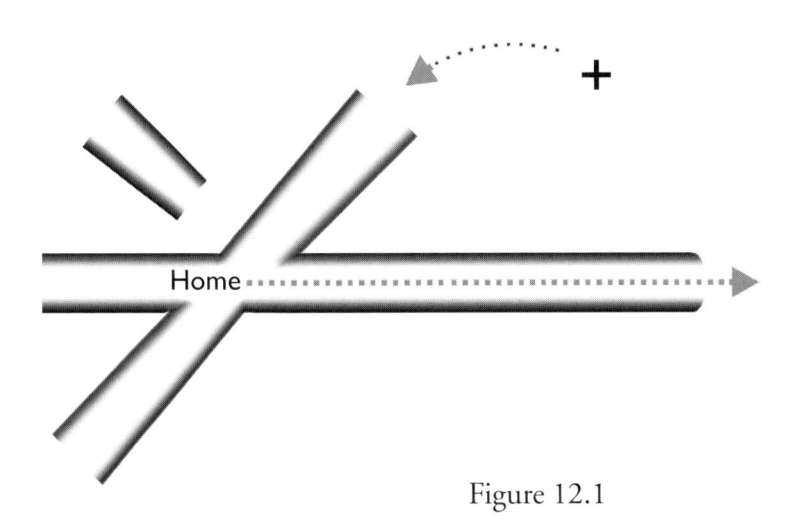

Figure 12.1

The mind is so good at making connections that wherever you start, you will track back and end up with one of the patterns leading into the focus area – but not the one you would have taken when working outwards from the focus area.

That is why we have stressed that it is essential to understand the type of information system operating in the brain in order to understand creativity and to design simple, usable creative tools. Nothing could be simpler than the random word.

Asymmetric patterns

Self-organising information systems set up patterns. The patterns are necessarily nonsymmetric or asymmetric as shown in Figure 12.2. This means that the route from A to B may be roundabout, but the route from B to A is direct. The way these patterns are set up is detailed in earlier books by Edward de Bono.

Asymmetric patterns are the basis of both humour and creativity. In both cases, we suddenly find ourselves on a sidetrack and immediately see the road back to the starting point or focus. In humour, the storyteller suddenly places us on a sidetrack. In creativity, we have to find ways of doing it ourselves.

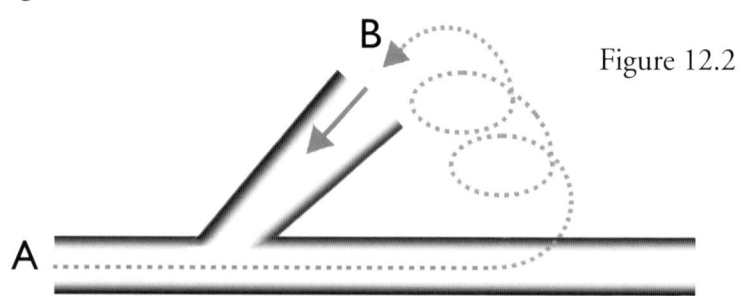

Figure 12.2

The history of science is full of examples of how chance events stimulated great ideas. There is the famous story, for example, of how Isaac Newton's idea of gravity as a force was triggered by an apple falling on his head as he sat reading under a tree.

In Figure 12.3, we can see that if we start off at the usual place, our thoughts will follow the traditional track from A towards C. If however we start at a totally new point N, then we might enter the sidetrack directly and then track back to A. *This becomes insight or the 'Eureka' moment. Suddenly we see things differently.*

Now we can sit around and under trees waiting for apples to fall on our heads, or we can deliberately shake the tree by using the formal random-word technique of lateral thinking. The random word provides the new entry point that would have to have been provided by chance.

Why do we have to rely on chance? Because if we select the new entry point, the selection will be based on our existing ideas and so will not get us to the new entry point. In certain cases, we can get a different starting point simply by directing attention from one part of the situation to another: let's start at this point. This process is also useful, but the random word has a much wider application.

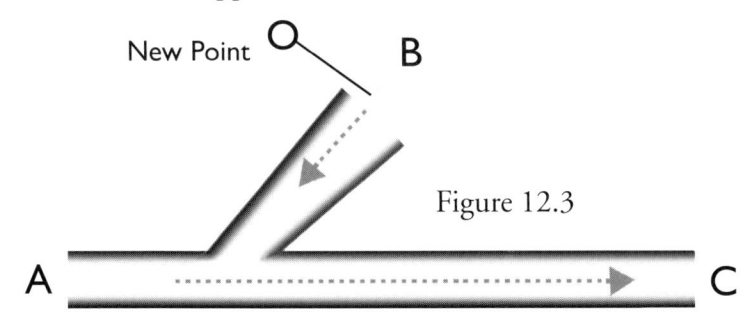

Figure 12.3

Provocation

There may not be a reason for saying something until after it has been said.

This is totally contrary to normal reason, where there should be a reason before you say something.

What is the point of saying 'police officers should have six eyes' or 'planes should land upside down'? They seem like total nonsense statements. In fact, they are logical statements, but it is the logic of patterning systems, not the logic of traditional passive-information systems.

Figure 12.4 shows that one of the ways of getting from the main track to the sidetrack is to set up a provocation and then to use this as an intermediate position in order to move on to the sidetrack.

Edward de Bono invented the word *po* to indicate a Provocative Operation. It deliberately allows us to say things that we have never

Figure 12.4

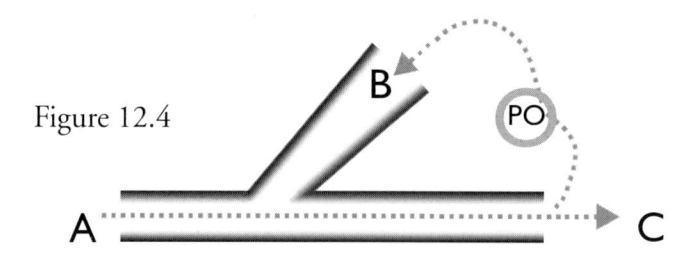

encountered in experience and, in some cases, could never encounter. The word *po* acts as a protecting signal to indicate that the statement is made as a provocation.

The very valuable concept of the hypothesis allows us to speculate and invent ideas, and then look at data through these ideas. The development of science is almost entirely due to the invention of the hypothesis. A hypothesis is an idea that is not yet proved, but which we hope to prove correct. *A provocation goes far beyond a hypothesis, and we make no pretence that it is correct.*

In chemical synthesis and in atomic physics, if there is a need to change from one configuration to another, it may be necessary to pass through an unstable intermediary before stabilising into a new configuration. A provocation has the same effect. In self-organising systems that always stabilise in some way – a way that may be less than the best way – *there is a need for destabilisation in order to settle down into a better stabilisation.* This point is well known mathematically.

There are various formal and systematic ways of setting up deliberate provocations. *One of the methods of setting up a provocation is simply to escape from something we take for granted.* For example, we take for granted that taxi-drivers know their way about, so we say 'po, taxi-drivers do not know their way around'.

Movement

Obviously, the process of provocation would never work if we were simply to use traditional judgement on the provocation. 'Po, taxi drivers do not know their way around' would be rejected on the basis that you could not possibly run a taxi service that way.

Many approaches to creative thinking talk about delaying, suspending or deferring judgement. Such processes are far too weak. Telling someone not to use judgement does not tell that person what to do.

We need to develop an active mental operation that we can use deliberately and specifically. Edward de Bono named this mental operation 'movement'.

The mental operation of movement is based directly on the 'water logic' of patterning systems. Movement is based on the word 'to': what does this flow to, what does this lead to? Movement is contrasted with traditional judgement, which is based on 'is' and 'is not'. 'Is this correct?' 'Is this in accordance with my experience?' 'Is this not going to work?'

They are several formal and systematic ways of getting movement. We can, however, get an idea of the process of movement by taking one of the provocations given above.

'Po, taxi-drivers do not know their way around.' The process of movement leads us to consider that the taxi driver might ask his or her passengers the way. This further leads to the concept that such taxis could indeed be used by city residents who know their way around. This leads to a two-tier taxi system in which one type of taxi (indicated by a question mark on the roof) is reserved for residents and a normal type is available for everyone else. Effectively, the customer is training the driver and some consideration could be offered for this service. A taxi-driver would only be able to pass from the resident's type to the general type after passing an exam on knowledge of the city.

The processes we have described here are not crazy but perfectly logical in a patterning system. They are essential in order to change perceptions rapidly. We can of course wait for mistake, accident or chance to provide provocations, or we can provide them ourselves – systematically.

We want to emphasise very strongly indeed that creativity is not just a matter of feeling free to have a crazy idea and hoping that maybe something useful will follow. That approach to creativity turns many people off. But once we can see that patterns take our thinking in one direction, then we can begin to see the logic of deliberate provocation.

The specific and formal techniques for setting up deliberate provocations and getting movement are described in full detail in Edward de Bono's book *Serious Creativity*.

How Gerry Harvey is seriously creative

Gerry Harvey has brought orderly retailing to categories in which previously there has been a great deal of chaos and corporate failure. He has won a dominant position, some would say too dominant, by choosing to be deliberately different. Like many other researched entrepreneurs he has achieved this position primarily through serious creative conceptual thinking, albeit applied intuitively rather than through a formal process. He constantly strives to challenge and if possible break industry 'rules' and norms:

- Fully franchising the traditional norm of a corporate department store

- Remaining the franchisees' landlord, when the norm among most franchisors is to mitigate that risk

- Focussing on the fundamental value drivers of franchisees and their staff, knowing that success with this critical motivation variable is the way to customer growth and loyalty

- Remaining his company's chief marketing officer, recognising that his company's success is fundamentally marketing-driven, when most public company chief executives choose to 'rise above' marketing

◗ Elevated cause

Like all franchisors, Harvey's principal customers for the most part are his franchisees. If he attracts, motivates and retains the right franchisees, then his business is reasonably assured. They will look after the customers and the business at the coalface.

Harvey aligns his cause closely with what is important to his franchisees, and to their staff who are his potential franchisees. He and other retailer entrepreneurs we've studied know how scarce good career people are in the retail industry. Sadly, many see retail as their last job preference. They are there simply because they need to earn a living.

◗ Outstanding value

Harvey is focussed on helping ordinary people, many of whom are limited in aspiration by self-imposed glass ceilings, to become the very best they can be and to achieve rewards commensurate with exceptional performance.

With his personal and organisational skills in retailing and promotion, and the buying and financial muscle his company now commands, Harvey is able to offer a very complete value bundle to his franchisees – one which is truly surpetitive in his categories.

◗ Replicable formula

With over forty years' retailing experience, Harvey has clearly formularised the basics of retailing – buying, merchandising, promotion etc. His formula for getting the best out of people is his constant work-in-progress, and has some clear signposts:

- Finding people suited to the retail business, frequently by growing them

- Giving people personal ownership and incentive to learn and stretch their horizons and performance

- Building people's skill and confidence and supporting them with a culture 'WHERE EVERYONE KNOWS YOU'RE TRYING TO GET THEM THERE ALL THE TIME'

With Harvey Norman, Harvey was almost certainly the first retailer in Australia to franchise every department in his department stores. Though acknowledging the great success of this innovation, his ever-learning mind continues to experiment with other models.

◗ Hero reputation

Few if any public company chief executives have Harvey's diverse reputation-building skills and track record. Yet, like Dick Smith, there is no magic to his formula.

Harvey creates controversy and news not only with his company's own initiatives but with his provocative statements on things retail. Wisely, he typically contains his commentary to things about which he is perceived to have above-average knowledge and track record. Even though he passes off his comments regarding the retailing competence of the board and management of arch rival Coles Myer as 'A BIT OF SHIT-STIRRING', many would accept his comments as based on reasonably expert opinion. His earthy style with the media, calling a spade a spade, seems to appeal to Australians and contrasts with the sanitised style of many of his corporate peers.

How Joe Saragossi is seriously creative

Joe Saragossi's external conservative appearance and demeanour belies a lifetime of serious creative conceptual thinking and doing which has reformed an industry. He is a classic example of the earlier mentioned prerequisite qualities for serious creativity – motivation, attitudes, focus and technique. Like many researched entrepreneurs, he uses other industries and disciplines to provoke new thinking in his own, to challenge and change entrenched thinking and doing habits.

◐ Elevated cause

Saragossi is passionate about continuous learning and improvement in whatever he or his organisation does. His personal reward yardstick is not to do with money but innovation, leadership and achievement. He is clearly hands-on, seriously creative, hard working and unassuming, and his organisation reflects those values. There is ample evidence of the truth of his statement: 'IF YOU'RE PASSIONATE ABOUT SOMETHING [HIS CAUSE], PEOPLE [HIS STAFF AND CUSTOMERS] WILL FOLLOW.'

Though he says 'I NEVER INVENTED ANYTHING', Saragossi's well-developed habit of adapting ideas and practices from other disciplines and industries, and frequently improving on them, is indeed inventive. Saragossi's methodology for conceptual creativity mirrors that of Dick Smith who says he 'FINDS THE BEST IDEAS FROM AROUND THE WORLD AND BRINGS THEM TOGETHER UNDER ONE ROOF [HIS PROJECT AT THE TIME].'

◑ Outstanding value

Early recognition of reality (the threat of aluminium frames to his traditional wood-framed window-making customers), and opportunity for his company (what that would mean for glass-handling, logistics and marketing), gave Saragossi a head start in making the major move from intermediary to direct supply – a courageous decision with which most companies wrestle often.

Being actively a first-mover on the ground floor of massive industry change and growth, first in the trend from small casement window glass panels to larger aluminium-framed glass panels, and eventually to complete glass curtain walling, Saragossi created outstanding value, and has been rewarded by his market.

◕ Replicable formula

'YOU DON'T HAVE TO WORRY ABOUT THE DETAIL IF YOU'VE GOT THE BIG PICTURE', is an important and telling comment from a man who also believes 'YOU DON'T ASK ANYONE TO DO ANYTHING YOU CAN'T DO YOURSELF.'

Saragossi brings real meaning and practicality to the often hollow-sounding text-book term 'the learning organisation'.

Further, his approach to much of that active learning being outside his industry has proven successful in enabling his company to profit from moving ahead of current industry thinking and practice (i.e. cross industry adaptation).

Having no dividend policy and re-investing 'IN YOUR OWN BUSINESS WHERE YOU HAVE CONTROL', thus funding growth internally and building corporate wealth, while controversial, has clearly been made to work in this family company.

Managing the risk of aggressive geographic expansion, by designing branch factories to have a fall-back position of rented warehouse, is as clever for its simplicity as much as for its effectiveness.

◗ Hero reputation

Saragossi has built his company's reputation primarily through innovation leadership, on-the-job performance, resulting relationships and arising word of mouth. Being first, or at least being early, coupled with being conceptually different invariably means being noticed.

Saragossi's plain talking is reflective of the value he places on up-front frankness and honesty. 'IT'S A FAMILY BUSINESS, SO I TREAT IT LIKE A FAMILY', seems to embrace staff and customers equally well. 'THEY SAY I'M TOUGH BUT I'M FAIR', is symptomatic of the highly individualistic, no-nonsense, roll your sleeves up reputation which clearly the company has built to its advantage.

How Paul Adler and Brad Bond are seriously creative

The creative conceptual thinking behind most sustained entrepreneurial success is achieved over time. Passion for the cause drives a vision of what could be in a more ideal world. This in turn drives the mental search for alternative concepts and ideas. What may appear to be quiet evolution is far more driven by creative conceptual thinking than the word 'evolution' usually implies. So it is and remains in the case of

Invizage. Paul Adler and Brad Bond's initial thinking focus was on concepts for enhancing crisis management, and it succeeded in taking their company through its first significant growth phase. However, they recognised at that point that a new concept was required to take it significantly further – a paradigm shift which meant first elevating their cause.

◗ Elevated cause

Adler and Bond are reforming the practices of an important emerging sector. SMEs are being forced to take computer technology very seriously. There is a rapidly increasing reliance on technology as their core business enabler. Without its successful application, they cannot hope to stay in business.

This reliance means SME support needs and expectations are changing rapidly. Inefficient use and failure of technology are becoming very costly and potentially a severe competitive disadvantage. For leading-edge smaller companies, intelligently leveraging business systems and processes using technology is proving a major competitive advantage in both productivity and customer satisfaction.

Adler and Bond have elevated the cause, from the sector norm of IT crisis management, to major productivity and convenience gains through technology for businesses who can't justify an IT department – a paradigm shift of major significance to the company and the client.

◗ Outstanding value

The value delivered to stakeholders – clients, staff and the company – is potentially much greater under the Invizage Support Plan model which manages IT proactively rather than in crisis response: leveraging productivity, reducing stress, increasing predictability, and facilitating longer and mutually more profitable relationships.

◗ Replicable formula

The Invizage business formula progressively integrates deeply with customers' values, gaining strength as it goes.

Support feeds the important and profitable "other half" of Invizage's business, contract work, including major installations and upgrades.

The trust and intimate knowledge that grows from providing competent support over time puts Invizage in the box seat to win clients' major contracts.

Not only is support a gateway to contracts, but the better the client's system becomes, the easier it is to provide efficient and profitable support.

◗ Hero reputation

Over half new client business is the result of referral from existing satisfied clients.

Practically all the company's major contract work flows from existing satisfied support relationships. Invizage's value delivery concept that predictably creates satisfied clients generates not only flow-on contracts from them, but enthusiastic referral to new clients as well – both at practically no marketing cost.

Chapter 13
BEYOND IDEAS TO CONCEPT DESIGN

In an earlier section, we suggested that surpetition is achieved through integrated values, serious creativity, and concept research and development. The suggestion is not exclusive and does not mean that surpetition cannot also be achieved sometimes through analysis and the use of product values.

Both integrated values and serious creativity have been considered in earlier chapters, and Concept R&D will be considered in the next chapter. In this chapter, however, we want to come back to concepts since we believe that in the future *concepts are going to be the most important source of surpetition and business success.*

Remember that a concept is a way of doing something that achieves a purpose and provides values.

Remember also the example of the car wheel clamp designed to discourage drivers from parking in the wrong places in cities. While the clamp could be described simply as a concept for preventing the use of the car until the authorities come to remove it after a parking fine is paid, the key concept behind the clamp is inconvenience. Inconvenience is usually a much greater deterrent than a fine. You have to wait by the car until it is released. Your schedule is wrecked, you are late for appointments, you can't go home. There is also a slight element of terror in the large yellow clamp that is attached to your car.

Thus a broader definition of the concept is that it is a way of using inconvenience as a deterrent to irresponsible parking. This broader definition enables us to look around for other specific ideas and for other ways of creating inconvenience.

Levels of concept

Let's suppose we wanted to do some creative thinking for ideas on raising money for the production of films. We might use the following provocation: " Po, a movie ticket should cost $100". From that provocation could come a specific idea that after seeing a film, a moviegoer could go back to the box office and invest $100 or more in that film. From that specific idea, we can proceed to extract the following concepts:

- A simple way for ordinary moviegoers to invest in films

- A way for people to invest in films after they have seen them; this is quite different from investing before the film has been made

- A way for some of the initial investors to sell out at a profit at an early stage (so encouraging initial investors)

- A way of getting moviegoers to recommend a film to others on a word of mouth basis. If they have invested, they will be more motivated to get others to see the film

- A way of using the cinema box office to collect small investments

Each of these five concepts can be carried out with a number of different ideas. The broadest concept is the first one.

An important point in concept design is to point out differences. The special value of a concept is often pinpointed by a comparison with an existing concept. In the above example, a key point of difference is that investors can invest after the film has been made and *after* they have seen it and pass their own judgement as to its likely success. This is crucially different from investing up-front.

Patent attorneys and agents are very good at describing different levels of concepts, because that is the essence of a patent application. They seek to protect an invention from being copied from the broader to the narrower applications of the concept. They must therefore explore different levels of concepts that others wishing to imitate the invention might subsequently try to use.

Defined needs

Much concept work starts from defined needs. 'We need something to carry out this function'. Let's take the area of security for example, and focus on ways to improve the security of access codes.

Most security systems have a weakness because, if there is a personal code, the person holding the code can provide access under pressure to someone else. We need a way of making sure that the person giving the code is not under pressure. That is the definition of the need, and it seems quite a difficult requirement.

Suppose we have a small television camera that records the pupil diameter of the guard's eye. The average and range of the pupil diameter are then filed. Under pressure, the pupil diameter would change in size and fall outside the normal range. So the code would become inoperative. There is also no way in which the pupil size could be brought back to normal. This concept is now in use commercially.

The asset base

Everything a bank does can be done by others. Cash can be dispensed by supermarkets. Credit cards are issued by many financial and even non-financial organisations. Stores extend lines of credit. Loans are obtained from many sources. Businesses can raise their own money in the market or from other sources. *Banks need to find new ways to make money.*

The asset base may not be money or financial know-how, but people and communication channels. Banks are attempting to make a business out of personal financial management for their customers. They can smooth the behaviour of their customers on a sort of insurance basis. Banks can act as guarantors and bulk purchasers for their clients. They can select groups of customers with very attractive profiles and give them special deals. Banks can act to set up joint-purchase schemes and provide intermediate holding positions when necessary. *Through providing bulking, selecting and channelling services, banks could charge permanent channel fees.* As the processes become more automated, the overhead costs on all these would keep going down.

Many major international airports today earn around half their revenue from retailing operations within the airport. How might one increase that revenue? The asset base is the large number of people using such airports.

How could we give people more shopping time? Instead of people using the spare minutes before the flight to shop, could they specifically come to the airport early in order to shop? Perhaps there could be a specific discount, depending on the time of the flight. If you shopped two hours before departure, you would get a ten per cent discount, if you shopped three hours before, you would get a fifteen per cent discount.

An overseas airport has a useful bulking asset. If you are going on holiday to a warm climate, the small town in which you live may not stock a large selection of suitable clothing because the local demand is low. But *thousands of people passing through the airport have much the same needs.* So there would be a point in selling specific destination clothing. When a customer bought a ticket from the local travel agent, the customer would be given a catalogue of the appropriate clothing for the destination. The needed items could be reserved by telephone and then picked up before departure.

Shopping at airports is also inhibited by the difficulty of carrying bulky items away with you in order to bring them back again. There could be ways of storing items to await your return. Or items could be selected and paid for, and then delivered by mail later on. In fact, airports could provide a mail-order catalogue with photographs of items that could be selected. Specific airlines could negotiate different discounts directly for their passengers or as part of a frequent-flyer scheme.

There are many ways in which airports can use their position for surpetition.

Concept extraction

Any existing idea has a concept behind it. The concept may have been designed to be there, or it may just have come about. It is also possible to extract a concept that the users of the idea have not noticed.

Chapter 13 – Beyond ideas to concept design

This concept extraction applies to ideas that are already in use or to the creative process itself.

From the fast-food business, we can pick out the following concepts:

- 1. Cheap and competitively cheap
- 2. Good standards of hygiene and service
- 3. Fast and convenient
- 4. You know what to expect
- 5. A meeting place for younger people
- 6. Bulk buying of standard items

Concepts 3, 4 and 5 have been extracted and put together to give the concept of 'expensive fast food'. There are oyster bars and seafood bars. You know what you are going to get. The service is fast and the standards high. But what you get is usually not cheap.

Tourists always complain that cafes in France seem to charge an exorbitant amount for a cup of coffee, whereas in the United States there is a bottomless cup. Of course, what the French cafes are charging for is time. You can sit for hours at a table and only have a cup of coffee. The overhead still has to be paid, and you are occupying an expensive piece of real estate.

One idea would be to charge by time. There would be a sort of parking meter in the centre of each table, and you would have to feed the meter. Otherwise, it would give out a loud and embarrassing whine. Your coffee could then be priced low. *This is a perfectly feasible idea, and a number of concepts can be extracted from it:*

- Customers are charged not for the item consumed, but for the *consumption of time and space;* a separately defined table charge could also be used, and this might vary at different times of the day

- Customers can assess how much they wish to pay; they *have control* over the costs

Marketing without Money

- ⇨ The establishment has some way of making a charge for time

- ⇨ The establishment has a way of getting a customer to *pay on an ongoing basis;* perhaps there might be a flat entry charge with a refund on leaving – depending on the time stamp

- ⇨ There is a way of making clear what is being paid for.

- ⇨ There is a concept of *charging for 'human parking'*

An even more practical idea would be to have a few tables with parking meters and others without. This would insure that some tables are always available for those who really need a short rest or a quick cup of coffee.

The concept could even be developed as an attractive environment to which customers brought their own food and drink, but were charged on a time basis for the use of tables and chairs.

The last concept could then be taken and developed in another way. *The customers could be made to pay not with money, but with attention.* The surfaces of the tables could be video screens showing advertising for various products or services. Advertisers would do the paying.

As suggested in Figure 13.1, *the creative conceptual thinking process is always a matter of moving backwards and forwards between ideas and concepts.* For this reason, it is often worth making the effort to put a concept into a practical form, because from this may arise a further concept.

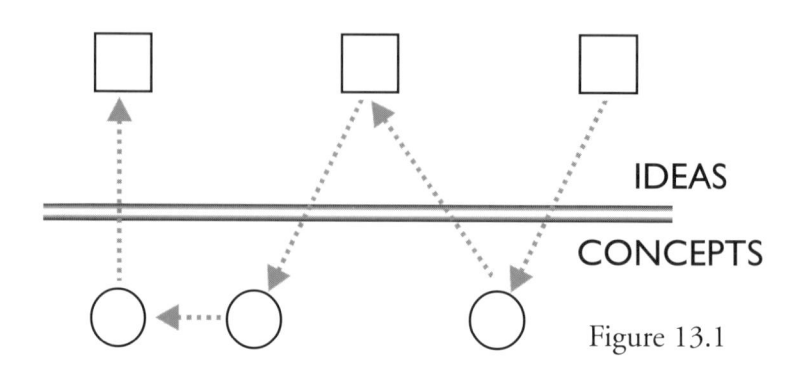

Figure 13.1

306 — John C Lyons and Edward de Bono

Surpetition

You are making a new film. How could you get some surpetitive advantage? You could deliberately incorporate some product and get joint advertising from the maker of that product. Television shows based on specific children's toys are a good example. The humorous use of the cleaning product *Windex* in the film *My Big Fat Greek Wedding* is another good example.

You could set up a telephone number dedicated to the film. This would automatically say something about the film and where and when it is showing in the neighbourhood. Of course, others could catch up with the idea, so you offer to do it for competing films as well. In this way, you control the market and keep your film at the top.

Insurance companies are very vulnerable to surpetition. As soon as an insurer gets big enough to cater to much of the market, then a newcomer comes along, picks out one section of the market, and offers better terms. Pensioners insurance is a good example. It is always possible to establish a surpetitive position by targeting a market and tailoring the product in this way.

If toothpastes offer to do everything possible for your teeth and gums, some one can come along with a new paste that promises only to make your teeth brighter. This specific function is now very credible. There is an unending cycle between promises of special functions, adding pieces to get a broader function, and then coming back again to special functions – and so on.

Improving concepts

If you design a concept, and there are obvious flaws in it, what do you do? Do you set about removing the faults and overcoming the weaknesses? This would be the approach of most design processes. With concepts however, it is usually better to try again and develop a parallel concept rather than try to overcome faults.

It is usually better to think in terms of alternatives, rather than attempting to polish the same gem over and over again.

How Graham Turner designs concepts

Graham Turner's achievement in concept design is not only world-class but, given that Flight Centre's achievement in market penetration outdistances that of arguably any comparable competitor in the world in its category, it is in a global *class of its own* – the mark of true surpetition. Turner and his management got it right by clear creative conceptual thinking focussed primarily on the *asset base*. Narrowing the product focus enabled efficient and replicable delivery. Concurrently, however, narrowing the *defined needs* served also enabled the company to become famous for its value because its communication focus via media and in store was made singular and simple.

Elevated cause

Turner believes the constraint to his company's growth is from the inside, not from the market. His primary cause appears to be devoted to maintaining the tight market focus of the business, its replicability and the motivation of staff.

Outstanding value

While Turner's business is predicated on providing outstanding value for money to its customers, his constant attention is focussed on providing value to his people who in turn make the business succeed by ensuring that customers are created and maintained. His seemingly homespun concepts of organisation structure show how deeply and creatively he thinks in providing a unique value bundle to his people.

◗ Replicable formula

Several key concepts are outstanding in Flight Centre's success formula:

- ◌ An unrelenting focus on discount flights and being famous for just one thing, in contrast with the traditional travel agency model of being all things to all people

- ◌ Focus and simplification as the key to a systems approach, thus turning a hotchpotch travel outlet into a well oiled, replicable machine, operable anywhere in the world in the same format

- ◌ A replicable formula for everything the business does, which means the business operates well with ordinary people (not neuro-surgeons!!), thus reducing human resource costs and ensuring continuity of supply in people

- ◌ Rewarding each individual 'ON THE OUTCOMES YOU WANT, RIGHT FROM THE START', demands that you have the 'RIGHT PEOPLE IN THE RIGHT PLACES' to produce those outcomes, that the outcomes are clearly measured, and that people are trained in exactly how to achieve those outcomes

- ◌ Pulling with human nature, not against it; applying sociology to business organisation structure, recognising that work is part of people's social structure, and if you pull against it, it is a lot harder

◗ Hero reputation

Even reputation-building is tightly formularised at Flight Centre. Turner openly resists complicating the company's simple advertising approach by changing it.

The consumer is promised, 'World's No.1 Discount Flight Specialists' and 'Lowest Airfares Guaranteed', and these ring in customers' ears because they have been repeated so many times in so many places for so long, and they are so simple. Even the advertising presenter seems ageless.

To the investor, Flight Centre's workmanlike, tell-it-as-it-is, pioneering reputation has been carefully cultivated. Corporate indulgence and waste are spurned. Results are what count and the company's growth and profitability track record is impressive.

How Jim McDonald designs concepts

Like many of his enterprising peers, Jim McDonald would probably never think of himself as a creative conceptual thinker. He may even spurn the label as jargon. Nonetheless, he designed, pioneered and proved concepts for sustainable outback drought management, low-cost production, quality and consistency of beef supply, and living with a hostile environment. While his creative focus was primarily on the *asset base*, the *defined needs* of his served market were never neglected.

◕ Elevated cause

Since 1946, McDonald has been dedicated to the cause of reliably and consistently producing low-cost, quality beef in the Australian outback. At age ninety-five, his accumulated learning is equivalent to that of two normal business lives.

His entrepreneurial creativity and persistence have enabled him to successfully manage, or at least live with, extraordinarily challenging variables which have proven too difficult for many who preceded or followed him.

◖ Outstanding value

McDonald has not only advanced the art and science of remote area beef production, and thereby contributed significant value to what is today Australia's world-class industry, but he has inspired, educated and helped many who have chosen to follow, or not follow his example.

◗ Replicable formula

Economies of scale and scope: MDH is designed to become not simply a large landholder and producer, but more importantly a sustainable business. As a drought-proofing formula, McDonald has chosen large open tracts of inexpensive land so that cattle can "follow the storms" on each property. In addition, the property portfolio is geographically diversified so that drought is highly unlikely to affect all properties at the one time. The addition of a feedlot is yet another hedge against drought preventing the finishing of cattle for market.

The right assets at the right price, judged on sustained performance. Emotional-decision-making and over-affection for some assets has been the downfall of many would-be-successful pastoral businesses. McDonald's intuitive use of business KPIs, long before the concept became fashionable even in business schools and city-based businesses, is another hallmark of his success formula. Critical variables such as land, cattle, people, management practices, and timing are chosen and managed based on performance.

◗ Hero reputation

Our deliberate sample of three long-experienced active entrepreneurs – Jim McDonald (ninety-five years), RM Williams (ninety-five years) and Joe Saragossi (eighty-three years) – is designed to extract from them the distilled essence of entrepreneurial success factors. In each and every case, "trustworthiness" and "your word is your bond" were at the top of their lists of key business success factors. They all see too little emphasis on trust as one of the big downfalls in business strategy today.

McDonald's chosen business demanded that he learn to live and do business in remote areas of Australia, which in the mid-twentieth century resembled the wild west and which still retain some of those characteristics today. His 'deterrence is better than litigation' approach to cattle duffers and 'contracts written on a handshake' approach to business transactions are other key hallmarks of his reputation and success.

How Peter Farrell designs concepts

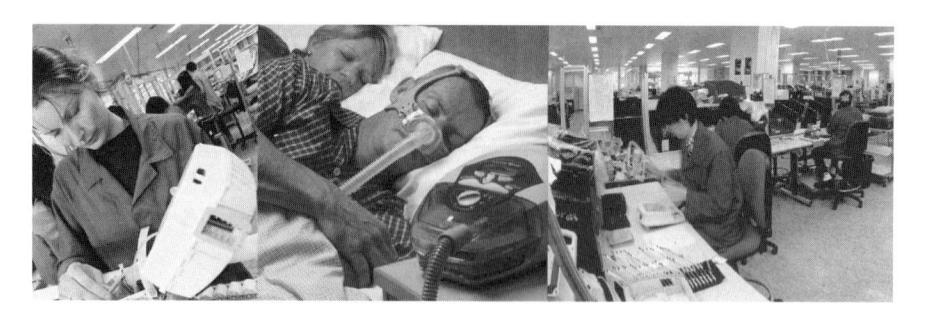

Peter Farrell's approach to concept design is formal and well advanced, no doubt driven by his scientific and academic backgrounds and by his desire to stand back and explore the big picture. He carefully balances his simultaneous focus on both the *asset base* and *defined needs*. He clearly thinks in concepts and is able to generate ideas from them. His formula for opportunity evaluation (below) is an important starting point, not a finish line. Alternative concepts and ideas are generated to find ways around barriers that arise when the checklist is applied.

◐ Elevated cause

Farrell's cause is an outstanding example of customers and their advisers not knowing what they want until they know what is possible, or even what is really happening in their lives.

Understanding by the medical profession and consumers of the huge damage caused by sleep disordered breathing is still in its infancy, even in the developed world. Hence, despite ResMed's outstanding commercial success, adoption of Farrell's cause by these audiences is still his greatest challenge.

The words of an early patient are a powerful example of Farrell's cause statement: 'IT SAVED MY LIFE; I CAN FUNCTION AGAIN; I'M BACK IN THE LAND OF THE LIVING; IT SAVED MY MARRIAGE; I'M ACTUALLY IN THE SAME BEDROOM AS MY WIFE; IT SAVED MY JOB.'

Outstanding value

Imagine how easily the sale and recommendation to others of ResMed products follows the effective communication to an affected consumer or practitioner of such a significant cause and solution.

Purchase and use of the product is insignificant compared to the value it provides – life itself or at least quality of life.

From a broader community perspective, the value is equally compelling when one considers that around ten per cent of people driving on our roads, and around eighty per cent of long-distance truck drivers, are a serious threat to everyone's lives because they suffer with chronic sleep deprivation.

Replicable formula

Farrell's simple and proven opportunity evaluation formula is an excellent blueprint for any entrepreneur's decision-making:

- Do we have a market that's accessible?
- Can we get the right people?
- Do we have the money to play the endgame?
- Does the timing make sense?
- Do we really understand the technology and what the competition and potential competition is, and the intellectual property terrain?
- Are we comfortable that we have something we can manage?

Hero reputation

Despite its impressive profitability, ResMed does not have the resources to take full and timely advantage of its head start in this growth category. If the company was already of a scale to afford a 'global' consumer communications campaign, it could doubtless create pull-through.

However, Farrell also understands deeply the conservatism of the health-care profession with whom product recommendation and implementation primarily rests. Overstepping the mark commercially is a risk to be managed with care.

To facilitate this, Farrell has assembled a highly credentialled, multi-disciplined ResMed Medical Advisory Board to help him and his executives carry the cause message around the world as fast as health professionals will listen.

Chapter 14
BEYOND TECHNICAL R&D TO CONCEPT R&D

We use the term Concept R&D to make a deliberate parallel with Technical R&D. The chemical and pharmaceutical industries worldwide spend billions of dollars on Technical R&D. So does the information technology industry. This money is spent because corporations know they have to invest seriously in technical research in order to stay in business.

Our point is that in the future, *concept development is going to be every bit as important as technical development.* We might even go further to say that concept development is going to be more important. You can copy or licence technology, but you need to have new concepts. Even if you adopt a "me-too strategy" and simply wait for others to develop a concept before following with the same concept, you will need some concepts of your own to follow successfully.

As mentioned earlier, *technology is fast becoming a commodity. What is really going to matter are the application concepts.* This is becoming true in the product area and has always been true in the service area, because service is directly a matter of concepts of value and concepts of organisation to deliver that value.

We need to begin to recognise that concepts are as vital to business as finance, raw materials, labour, and energy. Everyone knows this implicitly.

Any business, product or service is no more than a concept at heart. It will become necessary to recognise the importance of business concepts explicitly and seriously.

Good concepts, like good creative ideas, happen today as they have always happened. They come from talented individuals at a sufficiently senior level in an organisation to make things happen. Sometimes corporate strategy groups take on the task of developing concepts. Sometimes advertising agencies help with product concepts, and there are specific new product consultancies. Finally, copying is a much used source of concept change.

The purpose of a specific Concept R&D group is to treat the development of concepts much more seriously. Such a group would not be concerned only with the major strategic concepts and surpetition, but with production concepts, communication concepts, and concepts in every area within the organisation. *We are always using concepts. When we think we are not, it just means that we are carrying on with the old and traditional concepts – often without ever being aware of their nature.*

While it is perfectly true that the work of a corporate strategy group is mainly conceptual, this does not mean that it does or can do the work of the Concept R&D group. The purpose of corporate strategy is to look at the available options and at the world outside. From this base, a company can develop a number of possible options. One of these is chosen as strategy. *The purpose of corporate strategy is always reduction and selection for action.* That is what corporate strategy should be doing – it should be concerned with action.

Concept R&D, however, is a generative and expanding function, as distinct from the reducing function of corporate strategy. Just as Technical R&D opens up possibilities that are then fed into corporate strategy, so Concept R&D should also open up possibilities that are then fed into corporate strategy. Concept R&D is concerned with the possible. Corporate strategy must make a choice as to the most suitable. The two functions are synergistic. To expect the corporate strategy group to act as a Concept R&D group is to destroy its effectiveness. Corporate strategy needs to use a lot of black hat thinking (risks, concerns) and white hat thinking (information). Concept R&D needs to use green and yellow hat thinking.

Chapter 14 – Beyond Technical R&D to Concept R&D

Both marketing and Technical R&D, or specific new product development groups, do come up with concepts from time to time, but the focus and expertise of such groups is not directly on concepts as such. *There is a difference between having a development and then looking around for a marketable use for it, and having a use concept and then looking around for the technology with which to carry it through. Technical development can open up concept areas, but in the end the best results are led by concepts, not by technology.* In any case, the Concept R&D group should have a free-flowing interchange of people and ideas with marketing, Technical R&D, and product development.

It is important to emphasise here that even embryonic organisations should have what amounts to a formal Concept R&D group or function. Such a function need not be restricted to people actually working in the organisation. It may well benefit from the inclusion of outsiders. The important criterion is that thinking is being devoted to concepts that will drive the business forward. *Our researched entrepreneurs invariably penetrated markets without money because they investigated and developed better concepts.* They, frequently quite informally and subconsciously, used creative conceptual thinking and experiential learning to find and refine new and better concepts to deliver and become famous for their value.

The Concept R&D group should have four main functions:

1. Cataloguing
2. Generating
3. Developing
4. Testing

Function 1 Cataloguing

One of the main tasks of Concept R&D groups is to *extract, isolate and define* existing and past concepts.

Traditional concepts?

What have been the traditional concepts within the industry in general? What has been the essential nature of the industry as a whole? For example, it would be incorrect to say that the essential concept of the banking industry has been to channel funds from depositors to borrowers, because banks have taken a risk position. Channelling with channel fees has been more the function of investment banks.

Existing concepts?

What are the existing concepts within your organisation? How do these differ from the traditional industry concepts? What are the conscious points of change, and how much has happened through drift or incremental change? Is everyone aware of the concepts and agreed upon them?

Historic concepts?

Are there historic concepts that are no longer in use in your organisation? This need not apply only to the whole organisation but also to different parts. There are times when a change in conditions may make worthwhile the revival of traditional concepts. For example, computer communication and laser cutting is making the hand-tailored suit viable again.

Dying concepts?

What are the concepts that are dying either within the industry as a whole or within your own organisation? Sometimes people are conscious that a concept is dying (or suspect that it might be), but are unable to do anything about it. Perhaps the concept of large retail stores in city centres is dying. Perhaps the concept of printed newspapers is dying given the development of the internet.

Emerging concepts?

What concepts are beginning to emerge, either in the industry as a whole or in your own organisation? The concept of flexibility is beginning to emerge everywhere. The concept of joint marketing ventures overseas is beginning to emerge in the food-processing industry. The concept of shared basic research is beginning to emerge.

Competitors' concepts?

What new concepts are your competitors starting to use? Are these a matter of conscious choice, or have things just evolved that way? What are the strengths of these concepts, and what are their limitations? Is it worth adopting these concepts? What modifications or improvements are possible? How much surpetition is involved?

Indirect competitors' concepts?

Luxury fountain pens are beginning to compete with luxury watches as ways for men to wear jewellery. In the gift area, different products compete for the gift dollar. Bottled water is a competitor for beer and wine. *What are the new concepts that are emerging in your para-competitive fields?*

Other industries' concepts?

There is a need to look broadly at other industries that are not considered competitors in any sense. *There are times when some industries are forced by circumstances to move forward with a new concept faster than others. It is well worth looking to see what is happening.* They may be concepts of working more closely with suppliers. They may be concepts of off-shore research or off-shore data-processing.

The purpose of this cataloguing is to give an acute awareness of what is happening. The cataloguing can also suggest new concepts that are already in use elsewhere. The catalogue can focus attention on concepts that are dying and concepts that are emerging. *The catalogue is an attempt to produce a 'watch-list', just as conservation organisations produce a watch-list for endangered species.*

Function 2 Generating

The next task of a Concept R&D group is to generate new concepts.

> The generation of new concepts may arise in three ways:
> 1. *Pinpointing* specific need areas
> 2. *Perceiving* needed changes and developments
> 3. *A fresh look* at existing concepts

Pinpointing

A specific task of the Concept R&D group is to list specific areas of concept needs. These might be *bottlenecks, problems, high-cost areas, or areas of competitive disadvantage.*

These targets would be collected from all different departments. There might be concept needs in production, in personnel, in communications, and elsewhere. *In a sense, this is the formation of a Creative Hit-list.* At the end there is a clear sense of where concepts are urgently needed.

Changes and developments

There may be changes in the outside world such as a sudden rise in the price of oil, a government clamp-down on medical spending, or a new environmental bill. There may be changes in the internal world such as a new technical development from R&D, or a sudden rise in costs in one area.

Such changes provide focus areas for the development of new concepts. What are the defensive concepts that are needed, and what are the opportunity concepts that take advantage of the change? There might also be concepts of procedure: how is the new technical development going to be handled?

Fresh look

There is a high value in focussing from time to time on existing concepts or existing areas. This is not necessarily because the areas are problems or high-cost areas. You just want to focus on such areas. *There is often great potential for change in areas that are not problems. Because they are not problems, they may not have been examined for a long while.*

The Concept R&D group must always devote a part of its effort precisely towards a fresh look at existing concepts. *Call it a 'concept review' or 'concept reappraisal'. Even the most fundamental and successful concepts must not be immune to this review process.*

Once the focus areas have been determined in the above manner, there is the need to get on with generating new concepts.

New concepts can be designed by *borrowing an existing concept* and modifying it.

They can also be designed through the use of *information and analysis, followed by constructive thinking*. The normal design process can be used.

Finally, new concepts can be designed by *using serious creativity*.

There is a need for training in the skills and habits of concept design. With experience, the skills build up until working in concept terms becomes automatic. *The various tools, such as the tools of lateral thinking, are then used when appropriate, just as a carpenter uses whatever tools seem appropriate at the moment.*

In concept generation, it is important to remember that we are not problem solving. In problem solving, we are happy with the first solution that seems to solve the problem. *With concept generation, we should never be happy with the first concept, no matter how excellent it might be.* We put the first concept to one side and proceed to develop parallel concepts, as suggested in the section on concept design. It is never a matter of trying hard to modify a new concept so that it will work well. It is a matter of developing parallel concepts and then choosing the best one.

Concept generating work can be done through a Concept R&D group or can be carried out elsewhere in different departments. *The generation work may be carried out anywhere by individuals or by special task forces set up to focus on a specific concept.* All this potential activity is organised, supervised, and reviewed by the Concept R&D group. There should never be a suggestion, however, that all creative work has to be done by that group.

Concept R&D has the specific responsibility for seeing that the work gets done, but the work can be carried out in a variety of ways – including by outside consultants.

Function 3 Developing

Another key task of the Concept R&D group is to *develop* concepts.

The concepts to be developed may have been originated as part of the generating function of the Concept R&D group, or the concepts may have originated anywhere in the organisation. The responsibility of the Concept R&D group is to take note of the new concept and to facilitate its development. *This may be done by setting up contacts, by providing information, resources and technical help, and in any other way necessary.*

The originators of the concepts can be encouraged to continue to work on the concepts, or a concept can be taken over by the concept R&D group and an originator incorporated into the team working on that concept.

Members of the group must be very careful not to develop the 'not invented here' syndrome, which usually means a disdain for any new idea that has not originated within the group itself.

There comes a time when the concept is sufficiently developed to be handed over to another group such as Technical R&D or marketing. The Concept R&D group should still stay involved in order to see what happens and to record the progress of the concept. *If the concept fails to thrive, then it is worth noting why this has happened. The death of concepts should not pass silently.*

The skills of concept development differ from the skills of concept generation in the sense that there is a steady move from the possible to the practical. Account now has to be taken of practical constraints. There is much more attention to dangers and problems. There is a need to spell out benefits very clearly and to maximise them. There is still a need for creative thinking in overcoming difficulties, but the direction has been set, and there is the need to move solidly in this direction.

The benefits offered by a concept are much more important than the novelty. Novelty is a value to the originator of the concept; benefit is a value to the user of the concept.

Function 4 Testing

The way in which a concept can be tested is very much part of the concept design. It should not be a matter of designing a concept and then saying, 'how shall we now test this?' *The very design of the concept should build in the possibility of testing it. A concept that is not implemented, after all, is a wasted concept.* A concept is unlikely to be implemented if it cannot be tested. That is why it is important to design a concept not only for eventual use, but also for preliminary testing. A concept that can show its benefits in preliminary testing stands a better chance of getting used than one that cannot.

There are concepts that are so obvious and logical in hindsight that people want to use them right away. Cost-saving concepts can be like this: put a striking surface on one side of a matchbox instead of two.

There are concepts that do not need investments of money, but require investments of 'bother'. They require people to disrupt whatever they are doing in order to try out the new concept. This can work both ways. In the famous Hawthorne effect, we find that if enthusiastic people try out the new concept, the results may be immediately more favourable than they will be later on. *If a reluctant group tries out the new concept, the concept may be killed at once by the poor results arising from lack of enthusiasm.*

There are concepts that work well eventually, but not at first. Drink companies know that if you give a tasting panel a number of new drinks to try, they always prefer the sweeter drinks that subsequently fail in the market. If the benefits of the concept are potentially large, it is therefore important to insist on prolonged testing.

The design of testing involves the place, the people, and the method of measurement. Are you going to measure the savings of time, money, materials, energy, or what? How do you measure ease of working?

Quite often the testing of a concept needs to take place somewhere else – for example, in the Technical R&D department or in the marketing department. Nevertheless, the Concept R&D group should keep a watch on the concept, even though the concept has now passed to another department. If the concept fails to live up to expectations of benefits, then the Concept R&D group should compile a full report.

The design of testing procedures or situations may itself require a lot of creative thinking.

Even if the concept passes its tests and shows that it is both feasible and beneficial, this does not mean that the concept will necessarily be used. There may be other concepts that are even better. *The costs and risks of change may override the benefits of the concept, or the concept may not fit with corporate strategy.* The final question as to whether or not a concept is to be used ultimately passes out of the hands of the Concept R&D group.

On a strategy level, a corporate strategy group should now consider the concepts presented by the Concept R&D group. In internal matters – for example, production – the department involved would decide whether or not to use the concept. *In all cases, the Concept R&D group should record the history of the concept.*

Structure

What is to be avoided at all costs is a small in-house group that feels that no one else in the organisation should have ideas or generate concepts. That would be disastrous. *The Concept R&D group is there to focus, concentrate and supplement concept thinking throughout the organisation – not remove that function from all other areas.*

The size and structure of the Concept R&D group will obviously vary with the size of the organisation.

At its simplest, Concept R&D would be a person who is the nominated champion for concept development. Len Poulter began as this person at Lenard's. The person would then put together a group that could serve as the Concept R&D group. They would meet periodically to carry out the functions of Concept R&D. In a smaller organisation, all people involved would also have other line duties.

In a larger organisation, there should be a formal Concept R&D department. *There is a value in formality since if the grouping is informal it will only work when the members are not engaged in matters which seem (short-term) more urgent.* Concepts are so fundamental to an organisation's success that they merit formal attention. *If concepts could be developed by computers costing $5 million, many organisations would buy them.*

A small group of people would form the permanent core of the Concept R&D group. They would develop a high level of personal skill in dealing with concepts. Some would also develop training skills. The rest of the Concept R&D group would be formed from people who came into the Concept R&D group from other departments on a rotating basis. *People would come from marketing, research, production, human-resources, etc. They would spend time working directly with the Concept R&D group.* How long they spend there would depend on the size of the organisation and how long they can afford to be away from their usual duties. They would bring into the group their needs and their experience. *Along with people from other divisions and departments, they would work on concepts.* They would eventually go back to their own duties with more experience in dealing with concepts and with perhaps some new concepts to consider further. *In time, such people would set up subsidiary concept groups within their own departments.*

It is not to be expected that all individuals coming in from their own departments to the Concept R&D group will be equally comfortable with concepts. *At first, many of them will feel awkward and even might feel it is a waste of time. But like learning to ride a bicycle, the awkwardness wears off and skill develops.* The skill building and attitude changing is itself an important part of the function of the Concept R&D group.

In addition to this core group and its rotating members, there would also be other semi-permanent members of the Concept R&D group. These would be people who have shown particular talent and interest in concept development. They would be on call to take part in important discussions of the group and to take part in task forces set up to develop needed concepts. Many such people might also be involved in marketing, corporate strategy, product development, and Technical R&D. But they would need to change hats when working with the Concept R&D group, not simply carry over their other functions.

So the Concept R&D group should be loose and tight at the same time. It is tight in the sense that it has a definite existence, a definite role, and specific responsibilities. It would be loose in the sense that there are no hard boundaries that define who is within the group and who is not.

People

Who should the members of the Concept R&D group be?

There is a definite need to have some senior executives involved, otherwise the group will not have sufficient status and will be treated as subordinates. Ideally the Concept R&D group should have equal status with Technical R&D or marketing, even though the number of people will be fewer. If concepts are going to be treated seriously, the group has to be treated seriously.

The core members of the group must be energetic, good organisers and good at dealing with people. A lot of the work of the group in the first place will be to establish its identity and to interface with other departments without resentment. A lot of the work of the group will involve communication and liaison, so the people aspect is very important. It would be useless to fill the group with highly creative people who preferred to work on their own and did not get along with other people.

Although creativity is very important for the Concept R&D group, it must be remembered that much of the work of the group is not going to depend on creativity. There is also a danger with creative people that they are very judgemental of the ideas of others, and so may discourage the involvement of others in concept work.

It is more important that the members of the Concept R&D group be constructive and positive. The techniques of creativity can be learned, and the creativity of others can be encouraged.

A familiarity with concept work takes time to develop. Some people find it easier than others. The core group should contain members who are adept at concept work.

Again, we would like to emphasise that the Concept R&D group is not specifically a creative group or a new-idea group. There may be old and well-known concepts that require no creativity, but become the right concepts to use. Creativity is only one of the tools that need to be used.

We treat Technical R&D seriously because it requires scientists, laboratories and machinery. Concepts only require human brains aided sometimes by computers. However, this does not mean that Concept R&D is less important. In large organisations, *we would like to see at least five per cent of the Technical R&D budget spent on Concept R&D work. In other organisations, the percentage would be of the marketing budget.*

Often, concepts only work if there is a structure to support them. The serious attention that every business will have to pay to concepts in the future demands a structure like the Concept R&D group.

SUMMARY

Marketing without money is a vital skill not only for entrepreneurial organisations, but equally for established, better-heeled organisations who want to survive in business long term.

*There are four key points to be taken from the **Inspiration** section of this book.*

Key point 1: Marketing redefined

Marketing is simply defined as *'creating outstanding value and being famous for it'*. Business and marketing are one and the same. Business *is* marketing. In business, we create profits by creating value for stakeholders which exceeds the price they are prepared to pay in exchange for that value. If the value produced is outstanding, then all other things being commensurate, especially the cost of producing that value, profit will be outstanding. The creation of outstanding value for customers drives the delivery of outstanding value to shareholders. *Hence, marketing is too important and all encompassing to an organisation's success to be left to the marketing department.*

Key point 2: Marketing without money

There are two ways to increase the profit gap between revenue and cost. You can increase the revenue per unit produced and/or decrease the cost of producing each unit. A major part of what we include in the cost of production is the cost of marketing. Hence the concept of *Marketing without Money* is designed to underscore the absolute necessity to penetrate and serve markets as inexpensively and efficiently as possible and to maintain that penetration, and to grow it, at a lower than industry-average cost. *Successful entrepreneurs have mastered this skill.*

Key point 3: Entrepreneurial essence

Successful entrepreneurs typically enter markets against entrenched competition and, without the money normally required, build and sustain profitable market share. *What may appear to be masterstrokes of entrepreneurial brilliance and even extraordinarily good luck, are actually a replicable trail of opportunity recognition, creative concept development and thorough implementation, which others can follow.* Their concepts, though perfectly logical with the benefit of hindsight, usually elude conventional management thinkers because their minds are locked in to competitive, analytical and logical thinking – what we have termed "housekeeping".

Key point 4: Entrepreneurial concepts

While most business people are constrained by patterns of thinking to conformity with industry norms and practices, highly successful entrepreneurs deliberately challenge such convention, doggedly pursuing and pioneering new concepts which previously either had not been considered or were regarded as unpromising. *Their concepts cluster around four key directions:*

- **Elevated cause:** they search beyond *expressed needs*, identifying and *elevating a cause* which caters to the basic human desires of customers and other stakeholders

- **Outstanding value:** they rise above today's *competitive values* to create a *value monopoly* – a new race in which they can be undisputed leader rather than a follower

- **Replicable formula:** usually by narrowing the focus, they *simplify and make replicable* previously customised ways of producing value

- **Hero reputation:** they promote the cause, not their product; they use an authority position of *cause hero* as a powerful communication tool for reputation and brand building; their product follows

*There are **six key points** to be taken from the **Education** section this book.*

Key point 5: Housekeeping

Much of business thinking today is concerned with housekeeping. There is problem solving, cost control, quality management, and people care. These are all extremely important and have to be done. They are necessary, but they are not sufficient. Water is necessary for soup, but soup is more than water. *When you have a competent and efficient business machine, what is it going to do?*

Key point 6: Surpetition

Competition is necessary for survival. Competition is part of housekeeping and establishing the baseline. *We need to go beyond competition (seeking together) to surpetition (seeking above).* There is a need to create value monopolies. These will be the basis of success in the future. Surpetition is an attitude of mind and a matter of concept design.

Key point 7: Integrated values

Business has passed from the stage of product values to competitive values. The next stage is integrated values. *How does the value that you offer integrate into the complex life values of the buyer or consumer?* These are going to be the important values in the future. They are also the basis of surpetition.

There are four fundamental drivers of value with which we seek to integrate:

- **Convenience value** – how can we make it faster, simpler, easier, or just remove the problem and deal with it on the customer's behalf

- **Quality-of-life value** – how can we help the customer improve quality of life in such things as health, family, security and so on

- **Self-importance value** – how can we help customers increase personal self-esteem and others' esteem of them

- **Distraction value** – how can we create greater enjoyment for customers, either stimulating and entertaining them and/or relieving them of stress and other undesirable values

Key point 8: Serious creativity

We now know that in any self-organising information system, like human perception, there is an absolute mathematical need for creativity. *We need to move on from ineffectual methods of encouraging creativity, such as brainstorming and the release of inhibitions.* We can design specific creative-thinking techniques that can be used deliberately. We can understand and lay out the game of creativity and play it (conformists can play, too).

Key point 9: The importance of concepts

Technology is becoming a commodity: What now matters are the application concepts. Concepts are every bit as important as finance, raw materials, labour and energy. It is not enough to rely on "me-too" copying or the haphazard use of creative intelligence. *We need to take concepts very seriously indeed. Concepts are the basis of surpetition.*

Key point 10: Concept research and development

In order to take concepts seriously, there is a need for formal Concept R&D groups. These should be treated every bit as seriously as we now treat technical R&D or marketing. The concept function is not adequately handled by conventional corporate or business planning. *There are four key functions in Concept R&D:*

- **Cataloguing known concepts**: extracting, isolating and defining existing and past concepts so that they are generally recognised and agreed

- **Generating new concepts**: generating new concepts by pinpointing specific needs, perceiving needed changes, and taking a fresh look at existing concepts

- **Developing concepts**: facilitating the development of promising concepts – overcoming difficulties, minimising risks, maximising benefits, etc.

- **Testing concepts**: the design of the concept should build in the possibility of testing it; testing involves the people, the place and the method of measurement

Authors' final note

If, in reading this book, you came to the conclusion that you knew it all already – then consider the book an endorsement of your views. But beware of the complacency of the 'same as' trap.

If, however, after reading this book, you still feel that efficient housekeeping is all you need in an organisation, then we think the future will prove you wrong.

Appendix

SERIOUS CREATIVITY

Some introductory lessons

Creativity is a logical process and an essential part of thinking. It is a skill that can be learned and developed using tools, techniques and training.

It is important to understand the logic of creativity to use it effectively. We use perception to arrange the world so that we can use logic to make sense of it. But logic can only serve the perceptions that are given to it, and there are often many ways to look at the same situation. So often we make the mistake of trying to explain behaviour through logic in an inappropriate perspective. However, looking at a situation differently by changing our perception can give us many alternative ideas.

Changing perception is what we are particularly concerned with in creative thinking. How do we look at things differently?

Creative thinking is an essential skill for entrepreneurs and managers. This section introduces briefly the basic techniques of such thinking. The techniques are fully explained by Edward De Bono in his book *Serious Creativity*. While these materials provide a far greater depth of insight on the subject, it is our intention to at least provide a basic level of knowledge so as to assist you to begin to realise the benefits of a serious approach to creativity.

We begin by introducing one of the most basic purposes of creative thinking – finding alternatives.

LESSON 1
LOOK FOR ALTERNATIVES

The entrepreneurs profiled in this book all demonstrate the value of thinking creatively.

The search for *alternatives* is the most basic of all creative operations.

- Is there another way?
- What are the alternatives?
- What else can be done?

In some ways creativity can be defined as a search for alternatives. This is especially true when you set out to be creative about something that already exists.

Although the effort to find alternatives is so very basic to creativity, the process is not as easy as most people assume. Where do the alternatives come from? How do we get alternatives when we need them?

Good creative ideas are always logical in hindsight. But just because an idea is logical in hindsight does not mean you can use logic to discover it in foresight. The main danger to creative thinking is that we become too easily satisfied with obvious logical alternatives. Because standard solutions are obvious, we do not see other possibilities. Often we do not even conceive of an alternative because we are unable to look in a particular direction. We need creative thinking techniques to lead our mind in different directions.

Looking for alternatives and finding alternatives is the most basic part of creative thinking.

You should look for alternatives when:

1. There is an obvious need such as problem solving, design, planning or improvement required.

2. There are no problems, but we feel there may be a better way.

3. There is no need at all. Look for alternatives even though they do not appear necessary.

It is important to be disciplined in seeking alternatives. Create points in your thinking at which to stop and look for alternatives. Begin to seek new alternatives even though the way things are done appears satisfactory.

Management is sometimes defined as the ability to choose the right alternative. *Therefore, we believe, to succeed, management should place more emphasis on generating alternatives.*

Negativity is one of the worst habits when generating alternatives. *It is extremely important to separate the generation of alternatives from the judgement of alternatives.* You cannot improve the quality of your decisions by impoverishing your range of alternatives.

The concept triangle – a tool

The concept triangle is a simple way to generate alternatives:

1. Start by defining the purpose of your thinking. What is your ultimate goal?

2. Then suggest an idea to achieve this purpose.

3. Then extract the concept from the idea. "This idea is a way of doing what?"

    Continue to find alternative ways or ideas of carrying out this same concept. Repeat.

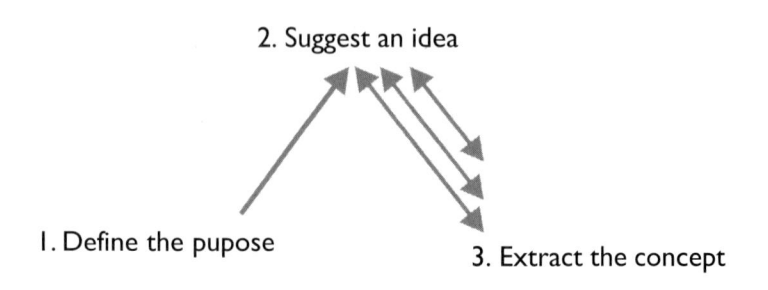

2. Suggest an idea

1. Define the pupose

3. Extract the concept

APPENDIX

ALTERNATIVE EXAMPLES

In establishing Flight Centre, **Graham Turner** identified a fresh alternative that would transform the travel industry. Most travel agencies of the time looked very similar; generalists, undifferentiated, famous for nothing in particular, and struggling to deliver a complex product. Turner says: 'MOST TRAVEL AGENTS PUT BULLSHIT IN THEIR WINDOWS, LIKE DISPLAYS WITH NICE POSTERS...AGENTS WEREN'T PREPARED TO PUT PRICES ON THEIR DESTINATIONS.' Seeing the opportunity for an alternative, Flight Centre began featuring clear and simple destination prices in Flight Centre shop windows and established a very prominent point of difference on which to build a reputation.

Gerry Harvey is continually on the look-out for new alternatives. In designing the business concept for Harvey Norman stores, he experimented with several alternatives to the traditional department store that was the dominant design of the time. He hit upon the idea of co-locating several franchisees within the one store. This simple concept had many profound effects. Harvey noted that: 'IF YOU GAVE THEM [THE FRANCHISEES] A PIECE OF THE BUSINESS, SUDDENLY THEY REACHED NEW LEVELS. THEY EMPLOY THE PEOPLE AND BUY THE STOCK, BUT THEY HAVE THE WISDOM AND STRENGTH OF A HEAD OFFICE STRUCTURE. IT HAS BEEN FANTASTIC, BY FAR AND AWAY A BETTER SYSTEM.'

LESSON 2
FOCUS YOUR THINKING

Focus means to be absolutely clear on what you are thinking about and what you are finding alternatives for, when you are thinking. Focus is one of the most difficult things to do in creative thinking because it seems easy, yet is often taken for granted. There are two types of focus.

Area focus

In *Area* focus we say we want ideas in a general area. We simply decide 'where' we want new ideas; we set out to generate ideas in that area. The focus area might be broad or tight. Because we have no desired outcome, we can find ideas that have a variety of outcomes. Area focus is important because it allows us to think about anything at all, without limiting our thinking.

Purpose focus

With *Purpose* focus there is a defined reason for our thinking. There is something we want to achieve. In purpose focus we decide 'why' we want new ideas – the purpose. What do we want to achieve with the ideas? We may wish to complete a task, make an improvement or reach a goal. When using purpose focus, it is very important to keep in mind exactly what we are trying to achieve.

An effective way of remaining focussed in your thinking is to make a *Creative Hit-list*. A Creative Hit-list defines focus targets for creative thinking effort. The Creative Hit-list is a tangible, visible and concrete target list that focuses and encourages creativity.

The list should include roughly one-third problems, some tasks or situations that could be improved, and some general area focuses. The List should include areas that have not been thought about for a long time, where there has been a change in technology or market circumstance, and some problems. The List should not have more than one-third problems, otherwise we just limit it to problem solving.

The purpose of the Creative Hit-list is to make visible to everyone in an organisation certain things about which there is a need or a desire to think creatively. There are many organisations where everybody says "we are very creative, now what should we be creative about?". This reverses that tendency by setting up a target list.

FOCUS EXAMPLES

Les Schirato encountered problems when, after some early success, he became unfocussed. He acknowledges that by deciding to narrow his focus, he was able to find alternative ways to better manage for profit. 'I WENT OUT AND CHOSE THE CLIENTS WE REALLY WANT TO DEAL WITH, AND THEN I WENT ON TO MANAGE THEM FOR PROFIT…WITH GOOD INTERNAL SYSTEMS THAT CAPTURED ALL THE COSTS OF DOING BUSINESS WITH THAT CLIENT…UMBRELLAS, PROMOTIONS, SERVICE ETC.…AND A GOOD SET OF KPIs. SOMETIMES I WISH I COULD ACT LIKE THAT WHEN WE ARE DOING WELL. I DON'T MAKE ANY EXCUSES NOW FOR BEING A BIT OF A CONTROL FREAK BECAUSE IT HAS MEANT WE'RE NOW SUCCESSFUL, STABLE AND SECURE.'

Peter Kazacos remains absolutely focussed on establishing a foundation customer in any new area of business he pursues. He first seeks the *right* customer, then searches for areas and alternatives where the application of technology may add value. At times adopting an *area* focus first and then a *purpose* focus, his process is one of discovery and learning. He frequently uses a foundation client as a springboard to decide on and gain access to others with similar needs.

LESSON 3
CHALLENGE EXISTING IDEAS

Without *challenge*, we would be very happy with the way things are. Challenge should never be seen as an attack or criticism as this would limit the challenge to items which are viewed as and agreed to be wrong. Instead challenge says 'Is THERE A BETTER WAY OF DOING THINGS?'

The challenge process is built on the word 'Why?' It says, 'THIS IS THE WAY IT IS. IT MAY BE THE BEST WAY. IT MAY SEEM THE ONLY WAY, BUT IS THERE A BETTER WAY?'

There are several steps to challenge.

1. **Do we really need to do this at all?**
   If something is not necessary then there is no point in doing it at all. Can we get rid of it altogether?

2. **Why do we do it? We do it because...**
   Look at the reasons why we do something the way we do. When we become conscious of the reasons we do something, we can effectively challenge those reasons, and in this way find alternatives to the reasons.

3. **Finding alternatives**
   What are the alternative ways of doing this?

The point of challenge is that things reach equilibrium where they are not a problem and we never think about them anymore. However, that equilibrium state may be far from the best, and now there is the possibility of doing things in a much better way. This may be the best way, it may be the only way, let me challenge it. Maybe there is another way.

Checklist of current thinking

Before we can begin to challenge existing ideas, we need to define our current thinking. We are often not aware of our current thinking so we take many things for granted. The checklist of current thinking provides a useful framework for understanding the norm.

It is very helpful before beginning a creative thinking session to categorise your current thinking using this checklist.

1. Dominating ideas

In this situation, which idea dominates our thinking? Perhaps we are unable to shift our thinking outside this idea. This idea may be totally valid, it is, however, important to be conscious of it. The dominating idea must be brought to the surface, so we can attempt to escape from it.

2. Boundaries

What boundaries are we working within? Become conscious of the boundaries of our thinking/problem so we know what to challenge.

3. Assumptions

What assumptions are we making? What are we taking for granted? Being conscious of our assumptions allows us to challenge them.

4. Essential factors

Essential factors are constraints or effects present in the situation. For example, an essential factor for an airline might be the safety of passengers.

5. Avoidance factors

Avoidance factors are situations that we always try to avoid when thinking about something. We should be conscious of all those things we are purposely trying to avoid. For example airlines would always avoid ideas that would make passengers frightened or sick.

6. Polarisations

Polarisations occur when you are fixed in your thinking between only two polar directions. For example, a business may think there are only premium or cut-price products in their market. What polarisations are normally used? How can we break from this rigid thinking?

CHALLENGE EXAMPLES

Through challenge, **Paul Cave** was able to sense and realise a large business opportunity that had been staring Australians in the face for as long as they have been driving across the Harbour Bridge. 'TELL ME WHY CAN'T PEOPLE CLIMB THAT BRIDGE?'

Therese Rein has created a valuable business, passionately challenging the traditional view that long-term unemployed people are simply a given in our society. 'I THINK THAT ENABLING PEOPLE TO RECONNECT WITH THEIR COMMUNITIES, TO RECONNECT WITH INDEPENDENCE, TO RECONNECT WITH THEIR POTENTIAL – I THINK THAT MATTERS'. Her conviction drove her to create the concept of "integrated human services" and to assemble a multi-disciplinary team of professionals with processes to deliver value to all affected stakeholders simultaneously.

LESSON 4
CREATE IDEAS FROM RANDOM ENTRY

Random entry is the simplest of all creative thinking techniques. Select a random word and use this word to stimulate new ideas.

To understand the random entry technique, we need to remember that the mind is a self-organising patterning system. Just as rain on a landscape quickly forms streams, the mind forms patterns, and thinking conforms to these patterns. The random entry technique opens up directions that would otherwise not be revealed by the brain's patterning system. It is important to choose entry points randomly because often the choice of new entry points is influenced by existing ideas.

The chaos of a random entry enables us to switch tracks in our thinking quickly. By using a random entry we increase our chances of finding a completely new track. One of the simplest ways of producing an entry point is to use a random word (use a noun from a dictionary for instance). The random word produces a concept that stimulates our thinking in a particular direction.

If you leave your house you will always travel along a road you are familiar with. But if you start in from the periphery of the town and find your way home, you are more likely to open up a new road. In the same way, random entry drops you at the periphery of a subject and as you move towards the centre you open up tracks, roads, paths you would never have taken on leaving the centre. It can be extremely powerful.

Mistakes using random words:

> 1. Don't wait for the perfect random word. If a word does not prove effective quickly, select a new random word. Take the random word and try your hardest to make it work. The purpose is to provoke a new line of thinking.

> 2. Don't list the attributes of the random word before beginning to think creatively. If you do so, you will quickly

focus only on the attributes that are closest to your existing ideas and miss the chance to discover new creative ideas.

3. Don't make too many jumps or associations from the random word to your new concept as nearly any concept can be moved to an existing idea given enough associations.

RANDOM ENTRY EXAMPLES

Euan Murdoch explains how a random and unforeseen extortion attempt actually benefited his business. Trade support increased markedly after the extortion attempt due to Herron's immediate national product recall and destruction of all stock, and rapid introduction of tamper-evident packaging, creating a good impression of the company. This random attack on normal practice forced Murdoch to challenge his traditional thinking and find better alternatives. It convinced skeptical trade and consumer customers that Herron was a serious player, and resulted in a doubling of market share.

For **Max Beck**, losing everything except his house was a random entry that changed his life. He moved further up the value chain from construction to development, and adopted a very different approach to business life. The survival and prosperity of Becton in a disaster-prone industry is due to his subsequent adoption of a very measured approach to opportunity, financial control and risk management. He always considers the down side.

LESSON 5
BE DELIBERATELY PROVOCATIVE

Normally we are only interested in ideas that are true or correct. With the creative thinking technique of provocation, we purposefully seek ideas that are absurd as a stimulus for the flow of new logical ideas. Provocation is used to help us move across the patterns that form in our minds that restrict our creative thinking.

In provocation we can say anything to provoke new ideas or new ways of looking at things. If we don't use provocation, we must always stay within the boundaries of our existing knowledge and experience. With provocation, we jump outside the boundaries; we take a step that is not fully justified in terms of our existing knowledge. *Provocations should not be challenged or attacked but instead used to provide conceptual movement to new ideas.*

There is now research proving that in any self-organising system, provocation is a mathematical necessity. The brain is a self-organising system which, with experience, organises itself into patterns and expectations. There is a real need for provocation to get us to move out of the usual patterns and increase our chance of opening up new patterns.

There are numerous ways of creating thought-provoking provocations.

Arising provocations: turning an idea into a provocation.

Escape provocations: escaping from the normal way of thinking; first list the things we already know about something, then make the effort to escape from these things; the escape becomes our provocation.

Reversal provocations: thinking in the opposite direction; making provocations by imagining the exact opposite of the logical situation.

Wishful provocations: using fantasy as a provocation; imagine a fantasy situation, something we don't really expect to happen; from this fantasy extract a provocation.

Distortion provocations: take a normal relationship and distort it, altering the relationship gives us the provocation; you can purposely try to get mental stimulation from a provocation in several ways.

Top of mind: means to run with any ideas that immediately spring to mind and follow the paths they create.

Extract a principle: means to take a principle that is at the core of the provocation and see how that principle can be applied to your problem.

Difference: means to focus on the difference between a provocation and a similar logical idea and extract this difference to form new ideas.

Moment to moment: means to stop and examine the path from a provocation to an end point idea and use the ideas that arise moment to moment.

Positive aspects: means to extract the positive features of the seemingly absurd idea (provocation) and see how these positives can spring new ideas.

Special circumstances: means to define some circumstances when the provocation might actually make some sense and see how these special circumstances give rise to new ideas.

PROVOCATION EXAMPLES

The examples in this book of provocation stimulating different thinking and action are numerous. Entrepreneurs are generally provocative by nature and reap the benefits of challenging traditional thinking every step of the way. They use or react to provocations, turning them to advantage or at least recognising the opportunities they present.

APPENDIX

Dick Smith has made provocation an art form, not only in his own mental processes, but as a means of reshaping how people perceive the status quo, and in provoking them to want to change things. Using Dickhead Matches as a product, a promotional tool and a means of pinpointing his cause (Fighting back for Australia) exemplifies the value of his creative conceptual thinking skills

Peter Farrell has put his cause, the criticality of healthy sleep, on the medical agenda as it has never been before. Stumbling over the technology that made it possible to measure and manage sleep apnoea certainly provoked him to think differently. Studies which showed the incidence (ten per cent of people, seventy-eight per cent of long-distance truck drivers) and seriousness (the major contributor to killers one and three – heart disease and stroke) of the condition have certainly provoked a major change of thinking in the health and medical professions.

LESSON 6
EXPLORE USING CONCEPT FANS

The concept fan is a powerful technique for generating alternatives. There are three levels of alternatives: directions, concepts, and ideas. Ideas are ways to implement concepts.

Concepts are routes for moving in alternative directions.

Directions are different ways of achieving a purpose.

To get broader directions and concepts ask: 'THIS IS A WAY OF DOING WHAT?'

To get detailed ideas ask: 'HOW CAN THIS BE ACHIEVED?'

Move up to broader or down to detailed in order to generate alternatives.

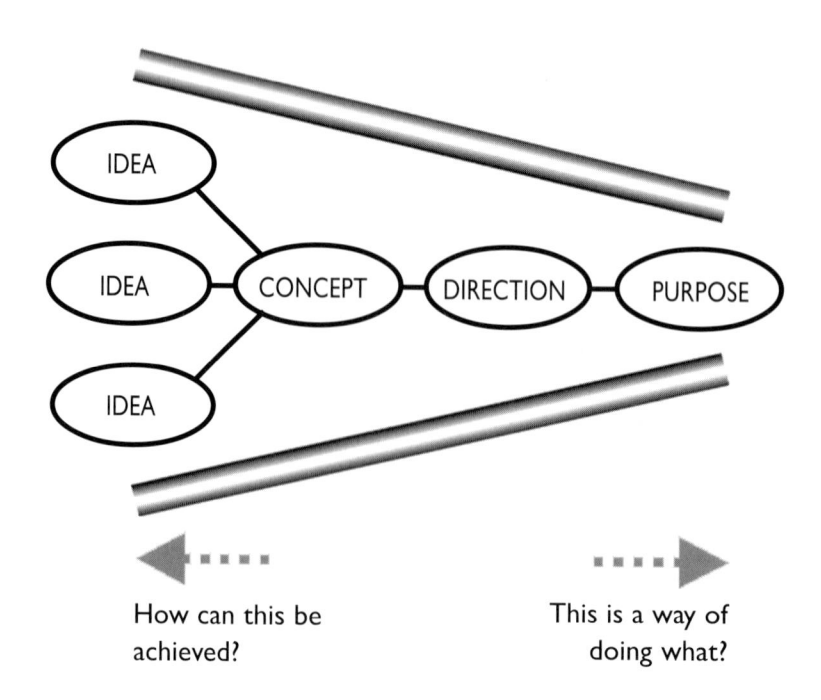

IDEA — CONCEPT — DIRECTION — PURPOSE

◄···· How can this be achieved? ····► This is a way of doing what?

CONCEPT EXAMPLES

Graeme Blackman achieved a surpetition by creating and monopolising his value in several different directions, using different concepts and ideas. One example is that:

- ⊃ From the *direction* of *limiting the competition*

- ⊃ Arises the *concept* of *restricted entry*

- ⊃ From which emerges the *idea* of *US FDA approval*

- ⊃ And the *idea* of *manufacturing* the APIs which IDT researches

- ⊃ And the *idea* of *specialising* in anti-cancer drugs

Paul Adler and Brad Bond achieved surpetition by creating and monopolising their value. For example:

- ⊃ From the *direction* of *scheduled versus crisis support*

- ⊃ Arises the *concept* of *packaging* broader value and price

- ⊃ From which emerges the *idea* of *Invizage Support Plans*

- ⊃ And the *idea* of *linking* service quality to installed quality

- ⊃ And the *idea* of *upgrade contracts* as a logical progression

LESSON 7
HARVEST YOUR THINKING

The specific technique of harvesting in creative thinking is used to identify exactly what has been generated by the creative thinking session. We use a **harvesting checklist** to gather the output of our thinking. At the end of a creative thinking session, we can review the ideas and concepts generated and categorise them in the following way.

Specific ideas: these are ideas that seem valuable, practical and usable. They may need further development, but we can recognise their potential. This is what we would normally seek in a creative thinking session.

Beginnings of ideas: the idea is far from usable, but there is something interesting or different about the idea.

Concepts: in recollection, it is possible to identify the concepts behind certain ideas. It is important to extract the concept as it then becomes possible to find alternative ways of putting that concept into practice.

Approaches: an approach is a broad way of looking at a problem or situation. At the end of our thinking we should be able to list the general approaches identified in our thinking.

Changes: it is worth noting definite changes that occur in our thinking – changes in our approach or concepts.

Flavour: It is important to record the flavour or essence of the creative thinking session primarily to ensure future sessions on the same purpose have a different flavour. On most occasions, all the ideas in a creative thinking session will be of the same general sort or flavour.

There are some concepts that are expressed directly during the thinking session. There are others that are indirect and behind the ideas that have been put forward. It is always worthwhile making an effort to extract the concepts behind the ideas, even if these concepts have not been expressed directly at the time.

Selection of ideas

Profile of idea: do you want a big idea with a big risk, or a small idea with a smaller risk? As you go through the ideas generated, you see what fits your exact profile of choice or need.

Best home for the idea: what is the best home for this idea? Is it a big company that dominates the market? Is it a good idea for a small company trying to enter the market? In the end, the purpose of creativity is to generate options and alternatives. Just as in a buffet dinner, where the food alternatives are displayed on the table, what you choose to eat depends on your profile of choice.

HARVESTING EXAMPLES

Successful entrepreneurs typically start with a concept, choose an idea which becomes the first stage of its implementation, and *discover* their way forward implementing other ideas progressively. In many cases, good ideas have been "warehoused" until their implementation could be afforded, or until the time for them became right in the marketplace.

Jim McDonald went to remote Australia in 1946 with the concept of using a large tract of cheap, parasite-free land to achieve economies of scale and, to some extent, as a drought-proofing strategy. Subsequently that concept has since been applied in acquiring geographically diverse properties and a feedlot for finishing cattle in dry times.

Len Poulter started with the concept of adding value to chicken meat in his butcher shop, then progressed that concept to a specialised chicken added-value retail franchise chain, and since has broadened the concept to total meal solutions.

LESSON 8
TREAT YOUR IDEAS

Some ideas are practical and usable as they are and are ready for assessment. Other creative ideas need to be subjected to a treatment process. Treatment involves modifying and improving ideas, making them simpler or less expensive.

There are some specific ways to make ideas more useful and usable.

In **shaping**, we change the idea to fit real-world constraints of cost, legality, technical feasibility, etc.

In **tailoring**, the idea is altered to fit the resources of the organisation. Sometimes the idea may not be practical, but concept extraction can be used to carry out the concept in a more practical way.

With **strengthening**, the idea is further improved by building on its power and benefits. The power of the idea relates to how easily, how quickly, and how widespread the benefits can be delivered, and the ability of the idea to change things.

We use **fault correction** to look at the faults, deficiencies, weaknesses or defects in an idea, and then attempt to remedy these faults.

Focus on the **difference** between ideas that are similar to previous ideas or to the way things are done now.

Remember that creativity is a skill that you can call on at any time. As you learn and practise the techniques of creative thinking your skill and confidence will build.

TREATMENT EXAMPLES

Jurgen Klein continues to generate, shape and tailor ideas to improve the quality of the Jurlique experience delivered in his retail outlets, particularly as this is where he aims to create long-term customers who will then purchase by mail, telephone or internet order. He has experimented with hiring health professionals versus experienced retail staff. With the objective of picking the most suitable staff early in the relationship, he continues experimenting with various mixes of staff induction. The retail end of his business is so challenging, and costly, because of the need to deliver an experience with many difficult-to-manage variables, that he may need to consider alternative concepts for generating new customers.

The RM Williams business concept has been shaped and tailored over time, apparently more by evolution and necessity than proactive idea generation. Discovering the need, then discovering direct mail and money-with-order, then expanding the product range, then opening retail outlets, and today broadening into a "city-bush" fashion statement market, all exemplify a progression of thinking and idea treatment, albeit one that has occurred over a period of some seventy years.

FURTHER INFORMATION AND TRAINING

Edward de Bono's techniques are now widely used throughout the world. They are simple and practical. They work. The techniques actually provoke and shape new concepts and ideas rather than simply allow them to emerge from the mind where some of them might be.

However, for full effect the techniques need to be learned in a disciplined way. Serious creativity is very different from sitting around and hoping that new concepts and ideas will just happen. It is very different from just brainstorming and withholding judgement.

Formal training in these techniques is available throughout Australia and New Zealand and may be obtained by contacting The de Bono Institute, 257 Collins Street, Melbourne 3000. Telephones (03) 9650 0822 or 1800 808 810.

Self-paced training combined with creative thinking software is available on the *Serious Creativity CD*. For information and orders, visit www.lyonsanddebono.com

INDEX

Accor Group 190
active pharmaceutical ingredient 67, 114, 135, 136, 137, 198, 278
Adler, Paul 26, 113, 121–6, 198, 298–9, 349
advertising 17, 55, 62, 64, 67, 69, 111, 168, 172, 222, 224, 232, 234, 245, 248, 250, 253, 268, 276, 278, 279, 306, 307, 309, 316
advertising, free 38, 89, 236
age of contraction 23
age of expansion 23
airlines 79, 143, 247, 265, 304, 341
airports 143, 265, 304
alternative therapies 95–8, 184, 197, 200, 255
aluminium 163, 165, 199, 297
AMP 103, 104, 164
analysis (of information) 22, 202, 203–5, 216, 234, 263, 283, 284, 301, 321
API, see active pharmaceutical ingredient
appeal values 268, 271
army, US 164, 165
Aspect Computing 103
asset base 28, 303–4, 308, 310, 312
assets 38, 57, 62, 135, 157, 173, 174, 178, 199, 208, 235, 240, 241, 242, 278, 311
    management 264, 265
    tangible and intangible 236
AstraZeneca 136
attitudes 285–6
Australian Administrative Services (AAS) 104
Australian Geographic Magazine 56, 61, 62, 63, 169, 195, 219
Australian ownership 57, 62, 170
Australian Roughriders Association 180, 240
automobile industry 246, 268
Avis 250

Bain, Ike 63–4
Baker's Delight 119, 144
ballpoint pens 263
banks 166, 244, 247, 303–4, 318
Barbaro, Ron 20–1
Bardwell, Paul 119
baseline 23–4, 27, 202–7, 226, 227, 229, 234, 256, 272, 329
Baxter Healthcare Inc. 73–4
Beck, Max, see Max Beck
Becton Corporation Pty Ltd 26, 187–93, 200, 241, 344
Bell, Alexander Graham 263
Benetton Corporation 212–13
Bertrand, John 9
Blackman, Dr Graeme 26, 113–14, 133–9, 198, 237, 349
Blundy, Brett 37
board, role of 17, 50, 86, 296

Body Shop 97, 213
Boeing 231
Bond, Brad 26, 113, 121–6, 198, 298–9, 349
borrowing 30, 163
brainstorming 28, 280–300, 330, 354
brand 26, 30, 32, 37, 38, 43, 44, 45, 46, 57, 62, 63, 67, 70, 119, 137, 168, 169, 170, 173, 180, 192, 220, 221, 222, 240, 245, 278, 279, 328
    hero 64
brand image 232, 233
brand lag 110
Branson, Sir Richard 79, 220
bread 119, 144, 223
BridgeClimb 25, 34, 37–9, 172, 194, 235–6, see also Cave, Paul
business
    concepts 63, 126, 137, 138, 140, 156, 212, 223, 237, 251, 257, 276, 316, 337, 353
    diversified 144, 167
    family 160, 167, 298
    focus of 108, 123
    formulae 80, 83, 90, 141, 142, 257, 275, 277, 300
    large 84, 129, 141, 149
    leadership 120
    mail-order 213, 240
    models 70, 104, 149, 151, 195
    new 61, 62, 84, 109, 139, 177, 196
    phases 20, 246
    plans 103, 330
    schools 22, 30, 31, 108, 232, 311
    skills 83
    small 84, see also small to medium enterprise
    structure 113, 119, 120, 223
    systems 15, 63, 89, 91, 113, 119, 124, 140, 141, 145, 151, 196, 199, 219, 221, 223, 236, 258, 299, 309, 337
    thinking 16, 18, 67, 68, 165, 202, 203, 206, 243
    vertically integrated 95
business and
    creating value 106, 142
    marketing 16, 327
    profit 15
business as cause 55, 131, 198, 258
business model 70, 104, 195
    replicable 15, 149, 151, 195, see also replicable business system
Business Review Weekly 124
Buxton, Michael 190–3
by-product values 261, 272, 273

Cadbury's 249
Cantarella Group 25, 34, 43, 44, 46, 194, 221
cashflow 125
    negative 118

catalogues 63, 173, 180, 219, 238, 240, 304
cataloguing concepts 317–19, 330
cattle 145, 146, 155–60, 177, 178, 179, 199, 311, 351
cause 25, 31–2, 34, 54–76, 79, 109, 123, 131, 198, 200, 220, 222, 253, 254, 255, 298, 313, 314, 347
   elevated 15, 25, 26, 57, 79, 126, 198, 219, 220–1, 222, 236, 237, 239, 241, 252, 254, 256, 258, 274, 276, 278, 295, 297, 299, 308, 310, 312, 328
cause hero 26, 31, 64, 168–93, 328
Cave, Paul 25, 34, 35–40, 172, 194, 235–6, 342
CEMAX 138
challenge 172–3, 285, 340
   convention 16, 67, 68, 206
   existing ideas 340–2, 344
chocolate marketing 248–9
Clairs, Reg 106
Clements 130
Club Mediterranee 245
Coles (Myer) 44, 107, 172, 296
commitment 31, 119, 120, 131, 173, 197, 255
commitment 197
commodity 27, 109, 226, 235, 315, 330
   price 17
   values 272
competitive values 33, 56, 243, 244–5, 246, 247, 249, 328, 329
competitors and competition 18–19, 20, 23, 26, 27, 30, 32, 44, 52, 53, 62, 68, 69, 76, 107, 108, 109, 110, 112, 137, 141, 150, 169, 170, 172, 195, 196, 198, 202, 204, 206, 207, 213, 222, 225–42, 244–5, 246, 251, 278, 313, 319, 328, 329
computer industry 231, 247
computers 18, 102, 123, 213, 234, 269, 272, 299, 318
concept 20, 21, 37, 63, 70, 90, 97, 98, 104, 106, 107, 112, 123, 126, 137, 138, 141, 149, 156, 197, 203, 206, 210–17, 218, 220, 223, 227, 228, 233, 234, 235, 237, 239, 245, 251, 256, 257, 265, 266, 267, 276, 292, 293, 299, 300, 301–14, 315–26, 328, 330–2, 337, 342, 343, 344, 350, 351, 353
   design 27, 28, 126, 217, 246, 301–14, 329
   examples 349
   extraction 304, 305, 352
   fans 348
   generating 218, 317, 319–21, 322, 324, 331
   research and development (concept R&D) 21–2, 27, 28, 32, 194, 234, 301, 315–26, 330–2
   triangle 336
concepts
   and Dick Smith 218
   and Les Schirato 220
   with flaws 165, 307
conceptual
   creative thinking, see creative conceptual thinking
   thinking 16, 22, 24, 25, 206, 218, 220, 222, 235
   work 217
context 79, 112, 213, 216–17, 241, 262, 263, 270, 274
contraction, age of 23

convenience 62, 126, 211, 212, 224, 250, 264, 266, 299
   value, see value, convenience
corporate strategy 28, 323, 325
   group 316, 323
cost of entry 232, 233
creative
   conceptual thinking 16, 25, 26, 30, 129, 207, 212, 236, 253, 294, 296, 297, 298, 306, 308, 310, 317, 347
   hit-list 286–287
   think tank 61, 326
   thinking 44, 105, 150, 206, 207, 208, 210, 218, 219, 235, 302, 322, 323
creativity 22, 24, 27, 28, 30, 31, 33, 37, 38, 44, 46, 64, 132, 207, 208, 209, 223, 234, 258, 259, 263, 278
   serious 22, 28, 234, 235, 280–300, 310, 321, 326, 330
CSIRO 75
customers
   desires and values 32–3, 54, 55, 56, 76, 79, 96, 111, 120, 138, 197, 221, 222, 243, 246, 251, 266, 300, 328
   foundation 103, 275, 379
   managing for profit 45–6, 52, 194, 195
   values 55

de Bono, Edward 9, 16, 19, 22, 290, 291, 293, 334, 354
debt 45, 95, 160, 179
defined needs 303, 308, 310, 312
delivery system 39, 124, 143, 144, 246
demand 179
desires, human 15, 26, 31, 32, 33, 54, 55, 56, 77–104, 106, 112, 222, 328, 339
developers 105, 190, 191, 212, 241, 281
Di Marco, Adrian 25, 34, 47–53, 141, 195, 255–7
Dickhead matches 172, 347
Dick Smith Foods 32, 57, 61, 64, 195, 219
distraction value, see value, distraction
dominance 226, 231, 241
drought 145, 146, 155, 178, 310, 311
drought-proofing 145, 146, 157, 311, 351

economies of scale 62, 143, 156, 199, 311, 351
Edwards, Jane 129
efficiency 24, 27, 33, 165, 202, 203, 226, 249
ego needs 78
Einstein, Albert 16, 209
empathy 89, 90, 138, 171, 196, 200, 220, 252
employment and training services 130
endometriosis 183, 184, 254, 255
environment 24, 95, 213, 226, 264, 265, 320
Ernst & Young 25
expansion 130, 146, 163, 166, 179, 199
   age of 23
extortion 69, 170, 230, 279, 344

INDEX

Fairfax 56, 62, 63
Farrell, Dr Peter 25, 32, 56–8, 71–6, 80, 196, 312–14, 347
fashion 89, 90, 91, 196, 213, 233, 252, 253 264, 353
   values 246, 271, 273
fast-food business 305
feedlots 146, 156, 157, 311, 351
feminists 185
fibroids 183, 184, 254
financial controls 145, 192, 200, 344
flanking 69, 107, 169, 195, 279
flexibility 53, 110, 120, 132, 141, 184, 198, 213, 218, 223, 318
Flight Centre Limited 26, 142, 143, 149–50, 199, 308–9, 337
Ford (UK) 19–20
Ford, Henry 15, 244
foreign ownership 57, 62, 172
foundation customer, see customer, foundation
franchisees 79, 85, 98, 113, 118, 119, 140, 141, 144, 223, 224, 277, 294, 295, 337
franchising 91, 95, 117, 118, 119, 120, 140, 294, 296, 351
franchisor 113, 118, 119, 223, 294, 295
Franklins 107
function values 272
fuzzy logic 247, 265

G James Group 26, 146, 163–5, 199
gateways 114, 126, 138, 237, 248, 269–70, 274, 276, 300
generating concepts, see concepts, generating
glass 163, 165, 166, 199, 260, 297
global companies, see multinationals
guerilla tactics 30, 43, 221, 279

Harvard Business School 232
harvesting 350–1
Harvey Norman 26, 81–6, 140, 196, 277, 296, 337
Harvey, Gerry 26, 79, 81–6, 91, 140, 141, 172, 196, 252, 294, 295, 296, 337
hat thinking, see six thinking hats
Hawke, Hazel 69, 169, 279
Heinz 232
hero reputation, see reputation
Herron Pharmaceuticals 25, 32, 57, 67–70, 169–70, 195, 277–9, 344
honesty 15, 173, 178, 179, 200, 239, 240, 298
housekeeping 23, 24, 27, 203, 205–7, 227, 229, 234, 235, 328, 329
humour 208, 290
hypothesis 283, 292

IBM 203, 231, 263
idea machine 205–6
IDT (Institute of Drug Technology Australia Ltd) 26, 114, 135–9, 198, 237–8, 349

implementation 16, 46, 52, 89, 107, 132, 142, 214, 222, 223, 257, 258, 284, 313, 322, 328, 351
in vitro fertilisation, see IVF
incentives 192, 241, 242, 257, 295
inconvenience 212, 265, 268, 301, 302, see also value, inconvenience
Inergise Australia 130
information analysis, see analysis
information system, self-organising 22, 208–9, 280, 290, 330
Ingeus 26, 113, 127–30, 198, 257
innovation 53, 132, 165–6, 199, 207, 213, 224, 228, 240, 258, 296, 297, 298
Institute of Drug Technology Australia Ltd, see IDT
integrated value, see value, integrated
intellectual property 70, 76, 138, 196, 230, 313
inventors 73, 169
investors 73, 129, 192, 205, 212, 241, 260, 302, 309
Invizage Technology 26, 113, 123–6, 198, 299–300, 349
IVF 26, 173, 183–6, 200, 253, 255

Japan 178, 207, 227, 247, 248, 265, 266, 267
Japanese 178, 207, 227, 231, 245, 246, 247, 265, 268, 282
Jennifer, Clair 26, 79–80, 87–92, 196, 233, 251–3
Johnson and Johnson 136
JRA Group 104
juice packaging 249
Jurlique International 26, 95–8, 197, 276–7, 353

KAZ (Group Ltd) 26, 102, 103, 104, 143, 197, 274
Kazacos, Peter 26, 79, 80, 99–104, 197, 274, 275, 339
Kidman, Sir Sidney 177, 179, 239
Kit Kat 250
Klein, Dr Jurgen 26, 79–80, 95–8, 197, 275–7, 353
Klein, Ulrike 95

lateral thinking 9, 20, 208, 285, 287, 288, 291, 321
leadership 17, 75, 120, 141, 145, 169, 197, 223, 297, 298
learning organisation 146, 298
Lenard's Pty Ltd 26, 113, 117, 119, 197, 222, 223–4, 324
life insurance 20–1
logic 16, 31, 171, 207, 208, 209, 280, 282, 283, 284, 285, 291, 293, 334, 335, see also fuzzy logic
logistics 164, 165, 297

magazines 56, 62, 63, 102, 169, 178, 219, 248
magazine publishers 247
mail order 173, 177, 178, 180, 213, 239, 240, 364
maintenance 22, 27, 125, 192, 198, 203, 205, 206, 217, 226, 229, 241, 260, 285
management 205
   asset 264, 265

case 132, 258
crisis 124, 125, 126, 299
drought 310
financial 51, 256, 303
human resource 51, 145, 240
injury 131
project 192
risk 344
manufacturers and manufacturing 19, 22, 23, 52, 57, 61, 63, 67, 68, 90, 112, 136, 137, 138, 139, 163, 164, 165, 178, 198, 238, 247, 257, 271, 278, 349
market
  accessible 75, 196, 313
  global 18, 44, 49, 50, 52, 74, 136, 143, 202
  new 16, 244
  vertical 51, 52, 195, 255, 256, 257
market entry 114, 138, 232, 237, 238, 275, 279, 328
market leadership 69, 171, 203, 226, 233
market penetration 17, 55, 123, 143, 150, 246, 256, 308, 317, 327
market position 18, 107, 110
market research 108, 111, 191, 207
market segment 89, 241, 250, 251, 270
market share 18, 23, 30, 67, 89, 107, 149, 223, 226, 250, 251, 278, 328, 344
marketing 16–17, 18, 23, 31, 34, 38, 39, 43, 49, 50, 51, 61, 64, 69, 70, 79, 108, 126, 136, 139, 145, 168, 192, 221, 230, 237, 238, 239, 245, 251, 257, 284, 286, 294, 297, 300, 317, 318, 322–7, 330
  definition 16–17, 327
Marks and Spencer 233, 247
Marx, Karl 267
Maslow, Abraham 77, 79, 112, 262
Maslow's hierarchy of needs 77–8, 79
Max Beck 15, 26, 173–4, 187–93, 200, 241–2, 344
Max Beck Constructions Pty Ltd 189
Mayne Pharma 138
McDonald,
  Alexander 155
  Bob 155
  Don 155
  Jim 26, 145, 153–60, 199, 310–11, 351
McDonald's 63, 110–11, 119, 123, 144, 232
MDH Pastoral Company 26, 145, 155, 159, 199, 311
media 33, 55, 56, 83, 169, 171, 172, 220, 253, 276, 296, 308
me-too approach 19, 21, 27, 32, 107, 207, 228, 315, 330
Microsoft 50, 231
mistakes 51, 109
Monash
  IVF 26, 183
  University 135
monopolising value, see value monopoly
Morton, Tex 180, 240
movement 292–3, 345
multinationals and global companies 68, 69, 70, 169, 170

multiple values, see value, multiple
Murdoch
  Euan 25, 32, 56–7, 65–70, 169, 172, 195, 277–9, 344
  Kaye 67

name recognition 230–1
NCP (National Car Parks) 19
needs 23, 26, 28, 31, 32, 77–9, 91, 102, 103, 105, 112, 113, 119, 124, 131, 169, 171, 191, 197, 198, 208, 218, 223, 251, 257, 258, 260, 262, 299, 304, 324, 328, 331, 339
  defined 303, 308, 310, 312
  concept 320, 323
  see also Maslow's hierarchy of needs
negative security value 278
negative value, see value, negative
Newton, Isaac 290
niches 43, 108, 203, 233, 251
Nokia 112
Norman Ross 83, 85

OCAL 102
outsourcing 104, 130, 136, 137, 144, 197, 237, 274
outstanding value, see value, outstanding

P&O 102
Panadol 67, 69, 169–70, 172, 279
paradigm shift 106, 126, 299
Parsonage, Brian 119
partners and partnerships 51, 101, 106, 113, 123, 125, 130, 132, 149, 183, 191, 238, 247, 254, 255, 256, 257, 274
passion 31, 53, 61, 69, 70, 76, 90, 92, 96, 109, 113, 166, 167, 168, 169, 183, 184, 195, 198, 218, 239, 241, 252, 258, 297, 298, 342,
patents 138, 230, 233, 263, 302, 303
patterns 208, 210, 211, 213, 280, 281–2, 289–90, 343, 345
  asymmetric 290
patterning systems 289, 291, 293, 343
perception 22, 28, 207–8, 210–12, 261, 267–8, 293, 330, 334
persuasion mode 54, 56
Pfizer 136
Philips 228
phone, see telephone
physiological needs, see Maslow's hierarchy of needs
Pizza Hut 246
po (provocative operation) 291–3, 302
positive value, see value, positive
Poulter, Len 26, 113, 115–20, 197, 222–4, 324, 351
problem-solving 132, 202–3, 206, 259, 321, 329, 335, 338
product 23, 27, 31, 32, 33, 43, 49, 50, 52, 54–8, 63, 64, 67, 70, 80, 95, 97, 105, 107, 110, 136, 138, 139, 144, 150, 151, 169–70, 173, 197, 205, 207–8,

219, 224, 233, 240, 243–59, 260–79, 307, 313, 316, 328, 353
    me too, 207
product development 52, 64, 141, 143, 166, 207, 257, 281, 317, 325
product differentiation 69, 234, 244, 245, 251
product recall 69, 170, 344
profit 15, 17, 49, 73, 101, 135, 149, 151, 166, 184, 327
    managing customers for 45, 194, 221, 339
    not for 135, 183, 200
provocation 171–2, 222, 282, 285, 288, 291–3, 302, 345–6, see also po
Prudential Insurance Company, Canada 20–1
publicity 33, 38, 61, 69, 168–70, 172, 279

quality 15, 23, 24, 40, 62, 96, 98, 106, 109, 119, 142, 144, 157, 173, 178, 179, 190, 194, 197, 199, 204, 207, 225, 233, 234, 239, 240, 241, 242, 244, 245, 247, 269, 336, 349
quality circles 283
quality management 23, 283, 329
quality of life 106, 111, 211, 212, 276, 313, see also value, quality of life value
Quilty Endurance ride 180, 240
Quilty, Tom 180, 240

Radio Shack 63
random entry technique 343–4
random-word technique 288–91, 343–4
Readers Digest 63
Rebel Sport 83, 85, 141
referral 52, 80, 98, 126, 172, 173, 252, 276, 300, see also word of mouth
rehabilitation 130
Rein, Therese 26, 113, 127–32, 198, 257–8, 342
reinvesting 92, 123, 166, 199
replicable business model 149, 151, 195, see also business model, replicable
replicable business system 63, 149, 219
replicable factory 26, 31, 33, 140–67
replicable formula 126, 132, 198, 219, 221, 223, 236, 237, 239, 241, 252, 254, 257, 258, 275, 276, 277, 278, 295, 297, 300, 308, 309, 311, 313, 328
replicable process 27
reproducible model 51
    systems 124, see also replicable
reputation 15, 30, 107, 109, 126, 132, 138, 151, 169, 173, 174, 177, 189–90, 192, 198, 220, 223, 232, 238, 242, 248, 253, 255, 257, 259, 272, 275, 277, 279, 296, 298, 300, 309, 311, 328, 337
    hero 33, 220, 221, 223, 236, 238, 240, 242, 253, 257, 259, 275, 277, 279, 296, 298
research and development (R&D) 49, 67, 73
    concept 21, 22, 27, 28, 32, 194, 329, 301, 315–26, 330
    technical 28, 234, 315–26
ResMed 25, 32, 58, 73–4, 196, 312–14

Revlon 55
Revson, Charles 55
risk aversion 231, 238, 241
risk, managing 146, 166, 193, 199, 200, 298, 313, 323, 344
Ritchie, Peter 144
RM Williams Outback magazine 178
Royal Adelaide Hospital 138

safety needs 77, 78, 79
Saragossi, Joe 26, 145, 146, 161–7, 199, 296-8, 311
Schirato, Les, 25, 34, 41–6, 194, 220–1, 339
security values, see values, security
segmentation 233
self-actualisation needs 78, 79
self-image values, see values, self-image
self-importance value, see value, self-importance
self-organising
    information system 22, 28, 208–9, 280, 281, 282, 290, 292, 330, 345
    patterning system 289, 343
serious creativity 20, 22, 28, 234, 235, 280–98, 301, 321, 330
shareholders 17, 37, 45, 119, 129, 135, 139, 166, 194, 218, 237, 327
shopping, types of 250
Sigma Pharmaceuticals 67
simplification 151, 199, 309
Singleton, John 111
six thinking hats 9, 316, 325
sleep 32, 76, 78, 313, 347
sleep apnoea 58, 196, 347
sleep disordered breathing (SDB) 58, 74, 76, 312
small to medium enterprise 113, 123, 124, 164, 299
SME, see small to medium enterprise
Smith Kline Beecham 67, 69
Smith, Dick 25, 32, 46, 56–7, 59–64, 69, 141, 169, 170, 172, 195, 218–20, 278, 296, 297, 347
social needs 78
software 49–52, 101–4, 124, 141, 143, 195, 197, 231, 256, 269, 354
Sony
    Betamax 250
    Walkman 227–8, 250
South Australian Insurance Commission 193
special value, see value, special
specialty stores 108
Stanbroke Pastoral Company 179
standardisation 110
starting up 61–2
stem-cell technology 185, 253, 254, 255
Stockman's Hall of Fame 178, 240
stockmen 156, 157, 158, 177
strategic
    concepts 316
    planning 70, 206
Sullivan, Professor Colin 73–4

supermarkets 44, 57, 61, 92, 108, 119, 170, 217, 220, 221, 303
supervision, personal 156–8, 199
supply chain 51, 52
support plan 113, 125–6, 299, 349
surpetition 19–20, 22, 24, 26, 28, 79, 112, 114, 126, 137–8, 140, 198, 206, 225–42, 243, 245, 246, 248, 250–1, 257, 263, 301, 304, 307–8, 316, 319, 329, 330, 349
Swatch 248
Swiss watches 248
Sydney Harbour Bridge 37, 38, 39, 172, 235, 236, 342
synergy 139, 270

teams 46, 50, 52, 68, 84, 120, 124, 135, 145, 152, 164, 183, 184, 194, 197, 223, 257, 279, 287, 322, 342
technical research and development (R&D), see research and development, technical
technology 22, 27, 50, 73–6, 80, 95, 101–2, 104, 113, 123–6, 143, 144, 146, 183, 196–8, 207, 214, 230, 231, 235, 244, 255, 265, 274, 299, 313, 315, 317, 330
Technology One Ltd 25, 49–53, 141, 143, 195, 255
telephone 247, 250, 263, 265, 272, 277, 304, 307, 353
television 227, 264, 267, 307
tenders 102, 130, 132, 259
testing concepts 191, 317, 322–4
trust 15, 30, 80, 97, 125, 135, 173, 178–80, 200, 238–41, 275–7, 300, 311
Turner, Graham 15, 26, 144, 145, 147–52, 199, 308–9, 337
typewriters 232, 263

unique value, see value, unique
uniqueness 39, 90, 173, 178, 194, 227, 229–31, 233, 236, 251, 252, 260
United States Food and Drug Administration (USFDA) 114, 136–8, 198, 230, 237–8, 349
University of New South Wales 74
University of Sydney 73
USFDA, see United States Food and Drug Administration

value
  by-product 261, 272, 273
  convenience 105, 106, 110, 111, 217, 233, 263, 265, 268, 274, 329
  definition 261
  distraction 106, 111, 263, 267, 330
  inconvenience 211, 212, 361
  integrated 19, 20–1, 27, 28, 33, 39, 56, 79, 137–8, 198, 214, 227, 233, 234, 235, 243–59, 301, 329
  multiple 261, 272, 273
  negative 80, 211, 261, 276, 278
  outstanding 15, 16, 17, 23, 26, 31, 33, 58, 77,

105–39, 198, 218, 236, 237, 239, 241, 252, 254, 255, 256, 258, 260, 262–3, 274, 276, 278, 295, 297, 299, 308, 310, 313, 327, 328
  positive 80, 212, 261
  quality of life 106, 111, 212, 217, 263, 264, 265, 274, 329
  self-importance 106, 112, 211, 212, 217, 263, 266
  special 90, 302
  unique 40, 50, 89, 91, 139, 196, 308
value bundle 79, 80, 106, 109–10, 112–14, 131, 212, 223, 239, 253, 258, 262, 263, 272, 276, 295, 308
value delivery 39, 91, 97, 126, 132, 141–3, 145, 198, 252, 277, 300
value monopolies 20, 26, 106, 110, 225, 226, 228, 229–33, 234, 237, 246, 250, 257, 264, 328, 329
values, product 27, 33, 54, 56, 137, 198, 234, 243–59, 301, 329
values, security 77, 78, 217, 270–1, 278, 329
values, self-image 266, 271
values, self-importance 106, 112, 211, 212, 217, 263–4, 266, 330
valufacture 22–3, 262, 263, 267, 268, 273
Variety Club Bash 64
VCR 228
Veberroth, Peter 9
vertical markets 51, 52, 195, 255, 256, 257
VHS 250
Virgin Airlines 79, 220
Vittoria coffee 43–4, 194, 220, 221

watches 226, 248, 269, 288, 319
Western Electric 263
Williams, RM (Reg) 15, 26, 173, 177–80, 200, 239–40, 311
Williams, RM, 175–80, 200, 238–40, 241, 353
windows 163, 165
Windows (Microsoft) 231, 257
Winton, Cleila 45
Wombat Enterprises 26, 89–90, 196, 233, 277
Wood, Carl 26, 173, 181–6, 200, 253–5
Woolworths 56, 62, 63, 106–7
word of mouth 34, 37, 38, 39, 64, 168, 169, 170–2, 173, 180, 220, 223, 224, 236, 240, 269, 298, 302, see also referral
word processing 269
Work Directions Pty Ltd 129, 130, 132
Wright Brothers 214
Wyeth 136

Xerox 263, 288

Young Presidents Organisation (YPO) 70

INSIGHTS

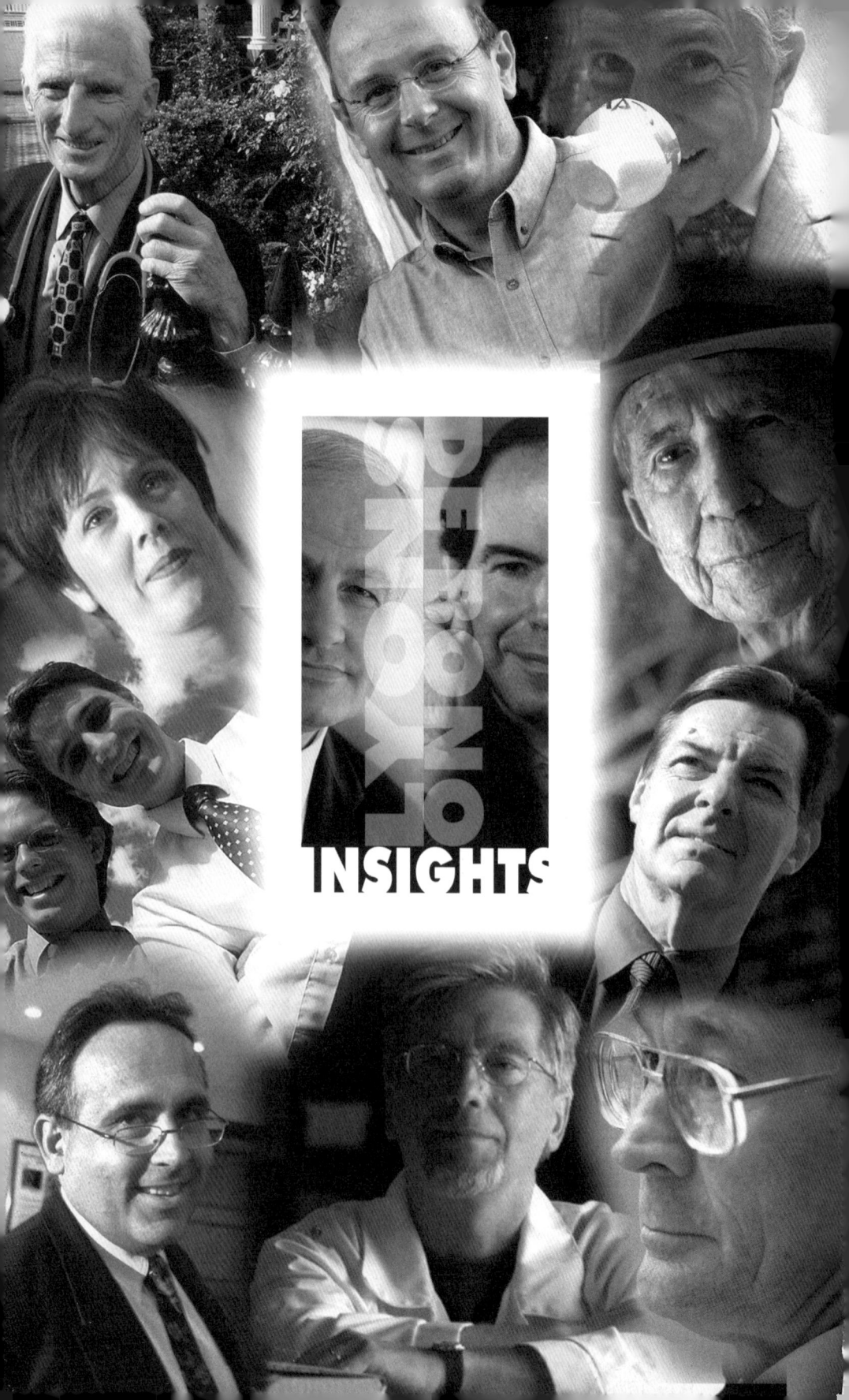